Fraud Auditi.
CAAT ɪ

Internal Audit and IT Audit

Series Editor:

Dan Swanson

Dan Swanson and Associates, Ltd., Winnipeg, Manitoba, Canada

The *Internal Audit and IT Audit* series publishes leading-edge books on critical subjects facing audit executives as well as internal and IT audit practitioners. Key topics include Audit Leadership, Cybersecurity, Strategic Risk Management, Auditing Various IT Activities and Processes, Audit Management, and Operational Auditing.

For more information about this series, please visit https://www.crcpress.com/Internal-Audit-and-IT-Audit/book-series/CRCINTAUDITA

Fraud Auditing Using CAATT

A Manual for Auditors and Forensic Accountants to Detect Organizational Fraud

Shaun Aghili

CRC Press
Taylor & Francis Group
Boca Raton London New York

CRC Press is an imprint of the
Taylor & Francis Group, an **informa** business

AN AUERBACH BOOK

CRC Press
Taylor & Francis Group
6000 Broken Sound Parkway NW, Suite 300
Boca Raton, FL 33487-2742

First issued in paperback 2022

© 2019 by Taylor & Francis Group, LLC
CRC Press is an imprint of Taylor & Francis Group, an Informa business

No claim to original U.S. Government works

ISBN 13: 978-0-367-14561-3 (hbk)
ISBN 13: 978-1-03-240155-3 (pbk)

DOI: 10.1201/9780429032325

Publisher's Note
The publisher has gone to great lengths to ensure the quality of this reprint but points out that some imperfections in the original copies may be apparent.

Visit the Taylor & Francis Web site at
http://www.taylorandfrancis.com

and the CRC Press Web site at
http://www.crcpress.com

Contents

Author

Shaun Aghili, DBA, CISSP-ISSMP, CISA, CIA, CCSA, CFSA, CGAP, CRMA, CFE, CMA, is a management associate professor and a veteran of the financial services industry. Dr. Aghili's academic research and professional interests revolve around internal audit, fraud prevention, and information systems assurance issues and considerations, especially within the financial services sector.

Shaun Aghili's academic achievements include a doctorate degree in business administration and the completion of a post-doctorate executive leadership training program through Cornell University.

Dr. Aghili also maintains a total of ten professional designations in internal and information systems auditing, management accounting, fraud examination, and information systems security management. On a global scale, Dr. Aghili is among the very few academic members of the Institute of Internal Auditors (IIA) to hold five internal auditing designations.

1

A PEDAGOGICAL APPROACH TO USING THIS MANUAL

The book that you are about to read is one of the many outputs of our collaborative research team in the Master of Information Systems Assurance Program (MISAM) at the Concordia University of Edmonton (CUE) in Alberta, Canada.

CUE's MISAM program got its start in September of 2013, thanks to the vision and hard work of Professor Ron Ruhl to whom this manual is dedicated. Ruhl was also the creator of our Master of Information Systems Security Program (MISSM) a few years earlier. I should also mention that MISSM was the first graduate-level information security program in Canada. Since then, the number of cybersecurity programs in both Canada and the United States has exploded, but as of this writing, MISAM is and remains the first and only graduate-level information systems assurance program in Canada.

Ruhl – who stepped down from the MISSM/MISAM chair position after 10 years of outstanding service in 2016 – was one of the best bosses I have ever had. He gave me full reign to take the MISAM conceptual plan (degree proposal) and design the MISAM curriculum based on my training and professional/academic teaching experience as a finance and accounting educator, a Certified Internal Auditor (CIA), a Certified Information Systems Auditor (CISA), and a Certified Fraud Examiner (CFE).

My objective in developing various course syllabi for the MISAM track was simple enough: to create MISAM graduates with a set of professional skills that would enable them to secure employment in a variety of enterprises. My vision was to provide our MISAM students with the Information Systems Audit and Control Association's (ISACA) recommended skill sets to perform typical information systems audit functions. I also wanted our students to develop additional skill sets so as to enable our graduates to also be able to serve as a Computer-Assisted Audit Tools and Techniques (CAATT) team contributor in various accounting or internal audit team audit projects. This meant that in addition to using ISACA's CISA certification task statements as a baseline I wanted our graduates to also develop additional competencies in financial accounting and fraud examination.

As such, we set up to incorporate CAATT training in various MISAM offerings, such as our Fraud Examination and Audit Theory and Application courses, so as to enable our students to build a solid CAATT foundational base. Currently, in MISAM, we use two CAATT vendor solutions: ActiveData and Interactive Data Extraction and Analysis (IDEA). As some of you may know, ActiveData is an Excel-driven CAATT software that may be a more suitable alternative for smaller audit shops due to its lower cost, whereas IDEA is essentially a more powerful (and expensive) CAATT alternative, better suited for organizations with more elaborate audit needs and deeper pockets. There are also other fine CAATT software solutions on the market such as Audit Command Language (ACL), which has managed to secure a CAATT market share lead, as well as Arbutus Analyzer. By using IDEA to demonstrate some audit tests in this manual, we are neither endorsing nor making a claim that IDEA is superior to any other CAATT solution. Promoting products or software is not what we are after in Academia. We have used IDEA for demonstration purposes for the simple reason that it is MISAM's chosen CAATT software for the purposes of training our assurance students.

Students have at times asked me why we use IDEA instead of ACL for training purposes. I answer this question using my word processing software experience as an analogy. I recall buying my very first personal computer circa 1990. It was an older model that I had purchased from a good friend that had *WordPerfect* already installed on it. For the next several years, like a lot of new personal computer users, I taught myself how to use *WordPerfect* for all my word processing needs. However, after a few years, it became apparent that *Microsoft Word* was fast becoming the most common word processing software in enterprises of all sizes. By 1995, just about every company that I was working with (or working for) had *MS Word* installed on their computer; it was time to say goodbye to *WordPerfect* and start working with *MS Word*! Surprisingly, I had a very easy time switching to

Word, because of my knowledge of *WordPerfect*. As a user, I did not find a significant difference between the two programs, although I am sure that both *CorelDRAW* and *Microsoft* could point out to a number of reasons why their word processing product is superior to the competition. The point that I am making is this: If you learn to work with just about any CAATT software solutions, switching to another CAATT software will most likely be a manageable change for most users. What makes a typical CAATT audit test reliable is not the software brand in most cases but the quality of the data used and the skill set of the auditor or fraud examiner to not only correctly apply the audit test but also be able to correctly interpret the ensuing audit results. In other words, an auditor needs to have the skill set necessary to pick up on the red flags revealed as the result of a test, and furthermore be able to recommend appropriate controls to help mitigate or prevent the occurrence of various fraud schemes.

Over the years, as we continued to use and further refine our pedagogical approach to CAATT technology, I noticed that our MISAM students could really use a supplementary CAATT-centric textbook, especially since many of the current CAATT-related book titles were quickly becoming old. As such, I decided to create a "research" project with the objective of creating a compendium of CAATT-centric audit tests aimed at training both students and audit professionals. Since an important MISAM graduation requirement is the completion of a research-based final paper, I created a five-part project aimed at using the Association of Certified Fraud Examiners' (ACFE) Fraud Tree as the base model, and then, with the help of my students, mapped as many CAATT-compatible audit tests to each of its 55 fraud tree schemes as we could find (Figure 1.1).

The intended audience for this manual is relatively large. It can be used as not only a training and reference tool for audit and fraud examination professionals but also a useful primary or supplementary textbook for graduate and undergraduate accounting and audit courses at various universities. In short, all students and professionals looking to become more proficient at CAATT testing are likely to benefit from this publication.

There are eight chapters in this compendium: Chapter 1 (the preface section that you are currently reading) provides the reader with some background information and the pedagogical approach used to

THE FRAUD TREE
OCCUPATIONAL FRAUD AND ABUSE CLASSIFICATION SYSTEM

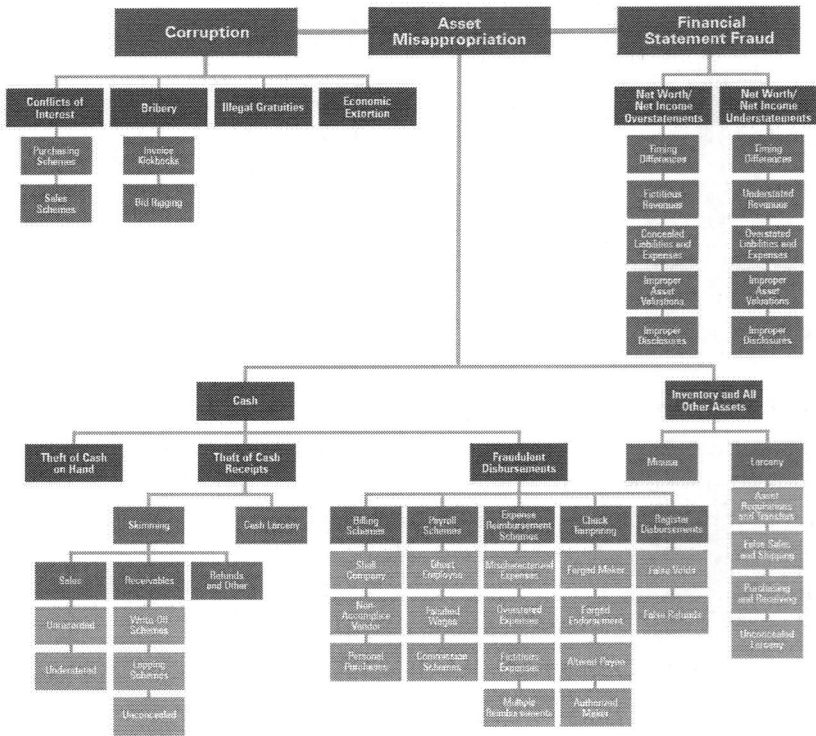

Figure 1.1   The ACFE Fraud Tree. (*Source:* www.acfe.com/fraud-tree.aspx)

develop this manual. Chapters 2 and 3 deal with fraudulent disbursements. Chapters 4 and 5 deal with financial statement fraud and corruption schemes. Chapter 6 presents a general discussion of CAATT, Chapter 7 provides step-by-step instructions on how to perform ten CAATT-based audit tasks and tests using IDEA V.10, and Chapter 8 outlines a "lab" exercise that I assign every semester in my own Fraud Examination course. I have found this to be a great class exercise, as it combines not only a research component, but is a very effective means of helping students better relate to my other course material. Finally, since the lab output is a group oral presentation deliverable, it provides students an opportunity to also exercise their group management and oral presentations skills.

In order for readers to derive maximum benefit from this publication, we followed a specific organizational format for each book section as follows:

a. *The Introduction Section*: Each section of this compendium starts out with an introduction section where we introduce the scope of discussion as it pertains to a particular section of the ACFE Fraud Tree. This section contains some relevant statistics taken out from the 2018 edition of the ACFE's Report to the Nations (RTTN) in order to provide readers some general norms and trends relevant to each type of organizational fraud. For those not familiar with ACFE's RTTN, this survey-based report provides fraud professionals with relevant trends and statistics derived by sending out RTTN survey forms to ACFE members and compiling responses in an organized and easy-to-read format. RTTN is currently published about every other year. According to my own observations of previous editions of the report, although its various statistics do change slightly from one edition to the next, most fraud scheme trends seem to remain the same in every edition. The 2018 RTTN is a compilation of various fraud statistics from 2,690 real cases of occupational fraud reported by ACFE members spanning over 125 countries and 23 industry categories. The 2018 RTTN statistics estimate global occupational fraud losses at over $7 billion with a median loss per case of $130,000. While these statistics are based on secondary sources of data (surveys completed by ACFE members, based on their own fraud investigation cases), it is nonetheless one of the most important sources for audit and fraud prevention professionals to gain an understanding of fraud norms and trends. As such, both professionals and students are highly encouraged to take the time to study each updated edition of the RTTN as an effective way to familiarize themselves with fraud facts, statistics, and considerations that are bound to come into play, especially during the planning stage of most audits and/or fraud investigations. RTTN can be accessed and downloaded for free at the ACFE site (www.acfe.com).

b. *Case Studies*: In each section, we have briefly identified and discussed several recent, real-life, related fraud cases. These case studies serve to better familiarize entry-level audit professionals and/or audit students with how a certain fraud scheme could work in the real world. Case studies have always been – and continue to remain – a very vital component of how we teach fraud examination to our MISAM students. Every few years, we identify a number of more recent fraud cases relating to a particular category on the ACFE Fraud Tree. We then ask our students to dig further into a number of these cases with the aim of analyzing the motivations of the perpetrators according to the Fraud Triangle theory, assess control failures that led to the occurrence of the fraud, and discuss the lessons learned from the occurrence of the fraud scheme. The study of real-life fraud cases enables both professionals and audit students to develop a better understanding of the nature and inner workings of each type of fraud scheme. The numerical citation system used in this compendium easily allows the reader to refer to the original source used by our team, as the first step for those interested in finding out more granular details about each case study. Educators or corporate trainers interested in incorporating case study assignments into their academic or professional courses can refer to the section entitled "Student Case Study Research and Oral Presentation Project" at the end of this manual for additional guidance on how to create such case study-based assignments.

c. *The Discussion Section*: This section is, in essence, the main body for each section aimed at providing a concentrated discussion of each major category of occupational fraud. When we were in the midst of completing each section of this project, I kept telling my MISAM students: "One of your important objectives for each section of this project is to create a relatively short and concentrated literature review section where you are running the reader through a 15- to 20-min crash course about the nuts and bolts of the occupational fraud category under study!" For those interested in a more expansive discussion of each major fraud category, there are a number of excellent books and articles available. Our primary "go to" guide continues to be ACFE's *The Fraud Examiners' Manual*, a comprehensive reference guide compiled and regularly updated by the ACFE.

d. *The Conclusion Section*: This wrap-up section provides the reader with statistics related to our mapping efforts for each section. For example, this section identifies how many related audit tests and controls were identified for each type of occupational fraud categories. This section can be regarded as the introduction section of the subsequent parts of each section, namely, the internal control/good practices and audit worksheet tables.

e. *Recommended Internal Controls and/or Good Practices Section*: This section is formatted as a series of tables where a number of recommended controls and/or good practices are presented and organized according to each fraud subcategory (scheme). Less experienced auditors are likely to find value in using these tables as a resource to formulate appropriate internal control recommendations for their audit reports.

f. *For Further Reading Section*: The numerical citation system seen at the end of most paragraphs used in this work refers to the source where various concepts or statistics discussed in those paragraphs were derived. Researchers and other professionals interested in further expanding their understanding related to the discussed concepts or topics in a paragraph can easily refer to this section to find more detailed information regarding various points discussed.

g. *Audit Worksheets*: This final part in Sections 2–5 is comprised of a series of small tables where relevant audit tests for each section are presented and discussed in a concise, yet easy-to-read manner. Information provided for each CAATT-based audit test includes the following: what occupational category/subcategory the audit test relates to; the purpose of the test; a quick explanation of the test itself including the test's overall procedure, explanation related to assertion that it aims to test, and the CAATT expression(s) to use; and finally, what fraud possible red flags to look for when reviewing/analyzing the results of the test.

As a graduate program research supervisor, I often ask my research supervisees what "contributions to knowledge" can be expected from their research proposal. The term contribution to knowledge is not solely limited to the synthesis of new knowledge. This is not what we intended to accomplish with this manual. Instead, the primary goal – as I mentioned before – was to compile and present the existing knowledge in a new format, one that I knew would be of benefit to audit students and/or audit professionals. It is my hope that this manual can act as an effective catalyst in encouraging both students and professionals to feel more comfortable in employing CAATT tests for their various audit projects.

In my audit and fraud examination classes, I always make it a point to emphasize the fact that as an educator, I can only aim at providing students with an overall understanding of how to use a certain technology to accomplish an information systems security or assurance objective. As such, just like learning a new language, it is highly unlikely that one can become fluent in a language, by simply taking a semester-long introductory language course. Learning a language can be both a fun and a manageable task, if an individual can have the discipline to study that language in frequent and short durations. I offer the very same advice to those who are interested in becoming more proficient with CAATT technology. Make sure to not only read this manual but also get a demo copy of your preferred CAATT software (if you do not have access to a fully functional version of it at work), and begin practicing with it in frequent and short practice sessions. It is fairly easy to choose one of the audit tests demonstrated step-by-step in the last section of this book and practice performing it within a 20- to 30-min self-study session. If you are interested in obtaining a demo copy of IDEA, please visit: http:// bit.ly/IDEA10EduDL.

Another point that I also keep repeating to my students is the idea that to become proficient at performing these CAATT audit tests, one must develop a thorough understanding and familiarity with not only the purpose of test but also the data to be used in conducting an audit test. As you look up various tests in the audit worksheet tables of each section, make sure to understand the purpose of each test and how the various CAATT expressions used for the test can help achieve its purpose. As mentioned before, the CAATT auditor must also understand what exact data – in terms of its content, range, currency, and relevancy – is needed to ensure meaningful results.

I could not possibly think about ending this introductory section without acknowledging the contributions of a number of individuals to the creation of this manual. First and foremost, a big thank you for the efforts of my former MISAM students for their research related to the various parts of this manual, namely, Anu Sudevan, Muhamed Sujjad, Khan Afsar, Anthoinette Nwaolisa, and Micheal Iroko Oluwatosin. Also, a special thank you to Athena Raypold for her editing services in converting the American Psychological Association (APA)-formatted research papers of the above-mentioned former MISAM students into a book manuscript format. I know this was probably not the most exciting editing project for a former English major, but she did an outstanding job at it. Last but not least, a special thank you to my esteemed colleagues Drs. Natasha Kinkahnina, Sergey Butakov, and Boby Swar in providing the extra research supervision needed to pull this project together.

I wish you all the very best in your auditing and/or fraud examination careers…

Shaun Aghili, DBA, CMA, CIA, CISA, CISSP, CFE
Associate Professor of Management
Concordia University of Edmonton, Alberta, Canada
Fall 2018

2

Compendium of CAATT-Based Audit Tests for the Detection of Asset Misappropriation (Cash and Inventory)

Introduction

To reiterate, according to the statistics derived from the 2018 Report to the Nations (RTTN), worldwide, organizations are losing over 5% of their revenue to occupational fraud each year – a loss that translates to over $7.1 trillion in 2018. As discussed in the introduction section, asset misappropriation accounted to around 7% of the 7 trillion losses attributed to occupational fraud for the banking and financial services sector and as much as 30% in the professional services sector [1]. Our research mapping of asset misappropriation (cash and inventory) fraud schemes to applicable audit tests reveal more than 100 audit tests and 43 internal controls.

Asset misappropriation is a type of occupational fraud where employees exploit the privileges their positions allow them to steal or misuse the organization's assets [2]. Employees perpetrate asset misappropriation fraud through cash or non-cash (inventory and all other assets) schemes. Cash schemes include skimming, cash larceny, and fraudulent disbursement. Non-cash schemes include misuse and non-cash larceny [3]. Because fraudulent disbursements is such a large category, this chapter focuses on all other asset misappropriation schemes, with fraudulent disbursements being covered in Chapter 3.

Case Histories

Asset misappropriation fraud's impact on victim organizations and society at large cannot be overemphasized given the widespread reports of huge economic losses. These schemes last for an average of eighteen (18) months before detection [4], and the longer the scheme lasts, the more losses it causes [1]. Virtually every organization loses revenue to asset misappropriation. This type of fraud happens all the time, with bigger losses reported in the news.

Nick's Roast Beef: Skimming

In 2017, Nicholas Koudanis and Nicholas Markos, co-owners of Nick's Roast Beef, along with Koudanis' wife and son were sentenced in U.S. federal court for skimming nearly $6 million in cash receipts from 2008 to 2013. The co-owners worked together to determine which funds they would skim and which they would deposit in the business' bank account. Together, the four skimmed $1 million in cash receipts per year, which they combined with false cash register receipts and using false financial statements to file income taxes. The Koudanis' accumulated $1.6 million in cash, which they kept in their home safe [5].

Calgary Transit: Theft of Cash on Hand

Former Calgary Transit employee, David John Hamilton, worked in fare collection services from 1984 to 2008 when he was fired and charged with theft over $5,000. Hamilton's job as a cash processor gave him daily access to coin payments from buses and ticket dispensers. His job was to sort, count, roll, and prepare cash for deposits. Hamilton grabbed coins off the conveyor belt, pocketed them, and then stashed them in his backpack, amassing over $375,000 of stolen cash from Calgary Transit (he likely stole more but that's the amount Calgary Transit could prove). Not only did Hamilton face criminal charges, but the City of Calgary also filed a civil suit to recover lost funds [6].

The City of Casper, Wyoming: Cash Larceny

Heather Kirkendall, former Casper employee, worked in the city's Community Development Division and Human Resources department from 2014 to 2017. During her time in the Community

Development department, Kirkendall sold permits. The city's Financial Service Director, Thomas Pitlick reviewed permit receipts and, from January to May of 2017, found 34 receipts for cash payments that weren't included in the deposits – Kirkendall was the employee who completed the paperwork and deposits. This discrepancy led to the City involving the Wyoming Division of Criminal Investigation (DCI) to review the receipt books and daily worksheets from December 2014 to October 2017. The DCI discovered 187 discrepancies between receipts issued and recorded (186 of which were cash payments) – in every instance, the employee that counted, signed, and sealed the deposit bag was Kirkendall – the discrepancies ended when she was transferred to Human Resources. Kirkendall has been charged with one count of cash larceny in the amount of $19,000 and faces up to 10 years in prison [7].

Discussion

The Association of Certified Fraud Examiners' (ACFE) 2018 RTTN survey estimates a 5% global loss of revenues to Occupational Fraud. The 2018 report is based on responses from 2,960 Certified Fraud Examiners in over 125 countries across the world, and the results affirm that asset misappropriation remains the most prevalent occupational fraud scheme, accounting for 89% of cases, with a median loss of $114,000 [1]. *The Corporate Fraud Handbook* indicates that 85.6% of cash misappropriation schemes have a median loss of $120,000. On the other hand, non-cash misappropriations amount to 20.3% of schemes with a median loss of $90,000 [8]. Similarly, another ACFE study disclosed that cash schemes are more prevalent than non-cash schemes [9]. Regardless, the longer the fraud schemes lasts, the greater the losses (Figure 2.1).

Asset Misappropriation Fraud Schemes (Cash and Inventory)

Cash Schemes

There are three types of cash schemes; in this chapter, we're only discussing skimming and larceny (fraudulent disbursement will be discussed in Chapter 3).

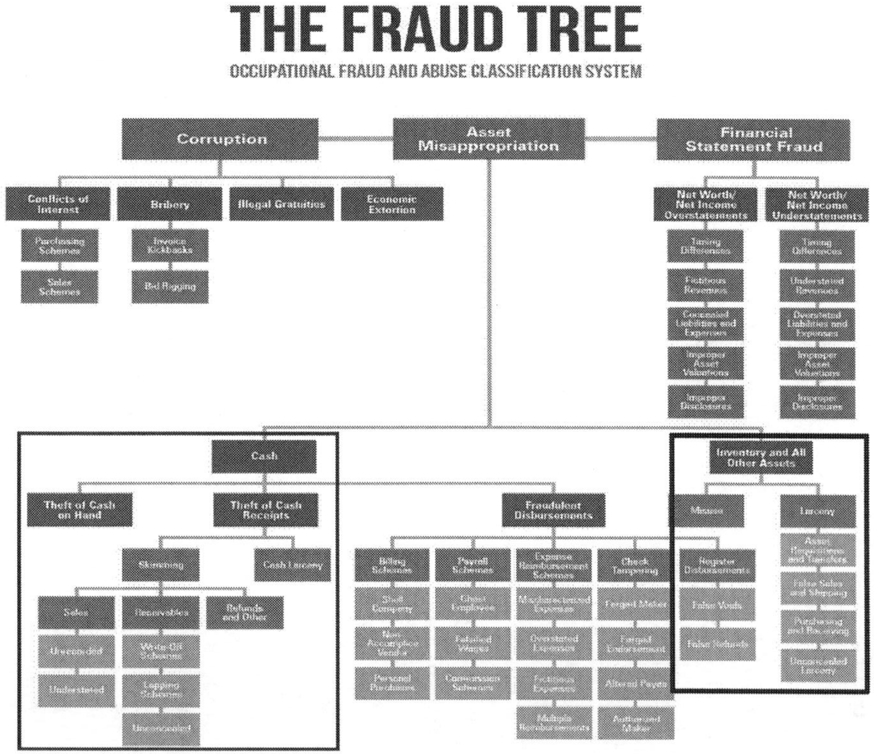

Figure 2.1 Asset misappropriation arm of the ACFE Fraud Tree depicting cash larceny, skimming, non-cash larceny schemes, and misuse. (Fraudulent disbursements is excluded and discussed in Chapter 3.)

Skimming   Often referred to as "off book fraud," skimming occurs when cash is stolen before it enters the accounting system; with no audit trail, it's difficult to detect that money has been stolen because there is no audit trail [10]. Skimming predominantly occurs in businesses where cash is accepted as a payment method [11].

Sales Skimming   Skimming is carried out by employees who take cash payments directly from customers for sales made or services rendered. There are two types of sales skimming: unrecorded and understated sales.

Unrecorded: Employees perpetrating unrecorded sales schemes collect payments from creditors but don't record the transactions in the books. Perpetrators can do this by manipulating the register, ringing a "no-sale," not issuing a receipt, destroying the store copy of the receipt, making sales during non-business hours, or by refraining from reporting off-site sales.

For example, a retail grocery store manager arrives at work by 7:00 am and opens the store (two hours before it's supposed to open at 9:00 am). The manager removes the register log, keeps the money from the sales made within those two hours, and destroys the register tape, leaving no trace of the transactions that occurred prior to store's official opening. The manager then starts at 9:00 am with a clean slate.

Understated: Employees perpetrating understated sales schemes record transactions at a value less than the actual collections. For example, an employee records sales at a discount (when no discount was actually given) and pockets the difference, or the employee prepares separate receipts for store records.

Skimming Receivables   When receivables are skimmed, the customer whose account was skimmed appears as delinquent in the company records. Skimming receivables schemes include write-offs, lapping, and unconcealed.

Write-Offs: To accomplish a write-off scheme, contra-accounts such as discounts, allowances, and bad debts expense accounts are used. For example, an employee authorized to write-off accounts could steal the incoming cheques from customers while making it appear as a write-off in the company's records. An employee could also intercept payments from a customer and then post the entries to a discount account, when no discount was actually granted to the customer.

Lapping: Employees running lapping schemes pocket received cash or cheques collected from one customer and cover up the payment with collections from another customer and so on. Figure 2.2 provides an example of a typical lapping scheme. Customer X's payment is pocketed by the accounts receivable clerk, and when Customer Y's payment is received, it replaces the payment for Customer X. Consequently, when Customer Z's payment is received, it replaces Customer Y's payment – this continues until the scheme is discovered.

Unconcealed: In unconcealed schemes, employees steal money without making any effort to conceal the theft.

Refunds and Others Refund schemes occur when an employee steals money from the register and rings in a refund, but no goods are actually returned. Another way to achieve this scheme is by overstating a legitimate refund and stealing the extra money [12].

Cash Larceny Cash larceny occurs when cash or cheques are stolen after the payment has been recorded in the books. It is an intentional

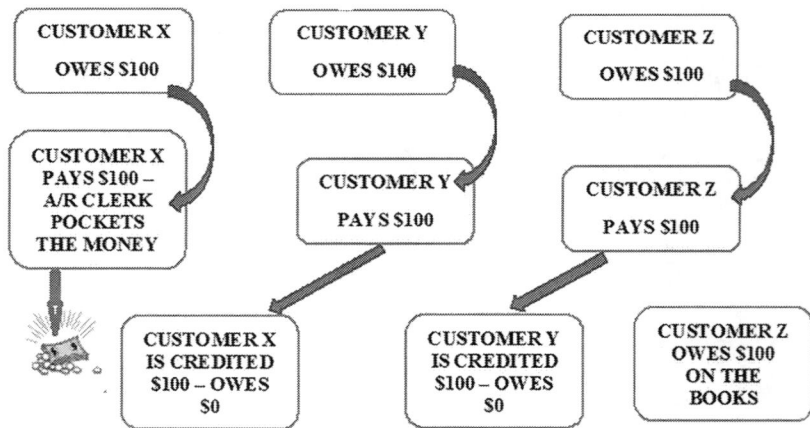

Figure 2.2 Lapping scheme illustrated. (*Source:* ACFE, 2011.)

removal of cash without an employer's consent or will. It includes theft of cash on hand, theft of cash from the deposits, and others [13].

Theft of Cash on Hand: Cash or cheque is stolen from safe deposits or from the vault which are still in the premises of the organization. For example, an employee steals cash from the register after ringing in a sale. Often, the employee may try to cover up his or her theft with a fraudulent disbursement scheme like a false refund or voided sale.

Theft of Cash from the Deposit (Theft of Cash Receipts): Cash or cheques already prepared for deposit to the bank are stolen while in transit before being deposited. For example, the closing employee prepares the deposit, takes money out of the bag, and alters the deposit slip to show a different amount.

Others: Depending on the type of business, an employee can devise various ways of stealing from the organization.

Inventory (and All Other Assets) Schemes

These schemes involve non-cash items such as company assets, confidential information, and inventory, which can be misused or stolen (non-cash larceny).

Misuse Nearly every organization provides assets to their employees for business use, for example, company vehicles, company phones, and company computers. These assets are misused when employees use them for personal reasons, for example, an employee who uses the company's vehicle to run a personal errand on company time or an employee who uses the company phone to make personal calls [14]. Another good example is an employee who uses company equipment to render the same kind of service to a client for personal gain. The company loses business to a competitor (the employee), and also loses money in terms of the company time used by the employee.

Non-Cash Larceny Non-cash larceny occurs when non-cash assets are stolen from an organization. Employees that perpetrate these schemes are typically those with direct access to inventory and supplies. Non-cash larceny is classified into the following subschemes: asset requisitions and transfers, false sales and shipping, purchasing and receiving, and unconcealed larceny.

> *Asset Requisitions and Transfers*: This scheme constitutes the falsification of documents from the organization to aid the theft of non-cash assets.
>
> *False Sales and Shipping*: For this scheme, the perpetrator sets up a fictitious address where goods are shipped to in order to steal the goods. The sales documents are usually destroyed to cover up this act. Another way to accomplish a false sales and shipping scheme is to have an outside accomplice who poses as a buyer. The employee will not ring up the sales but will have the goods delivered to the supposed buyer.
>
> *Purchasing and Receiving*: Purchasing and receiving schemes can be achieved by recording a shipment as a missing item and thereafter stealing the same item.
>
> *Unconcealed Larceny*: This scheme happens when an employee removes an asset from the organization without trying to conceal the absence of the stolen asset in the company's records. Unconcealed larceny results in an out-of-balance condition. Employees who commit unconcealed larceny are usually trusted employees who have unrestricted access to most areas of the business [8].

Conclusion Asset misappropriation remains the most prevalent type of occupational fraud. The ACFE's 2018 Report to the Nations on Occupational Fraud and Abuse's survey results estimated cash on hand, larceny, and skimming schemes at over 37% of all asset misappropriation cases, while non-cash schemes accounted for another 21%. Given that these schemes occur frequently, perpetrators can amass large sums of money or assets throughout each scheme's duration. As with all fraud, organizations with weak internal controls are at the highest risk of enduring asset misappropriation schemes [15]. Computer-Assisted Audit Tools and Techniques (CAATT) auditing, combined with work culture and internal controls, can mitigate these losses.

Recommended CAATT-Based Audit Tests

- The cash and inventory asset misappropriation fraud audit tests in this section address all of the schemes except for Fraudulent Disbursements.
- There are 105 CAATT-based audit tests for cash and inventory asset misappropriation fraud detection identified in our mapping:
  - 11 for Cash Larceny
  - 47 for Skimming
  - 39 for Non-cash Larceny
  - 8 for Misuse
- There are also 43 recommended internal controls for cash and inventory asset misappropriation schemes identified in this section:
  - 15 for Cash Larceny
  - 11 for Skimming
  - 12 for Non-cash Larceny
  - 5 for Misuse

Recommended Controls for Asset Misappropriation (Cash and Inventory) Fraud Risk Mitigation

1. Skimming	1. Customers are advised and encouraged to collect receipts for all payment forms.
	2. Sequentially numbered receipts and invoices are used for non-automated transactions.
	3. Every numbered receipt/invoice should be accounted for.
	4. The role of collecting process and depositing in the bank should be assigned to different employees.
	5. Daily deposits to the bank should be required.
	6. Remittances for products sold should match the remittances made by vendors for products purchased.
	7. Any adjustments to transactions should be investigated for repeated patterns by employee.
	8. Voids and no sale transactions should be investigated to ensure proper authorization and documentation.
	9. Write-offs should be properly authorized.

(Continued)

ACFE FRAUD TREE SUBCATEGORY	INTERNAL CONTROLS TO WATCH FOR DURING AN AUDIT PROCESS
	10. Exception reports should be mandated for any adjustments made to accounts receivables.
	11. Cash registers should be automated to ensure that every transaction is recorded and receipted.
2. Cash Larceny	1. Segregation of duties should be enforced. The roles of cash receipt and recording of cash should be separated.
	2. Cash registers should be closely located to discourage theft.
	3. Distinctive cash register access codes should be created for each employee.
	4. The roles of preparing deposit slips and taking the deposits to the bank should be separated.
	5. There should be an independent check for the tasks of cash receipt and recording of cash in the books.
	6. Ensure mail is opened in open space under clear view and supervision of management.
	7. Assign more than one employee to the job of opening and sorting daily mail.
	8. Install video surveillance cameras in areas where cash is handled.
	9. Conduct surprise cash counts.
	10. Employees should be mandated to use pre-numbered cash receipt forms to record all cash receipts.
	11. Mandatory vacations and job rotation should be enforced.
	12. Daily reconciliation between the total on cash receipt tapes and actual cash in each employee's till should be carried out at the end of the shift.
	13. All journal entries to the cash account should be checked regularly.
	14. Bank deposits should be verified against accounts receivable journal entries.
	15. Deposit slips should be made in triplicates and two copies should be left at the bank during a deposit. One of the copies should be stamped and returned to the organization periodically.
3. Non-cash Larceny	1. The job of requisition, receipt, disbursement, and conversion of inventory to scrap should all be performed by different employees.
	2. Shipment addresses should be matched against the address on the customer's file before any shipment is dispatched.
	3. Shipment address should be matched against employees' addresses.
	4. Unannounced inventory counts should be implemented.
	5. Every inventory shortage or shrinkage should be investigated.
	6. Delivery documents should be crosschecked with invoices before making payment to vendors.
	7. Amount on sales documents should match amount on payment voucher.

(Continued)

ACFE FRAUD TREE SUBCATEGORY	INTERNAL CONTROLS TO WATCH FOR DURING AN AUDIT PROCESS
	8. All equipment and inventories should be physically guarded.
	9. Only authorized employees should have access to inventory and equipment storage facilities.
	10. Access control logs should be implemented to determine which employee gained access to restricted areas, the purpose of their visit, and time of entry and departure from the restricted area.
	11. Authorized employees entering restricted areas should be monitored for departure from the norm.
	12. Security cameras should be installed in merchandise storage areas.
4. Misuse	1. Policies on what constitutes misuse of company assets (including time) should be enforced.
	2. Work schedules should be verified before authorizing request for use of company vehicles.
	3. Employee work schedules should be verified before travel claims are approved.
	4. Employee work schedules should be verified before wages are approved.
	5. Policies prohibiting an employee clocking in for another employee other than himself/herself should be enforced.

Audit Tests Worksheet Section

ACFE Fraud Tree Subcategory: Skimming schemes.

Purpose: To detect schemes related to unrecorded sales.

Audit Test Procedure: Report on gaps in the sequencing of invoices generated.

Explanation: To verify that all invoices generated are properly accounted for. Missing invoice numbers may be as a result of fraudulent transactions.

Assertion(s) Tested: Occurrence, Authorization, Accuracy, and Existence.

CAATT Expression: Gap.

Possible Red Flags: Missing invoice numbers.

ACFE Fraud Tree Subcategory: Skimming schemes.

Purpose: To detect schemes related to unrecorded sales.

Audit Test Procedure: Credits, receipts, and invoices not in proper sequence or range.

Explanation: To verify that all transactions are properly invoiced and appropriately matched to receipts.

Assertion(s) Tested: Occurrence, Authorization, Accuracy, and Existence.

CAATT Expression: Gaps or Sort.

Possible Red Flags: Missing receipt or invoice numbers.

ACFE Fraud Tree Subcategory: Skimming schemes.

Purpose: To detect schemes related to unrecorded sales.

Audit Test Procedure: Generate invoice summaries by customer or invoice amount.

Explanation: To verify that all invoices issued to customers are appropriately matched to payments.

Assertion(s) Tested: Occurrence and Existence.

CAATT Expression: Summarize.

Possible Red Flags: Missing invoices from account receivable ledger without record of payment.

ACFE Fraud Tree Subcategory: Skimming schemes.

Purpose: To detect schemes related to unrecorded sales.

Audit Test Procedure: Calculate average sales amounts by product, sales representative, or region.

Explanation: To verify that low sales generated by specific product are caused by other reasons not related to fraud.

Assertion(s) Tested: Occurrence and Existence.

CAATT Expression: Summarize and Expression/Equation.

Possible Red Flags: Lower revenue generation for specific product by employee or location compared to other employees or locations for the same product.

ACFE Fraud Tree Subcategory: Skimming schemes.

Purpose: To detect schemes related to unrecorded sales.

Audit Test Procedure: Calculate financial ratios, and changes, for sales/assets and debt/equity ratios.

Explanation: To monitor revenue generation by employee or region.

Assertion(s) Tested: Occurrence.

CAATT Expression: Expression/Equation.

Possible Red Flags: Lower revenue generation by employee or location in comparison with other employees or location.

ACFE Fraud Tree Subcategory: Skimming schemes.

Purpose: To detect schemes related to understated sales.

Audit Test Procedure: Calculate and compare variances in accounts between periods.

Explanation: To identify the reason for fluctuations in accounts for different periods.

Assertion(s) Tested: Accuracy and Completeness.

CAATT Expression: Summarize and Join/Relate.

Possible Red Flags: Unexplained variances in amounts generated in different accounting periods.

ACFE Fraud Tree Subcategory: Skimming schemes.

Purpose: To detect schemes related to understated sales.

Audit Test Procedure: Compare remittances to open receivables and report variances.

Explanation: To verify that remitted amounts tally with open receivables.

Assertion(s) Tested: Completeness and Accuracy.

CAATT Expression: Summarize.

Possible Red Flags: Inconsistency between amounts recorded as payments and corresponding expected open receivables.

ACFE Fraud Tree Subcategory: Skimming schemes.

Purpose: To detect schemes related to understated sales.

Audit Test Procedure: Generate sales and profitability reports by sales representative, product, and customer.

Explanation: To determine the contribution to revenue generation and profitability by employee, customer, and product.

Assertion(s) Tested: Occurrence and Accuracy.

CAATT Expression: Summarize.

Possible Red Flags: Lower revenue generation by employee or product in comparison with other employees for the same product.

ACFE Fraud Tree Subcategory: Skimming schemes.

Purpose: To detect schemes related to unrecorded sales.

Audit Test Procedure: Calculate sales by region, customer, and category.

Explanation: To determine the contribution to sales and revenue generation by employee, customer, and location.

Assertion(s) Tested: Occurrence, Completeness, and Accuracy.

CAATT Expression: Summarize.

Possible Red Flags: Lower revenue generation by customer with respect to past records.

ACFE Fraud Tree Subcategory: Skimming schemes.

Purpose: To detect schemes related to understated sales.

Audit Test Procedure: Compare current and previous periods to analyze sales trends.

Explanation: To identify the reason for fluctuations in sales for different periods.

Assertion(s) Tested: Accuracy, Occurrence, and Completeness.

CAATT Expression: Join/Relate.

Possible Red Flags: Considerable drop in targeted sales in comparison with previous periods.

ACFE Fraud Tree Subcategory: Skimming schemes.

Purpose: To detect schemes related to understated sales.

Audit Test Procedure: Summarize sales performance over time by product and sales representative.

Explanation: To identify the reason for consistent low sales by employee and product.

Assertion(s) Tested: Accuracy, Occurrence, and Completeness.

CAATT Expression: Expression/Equation and Trend Analysis.

Possible Red Flags: Considerable drop in targeted sales.

ACFE Fraud Tree Subcategory: Skimming schemes.

Purpose: To detect schemes related to understated sales.

Audit Test Procedure: Identify items selling for less than sales price.

Explanation: To verify why products are sold for amounts lower than indicated sales price.

Assertion(s) Tested: Accuracy, Authorization, and Completeness.

CAATT Expression: Filter/Display Criteria.

Possible Red Flags: Unexplained lowered prices for products.

ACFE Fraud Tree Subcategory: Skimming schemes.

Purpose: To detect schemes related to write-offs.

Audit Test Procedure: Identify bad debts and write-offs by customer or by department.

Explanation: To verify that write-offs of customer's account are a legitimate transaction and are properly authorized.

Assertion(s) Tested: Occurrence, Authorization, and Valuation.

CAATT Expression: Age and Summarize.

Possible Red Flags: Frequent write-offs of accounts by employee, customer, or location.

ACFE Fraud Tree Subcategory: Skimming schemes.

Purpose: To detect schemes related to write-offs.

Audit Test Procedure: Identify adjustments to discounts.

Explanation: To verify that adjustments made to discounts are genuine and properly authorized.

Assertion(s) Tested: Occurrence, Authorization, Valuation, Classification, and Completeness.

CAATT Expression: Filter/Display Criteria.

Possible Red Flags: Discounts granted on specific accounts greater than standard discount for that category.

ACFE Fraud Tree Subcategory: Skimming schemes.

Purpose: To detect schemes related to write-offs.

Audit Test Procedure: Examine bad debt account balances for increasing trends.

Explanation: To verify the reason for increasing trends in bad debt account balances.

Assertion(s) Tested: Occurrence and Authorization.

CAATT Expression: Join and Expression/Equation.

Possible Red Flags: Increasing trends in bad debt account balances.

ACFE Fraud Tree Subcategory: Skimming schemes.

Purpose: To detect schemes related to write-offs.

Audit Test Procedure: Identify large adjustments transactions.

Explanation: To verify that adjustments made to transactions are genuine and properly authorized. Adjustments could be as a result of trying to hide manipulations intended to cover up a fraud.

Assertion(s) Tested: Existence, Occurrence, and Authorization.

CAATT Expression: Filter/Display Criteria.

Possible Red Flags: Unexplained adjustments to transactions.

ACFE Fraud Tree Subcategory: Skimming schemes.

Purpose: To detect schemes related to write-offs.

Audit Test Procedure: Identify write-offs and bad debts.

Explanation: To verify that write-offs are properly authorized.

Assertion(s) Tested: Occurrence and Authorization.

CAATT Expression: Filter/Display Criteria.

Possible Red Flags: Frequent write-offs of accounts by employee or location.

ACFE Fraud Tree Subcategory: Skimming schemes.

Purpose: To detect schemes related to write-offs.

Audit Test Procedure: Calculate the number and value of write-offs and strike-offs by location.

Explanation: To verify that write-offs and strike-offs are properly authorized.

Assertion(s) Tested: Occurrence and Authorization.

CAATT Expression: Summarize.

Possible Red Flags: Frequent write-offs of accounts by employee or location.

ACFE Fraud Tree Subcategory: Skimming schemes.

Purpose: To detect schemes related to write-offs.

Audit Test Procedure: Identify write-offs and bankruptcies (by branch, by employee).

Explanation: To identify reasons for write-offs and their contribution to revenue generation. Also verify that write-offs are properly authorized.

Assertion(s) Tested: Occurrence, Authorization, Valuation, Classification, and Completeness.

CAATT Expression: Filter/Display Criteria and Summarize.

Possible Red Flags: Unusual write-off of loans that ought to have been paid by employee and location.

ACFE Fraud Tree Subcategory: Skimming schemes.

Purpose: To detect schemes related to lapping.

Audit Test Procedure: Generate confirmation letters to confirm customer balances.

Explanation: To verify the actual amount owed by customer.

Assertion(s) Tested: Existence and Occurrence.

CAATT Expression: Export and Mail Merge.

Possible Red Flags: Overdue account balances.

ACFE Fraud Tree Subcategory: Skimming schemes.

Purpose: To detect schemes related to lapping.

Audit Test Procedure: Calculate the days to payment by client, by sales representative, or by region, and calculate the carrying charges.

Explanation: To verify overdue accounts and to follow up on the collection process.

Assertion(s) Tested: Accuracy and Completeness.

CAATT Expression: Filter/Display Criteria and Summarize.

Possible Red Flags: Number of overdue uncollectible accounts exceeding the stipulated number allowed by credit policy.

ACFE Fraud Tree Subcategory: Skimming schemes.

Purpose: To detect schemes related to lapping.

Audit Test Procedure: Generate confirmation letters to verify customer payments.

Explanation: To verify the actual amount paid by customer.

Assertion(s) Tested: Existence and Occurrence.

CAATT Expression: Export and Mail Merge.

Possible Red Flags: Overdue account balances.

ACFE Fraud Tree Subcategory: Skimming schemes.

Purpose: To detect schemes related to lapping.

Audit Test Procedure: Highlight delinquent accounts by ranges of days aged.

Explanation: To verify that accounts that appear delinquent in the books have not already been collected.

Assertion(s) Tested: Occurrence, Valuation, Accuracy, and Completeness.

CAATT Expression: Filter/Display Criteria and Age.

Possible Red Flags: Increasing trends in the volume of delinquent accounts.

ACFE Fraud Tree Subcategory: Skimming schemes.

Purpose: To detect schemes related to lapping.

Audit Test Procedure: Identify loans where the terms were extended by more than the standard amounts.

Explanation: To verify that loans terms were properly authorized. Extension of loan terms could be an avenue to buy time to cover up lapping schemes.

Assertion(s) Tested: Occurrence, Authorization, Valuation, Accuracy, Classification, and Completeness.

CAATT Expression: Expression/Equation and Filter/Display Criteria.

Possible Red Flags: Unusual approvals outside regular authorized terms.

ACFE Fraud Tree Subcategory: Skimming schemes.

Purpose: To detect schemes related to lapping.

Audit Test Procedure: Calculation of late payment charges.

Explanation: To verify that customers' accounts that are overdue are properly billed for late payment. A customer that had already paid will likely complain about the billing for late payment charges.

Assertion(s) Tested: Occurrence, Existence, and Completeness.

CAATT Expression: Filter/Display Criteria and Expression/Equation.

Possible Red Flags: Communication from customers about receiving a reminder for a payment already made.

ACFE Fraud Tree Subcategory: Skimming schemes.

Purpose: To detect schemes related to unconcealed skimming.

Audit Test Procedure: Calculate the age and value of receivables by range of days (30, 60, 90, 120).

Explanation: To verify that customers' accounts that appear delinquent in the accounting records had not actually been paid. A follow-up on accounts that appear delinquent in the books (but may not be in reality) will result in customer complaint and merit further investigations.

Assertion(s) Tested: Occurrence, Existence, and Accuracy.

CAATT Expression: Age.

Possible Red Flags: Communication from customers about receiving a reminder for a payment already made.

ACFE Fraud Tree Subcategory: Skimming schemes.

Purpose: To detect schemes related to unconcealed skimming.

Audit Test Procedure: Calculate the average days from delivery of goods or services to billing date, to receipt of payment – by clerk and by customer.

Explanation: To verify prompt payments by customers within allowed credit period.

Assertion(s) Tested: Occurrence, Existence, and Accuracy.

CAATT Expression: Age and Summarize.

Possible Red Flags: Extended late payments by customer beyond allowed credit period.

ACFE Fraud Tree Subcategory: Skimming schemes.

Purpose: To detect schemes related to unconcealed skimming.

Audit Test Procedure: Calculate the days aged for receivables, by customer, to support contract negotiations.

Explanation: To verify customer's conformance to contractual agreement by making payments within allowed credit period.

Assertion(s) Tested: Occurrence, Existence, and Accuracy.

CAATT Expression: Age and Summarize.

Possible Red Flags: Extended late payments by customer beyond allowed credit period.

ACFE Fraud Tree Subcategory: Skimming schemes.

Purpose: To detect schemes related to unconcealed skimming.

Audit Test Procedure: Identify high-value credit notes, balances, and invoices – by customer and by clerk.

Explanation: To verify that credit notes issued by employee are genuine and properly authorized through the appropriate channel.

Assertion(s) Tested: Existence and Authorization.

CAATT Expression: Filter/Display Criteria.

Possible Red Flags: Unusual credit notes issued by employees.

ACFE Fraud Tree Subcategory: Skimming schemes.

Purpose: To detect schemes related to unconcealed skimming.

Audit Test Procedure: Identify high-value credit notes, balances, and invoices.

Explanation: To verify that credit notes issued by employee are genuine and properly authorized through the appropriate channel.

Assertion(s) Tested: Occurrence, Existence, and Accuracy.

CAATT Expression: Filter/Display Criteria.

Possible Red Flags: Unusually high-value credit notes and high balances by customer.

ACFE Fraud Tree Subcategory: Skimming schemes.

Purpose: To detect schemes related to unconcealed skimming.

Audit Test Procedure: Identify accounts with oldest activity for sales follow-up.

Explanation: To identify the reason for no activity in customer's account.

Assertion(s) Tested: Existence.

CAATT Expression: Age and Sort.

Possible Red Flags: Lack of activity for prolonged period in account belonging to regular customer.

ACFE Fraud Tree Subcategory: Skimming schemes.

Purpose: To detect schemes related to unconcealed skimming.

Audit Test Procedure: Identify credits/debits to dormant or unused accounts.

Explanation: To verify that dormant accounts are properly reactivated by following the appropriate procedures.

Assertion(s) Tested: Authorization.

CAATT Expression: Age and Expression/Equation.

Possible Red Flags: Sudden payments credited to dormant or unused accounts.

ACFE Fraud Tree Subcategory: Skimming schemes.

Purpose: To detect schemes related to unconcealed skimming.

Audit Test Procedure: Calculate defaulted loans or trade credit accounts (by branch, by employee).

Explanation: To verify the reason for defaults in loan/credit repayment. Confirm that outstanding amounts have not been already repaid.

Assertion(s) Tested: Completeness.

CAATT Expression: Summarize.

Possible Red Flags: Large volume of defaulted loan/credit repayments.

ACFE Fraud Tree Subcategory: Skimming schemes.

Purpose: To detect schemes related to unconcealed skimming.

Audit Test Procedure: Identify accounts past due, starting with the largest amounts.

Explanation: To ascertain reasons for accounts being past due and verify that the past due accounts have actually not been paid.

Assertion(s) Tested: Existence, Occurrence, and Completeness.

CAATT Expression: Age and Sort/Index.

Possible Red Flags: Increasing volume in the number of past due accounts.

ACFE Fraud Tree Subcategory: Skimming schemes.

Purpose: To detect schemes related to unconcealed skimming.

Audit Test Procedure: Identify dormant accounts.

Explanation: To verify reasons for accounts becoming dormant. A follow-up should be initiated to ascertain that accounts that appear dormant in the books are actually inactive.

Assertion(s) Tested: Authorization.

CAATT Expression: Filter/Display Criteria.

Possible Red Flags: Active accounts classified as dormant.

ACFE Fraud Tree Subcategory: Skimming schemes.

Purpose: To detect schemes related to unconcealed skimming.

Audit Test Procedure: Calculate the number and value of defaulted loans/trade credit balances by salespersons.

Explanation: To verify the reason for defaults in loan repayment. Confirm that loans have actually not been repaid.

Assertion(s) Tested: Completeness.

CAATT Expression: Summarize.

Possible Red Flags: High volume of defaulted loan repayments.

ACFE Fraud Tree Subcategory: Skimming schemes.

Purpose: To detect schemes related to refunds and others.

Audit Test Procedure: Identify credits given outside of management-approved discount terms.

Explanation: To verify the reasons for approval of discounts outside the stipulated terms. Also verify that all discounts are approved within stipulated terms.

Assertion(s) Tested: Authorization and Completeness.

CAATT Expression: Age and Filter/Display Criteria.

Possible Red Flags: Unusual discounts.

ACFE Fraud Tree Subcategory: Skimming schemes.

Purpose: To detect schemes related to refunds and others.

Audit Test Procedure: Compare year-to-date allowances to net sales by customer.

Explanation: To verify the contribution to net income generated by customers with high volume allowance. Allowances should be proportionate to volume of contribution made by customer's transactions and must be properly authorized.

Assertion(s) Tested: Accuracy, Authorization, and Completeness.

CAATT Expression: Summarize and Expression/Equation.

Possible Red Flags: Unusual allowances to customers with irregular transactions.

ACFE Fraud Tree Subcategory: Skimming schemes.

Purpose: To detect schemes related to refunds and others.

Audit Test Procedure: Identify cheques paid to more than one payee at the same address.

Explanation: To verify why more than one payee should have the same business address. The cheque payments could be going to a fraudulent employee or an accomplice.

Assertion(s) Tested: Occurrence and Existence.

CAATT Expression: Duplicates.

Possible Red Flags: Various cheques dispatched to the same address.

ACFE Fraud Tree Subcategory: Skimming schemes.

Purpose: To detect schemes related to refunds and others.

Audit Test Procedure: Compare the amount of allowances by store.

Explanation: To verify the reason behind high volume allowances by employee and location.

Assertion(s) Tested: Accuracy and Authorization.

CAATT Expression: Summarize.

Possible Red Flags: Unusual allowances by employee or location.

ACFE Fraud Tree Subcategory: Skimming schemes.

Purpose: To detect schemes related to refunds and others.

Audit Test Procedure: Identify duplicate return transactions.

Explanation: To verify that records exist for returned merchandise and that refunds are only given for items that are physically returned to the store.

Assertion(s) Tested: Existence, Occurrence, Completeness, and Accuracy.

CAATT Expression: Duplicates.

Possible Red Flags: Missing documentation for refund transactions.

ACFE Fraud Tree Subcategory: Skimming schemes.

Purpose: To detect schemes related to refunds and others.

Audit Test Procedure: Identify incomplete exchange transactions.

Explanation: To verify that records exist for exchanged merchandise and that items can only be exchanged when they are physically returned to the store.

Assertion(s) Tested: Existence, Occurrence, Completeness, and Accuracy.

CAATT Expression: Duplicates.

Possible Red Flags: Missing documentation for exchange transactions.

ACFE Fraud Tree Subcategory: Skimming schemes.

Purpose: To detect schemes related to refunds and others.

Audit Test Procedure: Identify price adjustments on returned merchandise (by department).

Explanation: To verify the reason for making price adjustments on returned merchandise. Any adjustments must be properly authorized.

Assertion(s) Tested: Existence, Occurrence, Authorization, and Accuracy.

CAATT Expression: Summarize.

Possible Red Flags: Improper documentation for price adjustments made on cash return transactions.

ACFE Fraud Tree Subcategory: Skimming schemes.

Purpose: To detect schemes related to refunds and others.

Audit Test Procedure: Identify credit card purchase and refund to different credit card.

Explanation: To verify why a transaction should be refunded to a credit card other than the one used for payment.

Assertion(s) Tested: Existence, Occurrence, Authorization, and Accuracy.

CAATT Expression: Expression/Equation and Summarize.

Possible Red Flags: Refunds to payment card other than the one used for original transaction.

ACFE Fraud Tree Subcategory: Skimming schemes.

Purpose: To detect schemes related to refunds and others.

Audit Test Procedure: Calculate the number and amount of refunds by clerk.

Explanation: To verify that refunds are genuine and properly documented and authorized.

Assertion(s) Tested: Existence, Occurrence, Authorization, and Accuracy.

CAATT Expression: Expression/Equation and Summarize.

Possible Red Flags: High volume of refunds by employee compared to other employees.

ACFE Fraud Tree Subcategory: Skimming schemes.

Purpose: To detect schemes related to refunds and others.

Audit Test Procedure: Identify refunds that are greater than selling price.

Explanation: To verify that refunds are genuine and properly documented and authorized.

Assertion(s) Tested: Existence, Occurrence, Authorization, and Accuracy.

CAATT Expression: Filter/Display Criteria.

Possible Red Flags: Refund value greater than selling price.

ACFE Fraud Tree Subcategory: Skimming schemes.

Purpose: To detect schemes related to refunds and others.

Audit Test Procedure: Identify claims for even amounts.

Explanation: To verify that expense claims submitted by employees are for actual official assignments and not merely falsified documents.

Assertion(s) Tested: Occurrence, Authorization, Accuracy, and Existence.

CAATT Expression: Filter/Display Criteria.

Possible Red Flags: Consistent even amounts submitted as expense claims by specific employee(s).

ACFE Fraud Tree Subcategory: Cash larceny schemes.

Purpose: To detect schemes related to theft of cash on hand.

Audit Test Procedure: Prepare trial balances and account reconciliation.

Explanation: To verify that for all ending balances in cash account, total debits equals total credits and also matches with the bank records. Ascertain that all receivables are properly recorded.

Assertion(s) Tested: Occurrence, Completeness, Accuracy, and Existence.

CAATT Expression: Summarize.

Possible Red Flags: Unbalanced journal entries. Difference between the total amount of debits and the total amount of credits.

ACFE Fraud Tree Subcategory: Cash larceny schemes.

Purpose: To detect schemes related to theft of cash on hand.

Audit Test Procedure: Comparison of no sale transaction to cash voided transaction (by clerk).

Explanation: To verify that voided transactions are due to legitimate errors. Void should be properly authorized.

Assertion(s) Tested: Occurrence, Accuracy, Authorization, and Existence.

CAATT Expression: Summarize.

Possible Red Flags: Frequent voided transactions by employee.

ACFE Fraud Tree Subcategory: Cash larceny schemes.

Purpose: To detect schemes related to theft of cash on hand.

Audit Test Procedure: Comparison of no sale transaction to cash voided transaction (by clerk).

Explanation: To verify that voided transactions are due to legitimate errors. Voids should be properly authorized.

Assertion(s) Tested: Occurrence, Accuracy, Authorization, and Existence.

CAATT Expression: Expression/Equation and Summarize.

Possible Red Flags: Frequent voided transactions by employee.

ACFE Fraud Tree Subcategory: Cash larceny schemes.

Purpose: To detect schemes related to theft of cash on hand.

Audit Test Procedure: Identify credit card purchase and cash refund.

Explanation: To verify that cash refunds are legitimate and properly authorized.

Assertion(s) Tested: Occurrence, Accuracy, Authorization, and Existence.

CAATT Expression: Expression/Equation and Summarize.

Possible Red Flags: Frequent cash refunds for credit card purchases by employee.

ACFE Fraud Tree Subcategory: Cash larceny schemes.

Purpose: To detect schemes related to theft of cash on hand.

Audit Test Procedure: Calculate the number and amount of voids by clerk.

Explanation: To verify that voided transactions are due to legitimate errors. Voids should be properly authorized.

Assertion(s) Tested: Occurrence, Accuracy, Authorization, and Existence.

CAATT Expression: Expression/Equation and Summarize.

Possible Red Flags: Frequent voided transactions by employee.

ACFE Fraud Tree Subcategory: Cash larceny schemes.

Purpose: To detect schemes related to theft of cash on hand.

Audit Test Procedure: Compare no sale to cash voided transactions by clerk.

Explanation: To verify that voided and no sale transaction occurring at the same time are due to legitimate errors. Voids should be properly authorized.

Assertion(s) Tested: Occurrence, Accuracy, Authorization, and Existence.

CAATT Expression: Expression/Equation and Summarize.

Possible Red Flags: No sale and cash voided transactions occurring at the same time by employee.

ACFE Fraud Tree Subcategory: Cash larceny schemes.

Purpose: To detect schemes related to theft of cash on hand.

Audit Test Procedure: Total cash disbursements by account, by bank, and by vendor.

Explanation: To verify that cash disbursements are legitimate and properly authorized.

Assertion(s) Tested: Occurrence, Accuracy, Authorization, and Existence.

CAATT Expression: Summarize.

Possible Red Flags: Unusual disbursements of cash by employee.

ACFE Fraud Tree Subcategory: Cash larceny schemes.

Purpose: To detect schemes related to theft of cash from the deposits.

Audit Test Procedure: Examine amounts "in transit" to bank deposits for increasing trends.

Explanation: To verify and confirm that "deposits in transit" are accounted for and truly exist.

Assertion(s) Tested: Occurrence, Authorization, Accuracy, and Completeness.

CAATT Expression: Join and Expression/Equation.

Possible Red Flags: Increasing trend of "deposit in transit" during bank reconciliations compared to normal transaction.

ACFE Fraud Tree Subcategory: Cash larceny schemes.

Purpose: To detect schemes related to theft of cash from the deposits.

Audit Test Procedure: Arrange accounts by account number – check first and last accounts.

Explanation: To verify all cheque payments that have been deposited to the company's account. Also verify that all deposits presumably made are reflected in the accounts.

Assertion(s) Tested: Existence, Occurrence, Classification, and Completeness.

CAATT Expression: Sort/Index.

Possible Red Flags: Inconsistencies between deposited cheque amounts and bank balances.

ACFE Fraud Tree Subcategory: Cash larceny schemes.

Purpose: To detect schemes related to theft of cash from the deposits.

Audit Test Procedure: Identify accounts with continual overdrafts or dormant activity.

Explanation: To verify reasons for accounts becoming dormant. A follow-up should be initiated to ascertain that accounts that appear dormant in the books are actually dormant.

Assertion(s) Tested: Occurrence and Existence.

CAATT Expression: Age and Filter/Display Criteria.

Possible Red Flags: Active accounts suddenly classified as dormant.

ACFE Fraud Tree Subcategory: Cash larceny schemes.

Purpose: To detect schemes related to theft of cash from the deposits.

Audit Test Procedure: Identify high-dollar cheque requests.

Explanation: To verify that high-dollar cheque requests are for legitimate transactions.

Assertion(s) Tested: Occurrence and Completeness.

CAATT Expression: Filter/Display Criteria.

Possible Red Flags: Frequent request of high-dollar cheques by employee.

ACFE Fraud Tree Subcategory: Non-cash larceny schemes.

Purpose: To detect schemes related to asset requisitions and transfers.

Audit Test Procedure: Calculate inventory reordering volumes by item, by warehouse, or by vendor.

Explanation: To verify adequate documentation is put in place for ordering and reordering of inventory. Proper authorization channels should also be adhered to.

Assertion(s) Tested: Occurrence, Authorization, and Existence.

CAATT Expression: Filter/Display Criteria.

Possible Red Flags: Missing documentation for inventory reorder.

ACFE Fraud Tree Subcategory: Non-cash larceny schemes.

Purpose: To detect schemes related to asset requisitions and transfers.

Audit Test Procedure: Calculate the turnover to determine usage and ordering efficiencies.

Explanation: To determine the contribution of a product to revenue generation and net income in comparison with the cost of acquiring the product. A fraudulent employee could falsify documents to aid the stealing of a product, thereby causing the product to run out regularly.

Assertion(s) Tested: Occurrence.

CAATT Expression: Age.

Possible Red Flags: Frequent request for reordering of a product that does not generate targeted income.

ACFE Fraud Tree Subcategory: Non-cash larceny schemes.

Purpose: To detect schemes related to asset requisitions and transfers.

Audit Test Procedure: Calculate the turnover by stock class and/or item.

Explanation: To determine the contribution of a product to revenue generation and net income in comparison with the cost of acquiring the product. A fraudulent employee could falsify documents to aid the stealing of a product, thereby causing the product to run out regularly.

Assertion(s) Tested: Occurrence.

CAATT Expression: Expression/Equation.

Possible Red Flags: Frequent request for reordering of a product that does not generate targeted income.

ACFE Fraud Tree Subcategory: Non-cash larceny schemes.

Purpose: To detect schemes related to asset requisitions and transfers.

Audit Test Procedure: Identify duplicate vendor numbers on vendor master file.

Explanation: To verify duplication of vendor number in order to rule out errors. Every vendor should be uniquely identified by their vendor number. A fraudulent employee could manipulate the vendor master file in order to steal inventories.

Assertion(s) Tested: Existence.

CAATT Expression: Duplicates.

Possible Red Flags: Duplicate vendor numbers.

ACFE Fraud Tree Subcategory: Non-cash larceny schemes.

Purpose: To detect schemes related to asset requisitions and transfers.

Audit Test Procedure: Identify vendors with more than one vendor number.

Explanation: To verify duplication of vendor number in order to rule out errors. Every vendor should be uniquely identified by their vendor number. A fraudulent employee could manipulate the vendor master file in order to steal inventories.

Assertion(s) Tested: Existence.

CAATT Expression: Duplicates.

Possible Red Flags: Duplicate vendor numbers.

ACFE Fraud Tree Subcategory: Non-cash larceny schemes.

Purpose: To detect schemes related to asset requisitions and transfers.

Audit Test Procedure: Identify vendors with names spelled or sounding similar to well-known vendors (e.g. FedEx, UPS, USPS).

Explanation: To verify that vendor names similar to well-known vendors are genuine and truly belong to a legitimate vendor. A fraudulent employee could open an account similar to well-known vendors doing business with the company in order to aid theft.

Assertion(s) Tested: Existence.

CAATT Expression: Soundslike() and Filter/Display Criteria.

Possible Red Flags: Similarity between vendor's name and well-known vendors.

ACFE Fraud Tree Subcategory: Non-cash larceny schemes.

Purpose: To detect schemes related to false sales and shipping.

Audit Test Procedure: Test for duplicate parts or descriptions.

Explanation: To verify any form of duplication in vendor documentation.

Assertion(s) Tested: Existence.

CAATT Expression: Duplicates.

Possible Red Flags: Duplicate documents.

ACFE Fraud Tree Subcategory: Non-cash larceny schemes.

Purpose: To detect schemes related to false sales and shipping.

Audit Test Procedure: Identify variances between delivery documents and contracted amounts.

Explanation: To verify that the amounts on the delivery documents match the amounts approved for payment. A fraudulent employee could lower the amounts on the receiving log and reverse the figures before it gets clearance from the accounts payable, such that the accomplice vendor is paid more.

Assertion(s) Tested: Occurrence, Authorization, Accuracy, and Existence.

CAATT Expression: Join/Relate and Filter/Display Criteria.

Possible Red Flags: Irregularities between figures on delivery documents and vendor's ledger.

ACFE Fraud Tree Subcategory: Non-cash larceny schemes.

Purpose: To detect schemes related to false sales and shipping.

Audit Test Procedure: Identify unusual delivery addresses.

Explanation: To verify that goods are delivered only to invoice addresses matching laid out criteria.

Assertion(s) Tested: Accuracy and Existence.

CAATT Expression: Summarize and Filter/Display Criteria.

Possible Red Flags: Unusual addresses violating specified criteria for addresses, for example, P.O. box addresses.

ACFE Fraud Tree Subcategory: Non-cash larceny schemes.

Purpose: To detect schemes related to false sales and shipping.

Audit Test Procedure: Match delivery addresses with employees' addresses.

Explanation: To verify that goods are not shipped to an address belonging to employees.

Assertion(s) Tested: Accuracy and Existence.

CAATT Expression: Join/Relate.

Possible Red Flags: Addresses matching employee address. Shipping documents not properly authorized through the regular channels.

ACFE Fraud Tree Subcategory: Non-cash larceny schemes.

Purpose: To detect schemes related to false sales and shipping.

Audit Test Procedure: Identify duplicate invoices, credits, or receipts.

Explanation: To verify that invoices, credits, or receipts are genuine.

Assertion(s) Tested: Existence.

CAATT Expression: Duplicates.

Possible Red Flags: Duplicate documents.

ACFE Fraud Tree Subcategory: Non-cash larceny schemes.

Purpose: To detect schemes related to false sales and shipping.

Audit Test Procedure: Variances between delivery documents and invoices.

Explanation: To verify that delivery documents are genuine and properly authorized.

Assertion(s) Tested: Authorization and Existence.

CAATT Expression: Join and Expression/Equations.

Possible Red Flags: Irregularities between delivery documents and invoice.

ACFE Fraud Tree Subcategory: Non-cash larceny schemes.

Purpose: To detect schemes related to false sales and shipping.

Audit Test Procedure: Identify customer accounts with no address or telephone information.

Explanation: To verify that goods are shipped to actual customers. A fraudulent employee could create a fictitious shipping document without an address. The presumed customer, who is an accomplice of the fraudulent employee, picks up the goods.

Assertion(s) Tested: Occurrence, Authorization, and Existence.

CAATT Expression: Expression/Equation.

Possible Red Flags: Customer accounts that have no address or telephone information.

ACFE Fraud Tree Subcategory: Non-cash larceny schemes.

Purpose: To detect schemes related to false sales and shipping.

Audit Test Procedure: Identify vendor records where address changes are frequent.

Explanation: To verify that goods are shipped to actual customers. A fraudulent employee could create a fictitious shipping document with varying addresses. The presumed customer, who is an accomplice of the fraudulent employee, picks up the goods.

Assertion(s) Tested: Existence and Occurrence.

CAATT Expression: Summarize.

Possible Red Flags: Frequent address changes by vendors.

ACFE Fraud Tree Subcategory: Non-cash larceny schemes.

Purpose: To detect schemes related to false sales and shipping.

Audit Test Procedure: Match vendor and employee names, addresses, and phone numbers.

Explanation: To verify that goods are not shipped to addresses belonging to employees.

Assertion(s) Tested: Existence and Occurrence.

CAATT Expression: Join/Relate.

Possible Red Flags: Vendor address matching employee address.

ACFE Fraud Tree Subcategory: Non-cash larceny schemes.

Purpose: To detect schemes related to false sales and shipping.

Audit Test Procedure: Match vendor and company phone numbers.

Explanation: To verify that contact information of vendor does not match that of any employee of the company or the company itself. Any matches should be properly investigated.

Assertion(s) Tested: Existence and Occurrence.

CAATT Expression: Summarize.

Possible Red Flags: Contact phone number in vendor's file matching company's phone number.

ACFE Fraud Tree Subcategory: Non-cash larceny schemes.

Purpose: To detect schemes related to purchasing and receiving.

Audit Test Procedure: Verify price compliance.

Explanation: To verify that customers are appropriately billed for goods sold. A fraudulent employee could manipulate sales documents and alter prices of goods purchased by an accomplice, hence having the accomplice payless.

Assertion(s) Tested: Occurrence, Authorization, Accuracy, and Existence.

CAATT Expression: Filter/Display Criteria.

Possible Red Flags: Discrepancies between prices on sales document and payment voucher.

ACFE Fraud Tree Subcategory: Non-cash larceny schemes.

Purpose: To detect schemes related to purchasing and receiving.

Audit Test Procedure: Report high-value items purchased by buyer.

Explanation: To verify that items are not purchased at inflated prices. The comparison should be made between the same items purchased by another employee in another location.

Assertion(s) Tested: Occurrence, Authorization, Accuracy, and Existence.

CAATT Expression: Filter/Display Criteria.

Possible Red Flags: Unusually high price for purchases by employee and location.

ACFE Fraud Tree Subcategory: Non-cash larceny schemes.

Purpose: To detect schemes related to purchasing and receiving.

Audit Test Procedure: Match stock receipts with vendor ledger and report variances.

Explanation: To verify that the received stock agrees with quantity and amount stated in the vendor's ledger.

Assertion(s) Tested: Occurrence, Authorization, Accuracy, and Existence.

CAATT Expression: Join/Relate and Expression/Equation.

Possible Red Flags: Disparity in received stock and vendor's ledger.

ACFE Fraud Tree Subcategory: Non-cash larceny schemes.

Purpose: To detect schemes related to purchasing and receiving.

Audit Test Procedure: Comparison of vendor and employee addresses and phone numbers.

Explanation: To verify that vendor contact information does not match any employee information.

Assertion(s) Tested: Occurrence, Authorization, and Existence.

CAATT Expression: Join/Relate.

Possible Red Flags: Vendor contact information matching an employee address.

ACFE Fraud Tree Subcategory: Non-cash larceny schemes.

Purpose: To detect schemes related to purchasing and receiving.

Audit Test Procedure: Total purchases by ordering clerk, by vendor.

Explanation: To verify that employee responsible for purchases does not include items intended for personal use in the company records. Also check to verify that items are purchased based on requirements.

Assertion(s) Tested: Occurrence, Authorization, and Existence.

CAATT Expression: Summarize.

Possible Red Flags: Shortage in received items.

ACFE Fraud Tree Subcategory: Non-cash larceny schemes.

Purpose: To detect schemes related to purchasing and receiving.

Audit Test Procedure: Check for purchasing more than required:
- Project requirements to contract
- Inventory remaining at end of project
- Order greater than quantity received

Explanation: To verify that employee responsible for purchases does not include items intended for personal use in the company records. Also check to verify that items are purchased based on requirements.

Assertion(s) Tested: Occurrence, Authorization, and Existence.

CAATT Expression: Join/Relate and Expression/Equation.

Possible Red Flags: Shortage in received items.

ACFE Fraud Tree Subcategory: Non-cash larceny schemes.

Purpose: To detect schemes related to purchasing and receiving.

Audit Test Procedure: Total number, and value, of contracts by contracting officer by vendor (bid rotation not followed).

Explanation: To verify that no particular vendor is favored over other vendors.

Assertion(s) Tested: Occurrence, Authorization, and Existence.

CAATT Expression: Summarize.

Possible Red Flags: A vendor seemingly favored over others gets more than usual contracts.

ACFE Fraud Tree Subcategory: Non-cash larceny schemes.

Purpose: To detect schemes related to purchasing and receiving.

Audit Test Procedure: Summarize large invoices without purchase orders (by vendor).

Explanation: To verify that proper documentation guidelines are adhered to for all purchases made. All invoices should be matched to a purchase order.

Assertion(s) Tested: Completeness and Existence.

CAATT Expression: Filter/Display Criteria and Expression/Equation.

Possible Red Flags: Irregular documentation for large amount invoices.

ACFE Fraud Tree Subcategory: Non-cash larceny schemes.

Purpose: To detect schemes related to purchasing and receiving.

Audit Test Procedure: Compare voucher or invoice amounts to purchase order or contract amounts.

Explanation: To verify that the amount on the invoice matches the amounts stipulated in the contract.

Assertion(s) Tested: Occurrence, Authorization, Accuracy, and Existence.

CAATT Expression: Join/Relate.

Possible Red Flags: Irregularities between invoice amount and contract amount.

ACFE Fraud Tree Subcategory: Non-cash larceny schemes.

Purpose: To detect schemes related to purchasing and receiving.

Audit Test Procedure: Isolate distributions to accounts not in suppliers' account ledger.

Explanation: To verify payments for purchased goods made to accounts that are not in the suppliers' account ledger. This could give a hint that something may be amiss and therefore prompt further investigations.

Assertion(s) Tested: Occurrence, Existence, and Completeness.

CAATT Expression: Join/Relate.

Possible Red Flags: Supplier details not found in supplier master list.

ACFE Fraud Tree Subcategory: Non-cash larceny schemes.

Purpose: To detect schemes related to unconcealed larceny.

Audit Test Procedure: Identify cheques issued to vendors with names that sound like known vendors.

Explanation: To verify that payments are only made to genuine vendors. A fraudulent employee could create a fictitious vendor account name similar to a genuine existing vendor and steal the cheque(s) thereafter.

Assertion(s) Tested: Occurrence, Authorization, and Existence.

CAATT Expression: Soundslike().

Possible Red Flags: Irregularities in documentation for purchases by employee or vendor.

ACFE Fraud Tree Subcategory: Non-cash larceny schemes.

Purpose: To detect schemes related to purchasing and receiving.

Audit Test Procedure: Total inferior goods (percentage returns by vendor).

Explanation: To verify that no particular supplier is favored over other vendors.

Assertion(s) Tested: Accuracy and Existence.

CAATT Expression: Summarize.

Possible Red Flags: Complaints from customers regarding lowered quality of goods sold.

ACFE Fraud Tree Subcategory: Non-cash larceny schemes.

Purpose: To detect schemes related to purchasing and receiving.

Audit Test Procedure: Check for purchases of more expensive items than required.

Explanation: To verify that items are not purchased at inflated prices. The comparison should be made between the same items purchased by another employee in another location.

Assertion(s) Tested: Occurrence and Authorization.

CAATT Expression: Summarize.

Possible Red Flags: Unusually high price for purchases by employee and location.

ACFE Fraud Tree Subcategory: Non-cash larceny schemes.

Purpose: To detect schemes related to purchasing and receiving.

Audit Test Procedure: Identify orders received without purchase order or contract.

Explanation: To verify that the items purchased match the items listed in the purchase order or contract.

Assertion(s) Tested: Occurrence, Authorization, Accuracy, and Existence.

CAATT Expression: Join/Relate.

Possible Red Flags: Irregular documentation for purchases.

ACFE Fraud Tree Subcategory: Non-cash larceny schemes.

Purpose: To detect schemes related to purchasing and receiving.

Audit Test Procedure: Identify duplicate purchase order numbers.

Explanation: To verify that purchase order numbers are not duplicated.

Assertion(s) Tested: Occurrence, Authorization, Accuracy, and Existence.

CAATT Expression: Duplicates.

Possible Red Flags: Irregular documentation for purchases by employee.

ACFE Fraud Tree Subcategory: Non-cash larceny schemes.

Purpose: To detect schemes related to purchasing and receiving.

Audit Test Procedure: Analyze overages and shortages (by vendor and by receiving clerk).

Explanation: To verify that purchased items are received in full and match the items listed in the purchase order or contract. Also verify that the items received match the items listed in the purchase order.

Assertion(s) Tested: Occurrence, Authorization, Accuracy, and Existence.

CAATT Expression: Expression/Equation and Summarize.

Possible Red Flags: Frequent shortages or overages while receiving purchased items by employee.

ACFE Fraud Tree Subcategory: Non-cash larceny schemes.

Purpose: To detect schemes related to purchasing and receiving.

Audit Test Procedure: Compare the items ordered to the items canceled (by employee).

Explanation: To verify that the items purchased match the items listed in the purchase order or contract.

Assertion(s) Tested: Occurrence, Authorization, Accuracy, and Existence.

CAATT Expression: Expression/Equation and Summarize.

Possible Red Flags: Frequent cancellation of orders.

ACFE Fraud Tree Subcategory: Non-cash larceny schemes.

Purpose: To detect schemes related to purchasing and receiving.

Audit Test Procedure: Reconcile receipts by comparing accrued payables to received items.

Explanation: To verify that the purchased items are received in full before payments are made.

Assertion(s) Tested: Occurrence, Authorization, Accuracy, and Existence.

CAATT Expression: Join/Relate.

Possible Red Flags: Irregularities in documentation.

ACFE Fraud Tree Subcategory: Non-cash larceny schemes.

Purpose: To detect schemes related to unconcealed larceny.

Audit Test Procedure: Compare physical stock count with computed stock counts.

Explanation: To verify that the items listed in the records are physically present. A stolen item may still be showing as available in the records. A physical stock count will reveal the actual state of inventory.

Assertion(s) Tested: Accuracy and Existence.

CAATT Expression: Summarize and Extract.

Possible Red Flags: Disparity between physical inventory count and computed records.

ACFE Fraud Tree Subcategory: Non-cash larceny schemes.

Purpose: To detect schemes related to unconcealed larceny.

Audit Test Procedure: Select items from perpetual stock for reconciliation.

Explanation: To verify that the items listed in the records are physically present. A stolen item may still be showing as available in the records. A physical stock count will reveal the actual state of inventory.

Assertion(s) Tested: Accuracy and Existence.

CAATT Expression: Sample.

Possible Red Flags: Disparity between physical inventory count and computed records.

ACFE Fraud Tree Subcategory: Non-cash larceny schemes.

Purpose: To detect schemes related to unconcealed larceny.

Audit Test Procedure: Reconcile physical stock levels to computed amounts.

Explanation: To verify that the items listed in the records are physically present. A stolen item may still be showing as available in the records. A physical stock count will reveal the actual state of inventory.

Assertion(s) Tested: Accuracy and Existence.

CAATT Expression: Sample.

Possible Red Flags: Disparity between physical inventory count and computed records.

ACFE Fraud Tree Subcategory: Non-cash larceny schemes.

Purpose: To detect schemes related to unconcealed larceny.

Audit Test Procedure: Compare the value of physical inventory to general ledger amounts.

Explanation: To verify that the value of items listed in the records agrees with the value of the items physically present.

Assertion(s) Tested: Accuracy and Existence.

CAATT Expression: Join/Relate.

Possible Red Flags: Disparity between the total value of physically counted items and the total value of computed records.

ACFE Fraud Tree Subcategory: Non-cash larceny schemes.

Purpose: To detect schemes related to unconcealed larceny.

Audit Test Procedure: Calculate (inventory items received minus items sold plus returns) and compare to inventory on hand.

Explanation: To verify that the items listed in the records are physically present. A stolen item may still be showing as available in the records. A physical stock count will reveal the actual state of inventory.

Assertion(s) Tested: Accuracy and Existence.

CAATT Expression: Expression/Equation.

Possible Red Flags: Disparity between the total value of physically counted items and the total value of computed records.

ACFE Fraud Tree Subcategory: Misuse schemes.

Purpose: To detect schemes related to misuse.

Audit Test Procedure: Calculate the stock turnover by item.

Explanation: To verify that inventory items that are regularly replenished are not being misused by employees.

Assertion(s) Tested: Completeness and Accuracy.

CAATT Expression: Age.

Possible Red Flags: Consistent request for replenishment of inventory item that does not generate high revenue by product and location.

ACFE Fraud Tree Subcategory: Misuse schemes.

Purpose: To detect schemes related to misuse.

Audit Test Procedure: Compare arrival and service times for field service representative.

Explanation: To verify that employees are actually using company time to carry out official duties and not using company time for personal business. To verify the actual time spent in an off-site location.

Assertion(s) Tested: Occurrence.

CAATT Expression: Expression/Equation.

Possible Red Flags: Employee absence at off-site location during an unannounced visit.

ACFE Fraud Tree Subcategory: Misuse schemes.

Purpose: To detect schemes related to misuse.

Audit Test Procedure: Calculate service call costs for labor, materials, and transportation by representative.

Explanation: To verify that employees are actually using company time to carry out official duties and not using company time for personal business. To verify that the actual time spent in an off-site location and the materials utilized for assigned job are within the range stipulated in the contract.

Assertion(s) Tested: Occurrence.

CAATT Expression: Summarize and Expression/Equation.

Possible Red Flags: Excessive use of materials to accomplish a task compared to employees in other locations.

ACFE Fraud Tree Subcategory: Misuse schemes.

Purpose: To detect schemes related to misuse.

Audit Test Procedure: Compare reported service time to time card hours from payroll.

Explanation: To verify that employees are actually using company time to carry out official duties and not using company time for personal business.

Assertion(s) Tested: Occurrence.

CAATT Expression: Join/Relate.

Possible Red Flags: Employee absence at off-site location during an unannounced visit.

ACFE Fraud Tree Subcategory: Misuse schemes.

Purpose: To detect schemes related to misuse.

Audit Test Procedure: Total material usage by work order and compare to plans to identify misused materials.

Explanation: To verify that the materials utilized for assigned job are within the range stipulated in the contract.

Assertion(s) Tested: Occurrence.

CAATT Expression: Summarize.

Possible Red Flags: Excessive use of materials to accomplish a task compared to employees in other locations.

ACFE Fraud Tree Subcategory: Misuse schemes.

Purpose: To detect schemes related to misuse.

Audit Test Procedure: Compare part requirements on contract with parts used on job.

Explanation: To verify that the materials utilized for assigned job are within the range stipulated in the contract.

Assertion(s) Tested: Occurrence.

CAATT Expression: Join/Relate.

Possible Red-flags: Employee absence at off-site location during an unannounced visit.

ACFE Fraud Tree Subcategory: Misuse schemes.

Purpose: To detect schemes related to misuse.

Audit Test Procedure: Identify duplicate time card or employee costs.

Explanation: To verify that the times entered by employees are the actual times worked.

Assertion(s) Tested: Occurrence.

CAATT Expression: Duplicates.

Possible Red Flags: High volume of hours worked and overtime entries by employee.

ACFE Fraud Tree Subcategory: Misuse schemes.
Purpose: To detect schemes related to misuse.
Audit Test Procedure: Compare completed work order quantities to materials ordered for the project.
Explanation: To verify that the materials utilized for assigned job are within the range stipulated in the contract.
Assertion(s) Tested: Occurrence.
CAATT Expression: Filter/Display Criteria and Expression/Equation.
Possible Red Flags: Excessive use of materials to accomplish a task compared to employees in other locations performing the same job assignment.

References

1. Association of Certified Fraud Examiners. (2018). Report to the Nations on Occupational Fraud and Abuse. Retrieved from https://s3-us-west-2.amazonaws.com/acfepublic/2018-report-to-the-nations.pdf
2. International Auditing and Assurance Standards Board (IAASB). (2010). International Standards of Auditing (ISA 240). Retrieved from www.ifac.org/system/files/downloads/a012-2010-iaasb-handbook-isa-240.pdf
3. Kranacher, M. J., Riley, R. A., & Wells, J. T. (2011). *Forensic Accounting and Fraud Examination*. Hoboken, NJ: John Wiley & Sons.
4. Tackett, J. A. (2013, May/June). Association rules for fraud detection. *The Journal of Corporate Accounting & Finance, 24*(4), 15–22.
5. United States Department of Justice. U.S. Attorney's Office, District of Massachusetts. (2017, April 26). Press Release: "Co-Owner of Nick's Roast Beef Sentenced for Skimming Nearly $6 Million in Cash." Retrieved from www.justice.gov/usao-ma/pr/co-owner-nick-s-roast-beef-sentenced-skimming-nearly-6-million-cash
6. Calgary Herald. (2008, June 20). City Suing Worker Who Stole $375,000. Retrieved from www.pressreader.com/canada/calgary-herald/20080620/281968898442800
7. K2 Radio. (2018, February 2). Former Casper City Employee Pleads Not Guilty to Stealing $19,000. Retrieved from http://k2radio.com/former-casper-city-employee-pleads-not-guilty-to-stealing-19000/
8. Wells, J. T. (2011). *Corporate Fraud Handbook: Prevention and Detection* (3rd Edition). Hoboken, NJ: John Wiley & Sons.
9. Association of Certified Fraud Examiners. (2014). *Fighting Fraud in the Government*. Austin, TX: ACFE.
10. Association of Certified Fraud Examiners. (2015). *Fraud Examiner Manual*. Austin, TX: ACFE.
11. Gee, S. (2014). *Fraud and Fraud Detection: A Data Analytics Approach*. Hoboken, NJ: Wiley Corporate F&A.
12. Telford, L. (2016). Tis the Season - for Fraud. The Fraud Examiner. Retrieved from www.acfe.com/fraud-examiner.aspx?id=4294970618

13. Andre, S., Pennington, A., & Smith, B. L. (2014). Fraud education: A module-based approach for all business majors. *Business Education & Accreditation*, 6(1), 81–94.

14. Albrecht, W. S., Albrecht, C. O., Albrecht, C. C., & Zimbleman, M. F. (2011). *Fraud Examination*. Boston, MA: Cengage Learning.

15. Albrecht, C., Kranacher, M.-J., & Albrecht, W. S. (2008). Asset Misappropriation Research White Paper for the Institute for Fraud Prevention. *The Institute for Fraud Prevention*. Retrieved from www.theifp.org/research-grants/IFP-Whitepaper-5.pdf

3

ASSET MISAPPROPRIATION II – FRAUDULENT DISBURSEMENTS

Introduction

As discussed in Chapter 2, asset misappropriation fraud occurs in a vast majority of reported fraud cases (89%), most of which are classified as fraudulent disbursements. Fraudulent disbursements are one of three ways a fraudster can misappropriate cash (the other two are discussed in Chapter 2 and include cash larceny and skimming); all fraudulent disbursement schemes are on-book schemes, which means funds leave the organization but are recorded in the books (which also creates a trail) [1]. Research mapping asset misappropriation (fraudulent disbursements) fraud schemes to applicable audit tests, testing management assertions, and applicable Computer-Assisted Audit Tools and Techniques (CAATT) expressions, as well as internal controls and associated red flags reveal more than 90 audit tests and more than 30 recommended internal controls.

Asset misappropriation is a type of occupational fraud where employees abuse their positions to steal or misuse company's assets [2]. Divided into cash or non-cash schemes, asset misappropriation encompasses fraud involving both asset types (e.g., inventory, supplies, vehicles, or information) and cash (including cheques). Fraudulent disbursement is a category of cash schemes which is broken down into five types of schemes: billing schemes, payroll schemes, expense reimbursement schemes, cheque tampering, and register disbursements. Because fraudulent disbursements cover so many schemes, this chapter focuses on it exclusively.

Case Histories

The Report to the Nations (RTTN) surveys seem to indicate that fraud-related issues involving asset misappropriations are further exacerbated by low detection rates: only 15% for internal audits and a mere 4% for external audits. Proactive detection methods, including a continual internal fraud auditing program, are essential in catching fraud as quickly as possible and thus minimizing the losses associated with it. Year after year, the survey results for the Association of Certified Fraud Examiners' (ACFE) RTTN clearly suggest that the longer frauds continue unnoticed, the more costly the losses. Among fraudulent disbursement schemes, billing and cheque tampering schemes pose the greatest risk due its frequency and subsequent losses; however, payroll schemes and expense reimbursement schemes occur just as frequently as billing and cheque tampering. Smaller organizations (<100 employees) fall victim to cheque tampering and payroll schemes twice as much as larger organizations. Fraudulent disbursement schemes occur most frequently in manufacturing, health care, education, non-profits, and government industries. Lastly, these schemes tend to be perpetrated by upper management and employees in accounting and finance departments [3].

Sheraton University Hotel

From 2008 to 2013, both the general manager and a chief engineer employed at the Sheraton University Hotel in Philadelphia used a billing scheme to misappropriate funds from their employer. The fraudsters amassed more than $3 million by creating a shell company called Cold Wash Zone LLC and using it to produce nearly 49 fake invoices for services that were never provided to the Sheraton University Hotel [4].

PACE Worldwide

For 7 years (2002–2009), Paul and Sandra Dunham were the executives for PACE Worldwide, which had offices in Maryland and North Carolina, as well as a division in Europe called PACE Europe Ltd. Both executives used an expense reimbursement scheme to steal $1 million using fictitious receipts, as well as submitting invoices for personal expenditures. The husband and wife team also made claims for reimbursement to PACE Europe Ltd. for business-related expenditures which were already paid by PACE Worldwide (dual reimbursements) according to the Federal Bureau of Investigation [5].

GMC Global

In 2014, a human resource executive, Jaslyn Chen Xiaohong, used a payroll scheme (falsifying payment instructions) in combination with asset misuse, larceny, and forgery that resulted in her employer depositing about $920,000 into her bank account over a period of 20 months. Xiaohong was ultimately charged with 29 counts of crimes and sentenced to 6 years in jail. Police were only able to recover about $207,246 [6].

Citizens Bank

A customer at a Providence branch of Citizens Bank noticed unauthorized transfers between his bank accounts along with cheques he didn't cash in June 2017. After he reported it, detectives discovered that a bank employee, Shantel Meza, was copying customer information and moving money into chequing accounts while her criminal partners (Monica Dossantos, Kareem Barros, Cindy Quiroa, and Jamal Mansaray) created and cashed counterfeit cheques with values up to $12,600. The team of five people, two of which were convicted felons, worked together to devise and perpetrate the scheme which police say stole hundreds of thousands from Citizens Bank customers [7].

Kilroy's Wonder Market

In Glen Rock, New Jersey, an employee of Kilroy's Wonder Market, Erin Marciniak, stole nearly $18,000 with a false refund scheme (register disbursement). Marciniak falsely entered items as returned and refunded and pocketed the cash herself. By the time the store's management noticed that the returned items were not in the inventory, they investigated and contacted police. The police investigation determined, through surveillance video, that Marciniak stole about $12,000 between January 2017 and March 2018 [8].

Discussion

Asset misappropriation fraud isn't just the most common fraud on its own (57%), but it's also commonly paired with corruption (23%) in addition to coupling with financial statement fraud (4%) or a combination of all three types (3%) [3]. On-book schemes, fraudulent disbursement schemes pay for activities which have no requirement and are never accomplished to add value to the organization [9].

The Impact of Asset Misappropriation Fraud

As discussed in Chapter 2, occupation fraud accounts for about 5% of lost global revenues, with asset misappropriation schemes remaining the most ubiquitous. Within asset misappropriation, fraudulent disbursement schemes such as billing, expense reimbursement schemes, and cheque tampering are the most frequent [3]. In most cases, 40%–50% of targeted companies aren't able to recover lost funds money from asset misappropriation perpetrators [10]. However, since fraudulent disbursements are on-book schemes, an audit trail exists [11] (Figure 3.1).

Asset Misappropriation Fraud Schemes (Fraudulent Disbursements)

Billing Schemes

A billing scheme targets a company's purchasing function by "buying" nonexistent, overpriced, or unnecessary goods and services. Primarily, the purpose of a billing scheme is to amass cash, resulting in an illicit gain to the perpetrator [11]. There are three billing schemes:

> *Shell Company*: An entity (typically no more than a name and P.O. Box) created by an employee (and accomplices) to commit fraud. Usually, the company's owner is listed as someone other than the employee such as a spouse, friend, or fictitious person. Employees running billing schemes can authorize purchases, approve purchase payments, and supervise employees who authorize or pay invoices. A shell company billing scheme usually relies on overbilling or false billing where the shell company is paid for goods or services that

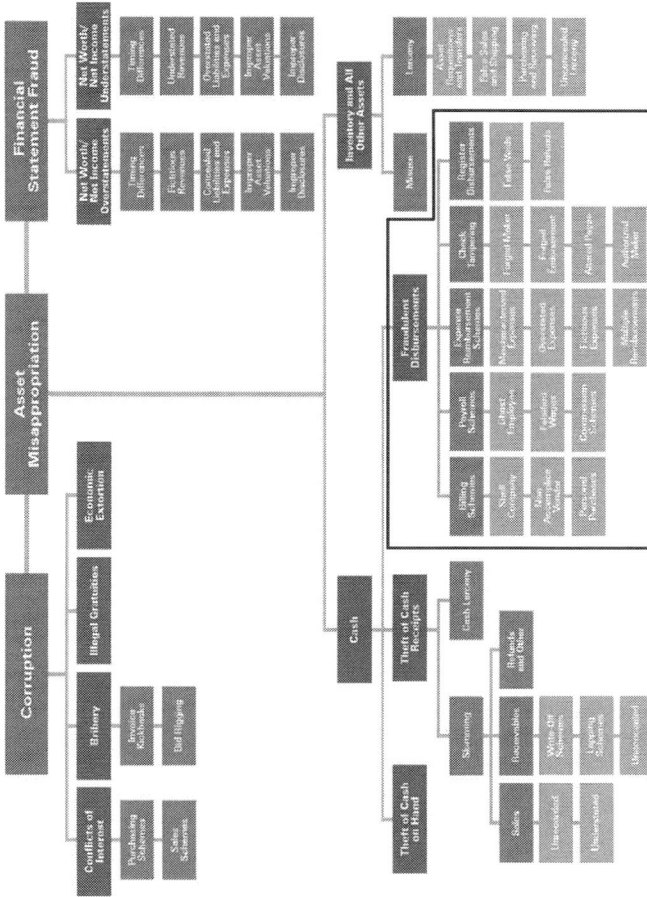

Figure 3.1 Visual graphic of Fraudulent Disbursement scheme. (*Source:* mukhsonrofi.wordpress.com, 2013.)

were never received. To minimize detection, the fraudster opens a bank account in the shell company's name to receive payments [12].

Non-accomplice Vendor: This scheme involves paying a legitimate seller twice, overpaying a legitimate seller, or making payment to the wrong seller. In each situation the returned cheques are intercepted and cashed by the perpetrator for his personal benefit [13].

Personal Purchases: With this scheme, an employee purchases items through the company for personal use, for example, tools, computers, parts, or supplies. Sometimes, fraudsters purchase these items through the company and resell them for financial gain [14].

Expense Reimbursement Schemes

A common target for fraud are travel and expense budgets. Perpetrators can falsify information by mischaracterizing receipts as business expenses, overstating business expenses, creating fictitous expenses, or submitting the same expense multiple times.

Mischaracterized Expenses: Here, an employee provides personal receipts for reimbursement by the organization [15].

Overstated Expenses: This scheme happens when an employee inflates the actual business expenses, for example, altered receipts, overpurchasing and overstating another employee's expenses [16].

Fictitious Expenses: To commit this scheme, the perpetrator submits an expense claim for an invented item which is fictitious and needs to be reimbursed [9].

Multiple Reimbursements: For this scheme, an employee submits the same claim repeatedly to obtain reimbursement numerous times [15].

Payroll Schemes

Payroll schemes happen when an employee fraudulently receives over-compensation. Like billing schemes, the overcompensation occurs as the result of false documentation: payroll records, timekeeping, or other payroll functions [11].

Ghost Employee: A ghost employee is someone, either real or fictitious, who doesn't actually work for the organization. The fraudster or accomplice sets the ghost employee up in the human resources, timekeeping, and payroll systems so that falsified record can be created to generate paycheques, which are then reallocated to the fraudsters. If the ghost employee is a real person, that individual is "hired" by the fraudster and paid but not actually working there [17].

Falsified Wages: This scheme is an overpayment of wages by fraudulently inflating hours worked, salary, or wages [18]. Fraudsters might overstate hours worked on time-cards, or payroll personnel manipulate pay rates or hours worked. In some cases, fraudsters will even pay themselves bonuses [19].

Commission Schemes: To enact this scheme, an employee misrepresents their sales figure or enhances their commission rate. Fraudsters may create false sales amounts by generating fictitious sales, altering sales, or converting the sales of others [20].

Workers Compensation Schemes: These schemes involve an employee fraudulently recceiving disability-related payments from the organization when there is no injury [21].

Register Disbursement Schemes

When a customer returns an item to a store, the transactions are either processed as refunds or voids. Register disbursement schemes occur when an employee fraudulently refunds or voids transactions in order to take the refund. With these schemes, the refunds are recorded, showing the money was disbursed from the register to the customer. This type of fraud is a cross between cash theft and fraudulent disbursements, but because they are recorded on the register, leaving an audit trail, it's classified as fraudulent disbursement instead of a cash larceny scheme [11].

False Refund: A false refund occurs when a fraudster enters a return into the register, but no merchandise has actually been returned. Then they refund the dollar amount of the supposed merchandise to themselves.

False Void: In false void schemes, the perpetrator uses a buyer's receipt to void a sale and takes money from the register as if the money was given back to the buyer [13].

Cheque Tampering

A more direct form of fraud, cheque tampering schemes occur when a fraudster enters false information on a company cheque to illegally obtain funds. This type of fraud is dependent upon access to company checkbooks, bank statements, and forging signatures – and it's committed by those who see a weakness in the company's cheque writing process and choose to exploit it [11].

Forged Maker Scheme: Involves an employee without signatory power in an organization who misuses a company cheque by forging the signature of an approved signer [9].

Forged Endorsement Scheme: This scheme is committed by an employee who diverts an organization's cheque meant for a third party and cashes it by signing the third party's name, or signing his name as another endorsee [16].

Altered Payee Scheme: To committ this scheme, an employee diverts a third-party cheque and changes the recipient's designation by inserting his name or another's name making it possible for the perpetrator or his partner to cash the cheque [9].

Concealed Check Scheme: When a fraudulent cheque is submitted along with a stack of other genuine cheques to a manager for signature, this scheme occurs. Absent a proper cheque by verification, the signing authority may sign the fraudulent cheque [9].

Authorized Maker Scheme: This scheme involves a person with approval power in an organization who makes and writes fake cheques for personal benefit [16].

Conclusion

Most asset misappropriation fraud cases tend to fall under fraudulent disbursement schemes, but internal and external audits combined contributed to just 19% of fraud detection [3]. Given the median duration of these schemes, together with their frequency, organizations lose a significant amount of revenue to these schemes – losses they're not likely to recover. As per the fraud triangle, occupational fraudsters must have a financial need, perceived opportunity, and rationalization to commit fraud. Internal controls can remove fraudsters' perceived opportunity, making detection the most powerful factor in fraud prevention and loss mitigation.

Recommended CAATT-Based Audit Tests

- Asset misappropriation (fraudulent disbursements) fraud audit tests address all of the schemes in this category.
- There are a total of 92 CAATT-based audit tests identified for fraudulent disbursements fraud detection:
  - 32 for Billing schemes
  - 18 for Expense Reimbursement schemes
  - 32 for Payroll schemes
  - 10 for Register Disbursement schemes
  - 0 for Cheque Tampering*
- There are 36 recommended internal controls for fraudulent disbursements fraud:
  - 11 for Billing schemes
  - 9 for Expense Reimbursement schemes
  - 9 for Payroll schemes
  - 7 for Register Disbursement schemes
  - 0 for Cheque Tampering*

*Given CAATT-based auditing technologies' current limitations in reading scanned documents (e.g., .pdf or .jpeg files), physical inspections of cheques offer a better means of detecting cheque tampering or alteration schemes. Such non-CAATT-based techniques for fraud detection includes a close inspection of physical security controls such as watermarks, void pantographs, chemical voids (chemicals used to make changes to check), high-resolution micro printing, reflective holograms, and security inks. Furthermore, responsibilities involved in check approval, preparation, and signing must be segregated.

Recommended Controls for Asset Misappropriation (Fraudulent Disbursements) Fraud Risk Mitigation

ACFE FRAUD TREE SUBCATEGORY	INTERNAL CONTROLS TO WATCH FOR DURING AN AUDIT PROCESS
1. Billing schemes	1. Liability must be entered in the books and cash disbursements must be completed after a comparison check of seller invoice, delivery documents, and procurement details.
	2. For all vendor companies, conduct a background check by checking the directory and verifying the validity of those with just a P.O. box address or company names that are initials.
	3. Purchasing duties, accounting duties, invoice handling, and payments to vendor must be segregated and performed by different personnel.
	4. Check for the matching of worker and seller addresses by authorized personnel before adding new sellers to company records.
	5. Cash disbursements to sellers must only be made after verifying the source document for the purchase order and invoice details, and after obtaining approval from a manager or department head.
	6. Cheque disbursements must not be completed for sellers who have either P.O. Box addresses or no street address in the company records.
	7. There must be an enterprise approved business partner list (suppliers and clients) that is regularly updated. All trade credit sales and purchases must be conducted with a company revised and approved business partner.
	8. Purchases must be made only after obtaining the approval from manager or department head.
	9. Purchase orders must contain a detailed explanation about the goods purchased, date, time, quantity, price, etc.
	10. Purchase and sales invoices and supporting documentation should contain a detailed information about the items purchased or sold, quantities, unit prices, and dates of the transactions.
	11. Smaller invoices from a seller (below the authorization limit) must be checked against original source documents before making a cash disbursement.

(Continued)

ACFE FRAUD TREE SUBCATEGORY	INTERNAL CONTROLS TO WATCH FOR DURING AN AUDIT PROCESS
2. Expense Reimbursement schemes	1. Before reimbursing employees, employee work days or hours must be cross referenced with vacation, sick leave, or days off in the calendar.
	2. Before reimbursing employees, original receipts must be submitted by employees.
	3. The original copy of business travel receipts submitted by employees must contain a detailed description of the total costs incurred for the business travel along with dates, times, places and total money spent.
	4. Organization credit card must be used instead of personal credit card for business expenses.
	5. Set time frames for expense reimbursement schemes to avoid multiple reimbursement claims by employees.
	6. Manager or department head must check the number of reimbursements made to employees. Source documents for multiple smaller reimbursement (below the minimum approval limit) may also need to be analyzed.
	7. Organization credit card statements must contain an explanation of the items purchased and costs incurred by the employee when making a reimbursement claim.
	8. Additional scrutiny is warranted if business purchases are done using a personal credit card or if personal credit card billing details are submitted.
	9. Every employee must have expense reimbursement schemes approved by respective department heads.
3. Payroll schemes	1. Different individuals should handle various HR functions, such as payroll generation, time sheet preparation, payment, and pay cheque delivery functions.
	2. Before making commission-related payments, check for linear relation between sales and commission earned by employees.
	3. A review must be done for the commission amounts due and method used to calculate commissions before making the payments to employees.
	4. Workers must be hired by the HR department after checking educational details, employment history, and other documentations against submitted resumes.
	5. Payroll file must be analyzed for name, hours, and rate of pay for workers before making payments.
	6. There must be an activity log for changes made to organization records by employees.

(*Continued*)

ACFE FRAUD TREE SUBCATEGORY	INTERNAL CONTROLS TO WATCH FOR DURING AN AUDIT PROCESS
	7. When making overtime-related payments to employees, the source documents must be checked and approval must be obtained from a manager or department head before processing.
	8. Employees who leave the organization must be removed from the payroll records immediately, and new employees must be added to the payroll list at the respective dates with approvals from the manager or department head.
	9. After obtaining approval from manager or department head for time sheets, these must be sent to payroll. Computerized time sheets must be made "read only" after approval.
4. Register Disbursement schemes	1. There should be different individuals responsible for inventory counting, cash register handling, and calculating total register sales.
	2. Register tapes must be reviewed to check if all the transactions are properly arranged and an analysis must be done for credit transactions.
	3. Manager approval must be required for refunds.
	4. In order to cancel or void employee sales, manager authorization must be made compulsory.
	5. Proper documentation details must be maintained for refund and void transactions.
	6. Horizontal analysis must be performed on gross sales, refunds, and voids to check for any deviations in trends or variations in the transactions.
	7. Manager approval is required before processing duplicate refunds or voids within the threshold range.

Audit Tests Worksheet Section

ACFE Fraud Tree Subcategory: Billing schemes.

Purpose: To detect schemes related to shell companies.

Audit Test Procedure: Summarize large invoices without purchase orders (by vendor).

Explanation: Large invoices without any purchase orders might be issued by employees themselves on behalf of shell companies to perpetrate fraud. Summarizing large invoices without any purchase orders helps to determine the validity of the transactions which are of higher amounts. If the transaction has taken place without obtaining proper approval by a manager or department head, then it may indicate a shell company scheme.

Assertion(s) Tested: Occurrence and Authorization.

CAATT Expression: Filter/Display Criteria and Expression/Equation.

Possible Red Flags:
- Purchases done without obtaining approval from the manager or department head.
- Presence of large invoices without any purchase orders in the organization's records.

ACFE Fraud Tree Subcategory: Billing schemes.

Purpose: To detect schemes related to shell companies.

Audit Test Procedure: Identify duplicate purchase order numbers, credits, and invoices.

Explanation: Duplication of purchase order number, credits, and invoice transactions can be recorded to perpetrate a shell company scheme. If the transactions are recorded without checking the related documents, then duplication can be done by employees to perpetrate fraud. Also, if the same employee is handling various duties in an organization, then duplicate transactions can be recorded to perpetrate shell company schemes.

Assertion(s) Tested: Occurrence.

CAATT Expression: Duplicates.

Possible Red Flags:
- Liability entered in the books without doing a comparison of seller invoice, delivery documents, and procurement details.
- Same person handling the purchasing duties, accounting duties, invoice handling, and vendor payments.
- Presence of duplicate purchase order numbers, credits, and invoices in the organization records.

ACFE Fraud Tree Subcategory: Billing schemes.

Purpose: To detect schemes related to shell companies.

Audit Test Procedure: Identify checks issued to vendors with names that sound like known vendors.

Explanation: In a shell company scheme, an employee can fabricate phoney vendor names similar to real vendors in order to generate a cheque and avoid suspicion. This happens due to fictitious vendors in the organization's records without obtaining approval from a manager or department head.

Assertion(s) Tested: Occurrence and Authorization.

CAATT Expression: Soundslike().

Possible Red Flags:
- Manager or department head authorization not necessary before adding new suppliers to company records.
- Organization not keeping a list of authorized sellers.
- Unusual suppliers (with identical names) present in company's records.
- Supplier information missing in the database such as contact number and taxpayer ID details.

ACFE Fraud Tree Subcategory: Billing schemes.

Purpose: To detect schemes related to shell companies.

Audit Test Procedure: Identify high-value credit notes, balances, and invoices.

Explanation: Large invoices might be issued by employees themselves on behalf of shell companies to perpetrate fraud. Transactions which are of higher amounts, like large invoices, must be reviewed to check the validity. If the transaction has taken place without obtaining proper approval from a manager or department head, then it may indicate a shell company scheme.

Assertion(s) Tested: Occurrence and Authorization.

CAATT Expression: Filter/Display Criteria.

Possible Red Flags:
- Purchases done without obtaining approval from the manager or department head.
- Presence of large invoices without any purchase orders in organization records.

ACFE Fraud Tree Subcategory: Billing schemes.

Purpose: To detect schemes related to shell companies.

Audit Test Procedure: Summarize invoice amounts by account.

Explanation: Summarizing invoice amounts by account helps in detecting vendors with larger deviations in activity compared to other vendor companies. Shell companies will have purchases which will be different compared to genuine sellers and an analysis of the purchases can detect fraud.

Assertion(s) Tested: Occurrence.

CAATT Expression: Summarize and Sort.

Possible Red Flags:
- Organization makes frequent buying from a single supplier compared to others.
- Organization is receiving many invoices from a supplier in a month.

ACFE Fraud Tree Subcategory: Billing schemes.

Purpose: To detect schemes related to shell companies.

Audit Test Procedure: Identify instances where one clerk has processed all the invoices for the account.

Explanation: If a particular clerk processes all invoices for an account and the organization does not have duties segregated, then shell company schemes can be perpetrated. An employee working in purchase department can manipulate records in accounting, receiving, or shipping divisions to conceal shell company fraud. If a particular clerk processes all the invoices for an account which belongs to a shell company, then the employee may try to conceal the deviation in activity for shell company.

Assertion(s) Tested: Occurrence.

CAATT Expression: Cross Tab/Pivot Table.

Possible Red Flags:
- Same person handling the purchasing duties, accounting duties, invoice handling, and vendor payments.
- Organization is frequently buying from a single supplier compared to others.
- Organization is receiving many invoices from a supplier in a month.

ACFE Fraud Tree Subcategory: Billing schemes.

Purpose: To detect schemes related to shell companies.

Audit Test Procedure: Identify duplicate purchase order numbers.

Explanation: Duplication of purchase order numbers can be recorded to perpetrate shell company schemes. If the transactions are recorded without checking the related documents, then duplication can be done by employees to perpetrate fraud. Also, if the same employee is handling various duties in an organization, then duplicate transactions can be recorded to perpetrate shell company schemes.

Assertion(s) Tested: Occurrence.

CAATT Expression: Duplicates.

Possible Red Flags:
- Liability entered in the books without doing a comparison of seller invoice, delivery documents, and procurement details.
- Same person handling the purchasing duties, accounting duties, invoice handling, and vendor payments.
- Presence of many identical purchase orders in organization records.

ACFE Fraud Tree Subcategory: Billing schemes.

Purpose: To detect schemes related to shell companies.

Audit Test Procedure: Comparison of vendor and employee addresses and phone numbers.

Explanation: An employee and vendor cannot have exactly the same address or phone number in an organization's records. Presence of similar addresses or phone numbers for both employee and vendor indicates an employee adding fictitious vendors to company records without obtaining approval from a manager or department head.

Assertion(s) Tested: Occurrence and Authorization.

CAATT Expression: Join/Relate.

Possible Red Flags:
- Supplier and employee share the same address or phone number in the organization's records.
- Manager or department head authorization not necessary before adding new suppliers to company records.
- Organization not keeping a list of authorized sellers.
- Supplier information missing in the database (e.g., contact number, taxpayer ID details).

ACFE Fraud Tree Subcategory: Billing schemes.

Purpose: To detect schemes related to shell companies.

Audit Test Procedure: Identify duplicate vendor numbers on vendor master file.

Explanation: Each vendor must have a unique vendor number in the organization's records. Duplication of vendor numbers can be done by employees to add shell companies in the records. Employee could add fictitious vendors with duplicate vendor number to company records without obtaining approval from manager or department head to perpetrate shell company scheme.

Assertion(s) Tested: Occurrence and Authorization.

CAATT Expression: Duplicates.

Possible Red Flags:
- Manager or department head authorization not necessary before adding new suppliers to company records.
- Organization not keeping a list of authorized sellers.
- Presence of dual vendor numbers in the organization's records.

ACFE Fraud Tree Subcategory: Billing schemes.

Purpose: To detect schemes related to shell companies.

Audit Test Procedure: Identify vendors with more than one vendor number.

Explanation: Each vendor must have a unique vendor number in the records. Presence of vendors with more than one vendor number may indicate fraud. Additional numbers for the same vendor may indicate fraud.

Assertion(s) Tested: Occurrence and Authorization.

CAATT Expression: Duplicates.

Possible Red Flags:
- Manager or department head authorization not necessary before adding new suppliers to company records.
- Organization not keeping a list of authorized sellers.
- Presence of dual vendor numbers in organization records.

ACFE Fraud Tree Subcategory: Billing schemes.

Purpose: To detect schemes related to shell companies.

Audit Test Procedure: Identify vendors with P.O. Box addresses.

Explanation: To perpetrate a shell company scheme, employee could add phoney vendors with just P.O. Box address to company records in order to avoid easy detection without obtaining approval from manager or department head. Presence of vendor with just P.O. Box address could be an indication of shell company.

Assertion(s) Tested: Occurrence and Authorization.

CAATT Expression: Filter/Display Criteria.

Possible Red Flags:
- Presence of suppliers with only P.O. box details in organization records.
- Manager or department head authorization not necessary before adding new suppliers to company records.
- Organization not keeping a list of authorized sellers.
- Supplier information missing in the database such as contact number and taxpayer ID details.

ACFE Fraud Tree Subcategory: Billing schemes.

Purpose: To detect schemes related to shell companies.

Audit Test Procedure: Identify vendors with names spelled or sounding similar to well-known vendors (e.g., FedEx, UPS, USPS).

Explanation: In a shell company scheme, employee can fabricate phoney vendor names spelled or sounding similar to well-known vendors in order to generate a cheque and avoid suspicion.

Assertion(s) Tested: Occurrence and Authorization.

CAATT Expression: Soundslike() and Filter/Display Criteria.

Possible Red Flags:
- Manager or department head authorization not necessary before adding new suppliers to company records.
- Organization not keeping a list of authorized sellers.
- Unusual suppliers (with identical names) present in company's records.
- Supplier information missing in the database such as contact number and taxpayer ID.

ACFE Fraud Tree Subcategory: Billing schemes.

Purpose: To detect schemes related to shell companies.

Audit Test Procedure: Match vendor and employee names, addresses, and phone numbers.

Explanation: Employee and vendor details must be distinct, any similarities found may indicate false vendors. Fictitious vendors can be added to organization records by employees without obtaining approval from manager or department head to perpetrate shell company scheme. If there is a similarity of employee information with vendor, then it may indicate a shell company.

Assertion(s) Tested: Occurrence and Authorization.

CAATT Expression: Join/Relate.

Possible Red Flags:
- Unusual suppliers (with identical names) present in company's records.
- Manager or department head authorization not necessary before adding new suppliers to company records.
- Organization not keeping a list of authorized sellers.
- Supplier and employee with same address or phone number present in the organization records.
- Supplier information missing in the database such as contact number and taxpayer ID.

ACFE Fraud Tree Subcategory: Billing schemes.

Purpose: To detect schemes related to shell companies.

Audit Test Procedure: Identify vendor with significant changes in activity (increase or decrease).

Explanation: Vendors with larger deviations in activity compared to other vendors may indicate a fictitious vendor created by employee. Shell companies will have purchases with variations compared to other sellers and an analysis of the purchases can detect fraud. If there are more purchases from shell companies, then there will be deviation in the actual and budgeted cost, which may indicate fraud.

Assertion(s) Tested: Occurrence.

CAATT Expression: Summarize.

Possible Red Flags:
- Organization makes frequent purchases from a single supplier compared to others.
- Organization receiving many invoices from a supplier in a month.
- Large deviation in actual and budgeted costs.

ACFE Fraud Tree Subcategory: Billing schemes.

Purpose: To detect schemes related to shell companies.

Audit Test Procedure: Match vendor and employee phone numbers.

Explanation: Employee and vendor details must be distinct; any similarities found may indicate false vendors. Fictitious vendors can be added to organization records by employees without obtaining approval from manager or department head to perpetrate shell company scheme. If there is a match of employee information with a vendor's, then it may be a shell company.

Assertion(s) Tested: Occurrence and Authorization.

CAATT Expression: Join/Relate.

Possible Red Flags:
- Organization not keeping a list of authorized sellers.
- Manager or department head authorization not necessary before adding new suppliers to company records.
- Supplier information missing in the database such as contact number and taxpayer ID.
- Supplier and employee with the same address or phone number present in the organization records.

ACFE Fraud Tree Subcategory: Billing schemes.

Purpose: To detect schemes related to shell companies.

Audit Test Procedure: Total cash disbursements for consulting and professional services.

Explanation: Consulting and professional services are intangible items which cannot be easily quantified, and therefore easy to perpetrate shell company fraud. Total cash disbursements for consulting and professional services must be summarized and checked with budgeted cost to detect fraud.

Assertion(s) Tested: Occurrence.

CAATT Expression: Summarize.

Possible Red Flags:
- No proper explanation for vague consulting or any other services.
- Large deviation in actual and budgeted costs.

ACFE Fraud Tree Subcategory: Billing schemes.

Purpose: To detect schemes related to non-accomplice vendor.

Audit Test Procedure: Reconcile cheque register to disbursements by vendor invoice.

Explanation: Discrepancy between cheque register and vendor invoice may indicate manipulation in the cheque register, which could result in an incorrect cheque disbursement to vendors in order to convert the returned cheque. Incorrect cash disbursement to vendors without manager or department head approval can enable an employee to perpetrate a non-accomplice vendor scheme.

Assertion(s) Tested: Accuracy, Occurrence, and Authorization.

CAATT Expression: Join/Relate.

Possible Red Flags:
- Same person handling the purchasing duties, accounting duties, invoice handling, and vendor payments.
- Organization not keeping a record of all bill payments to seller.
- Many cheques disbursed for the same invoice to different sellers.
- Manager or department head authorization not necessary before making cash disbursement to seller.

ACFE Fraud Tree Subcategory: Billing schemes.

Purpose: To detect schemes related to non-accomplice vendor.

Audit Test Procedure: Identify duplicate purchase order numbers, credits, and invoices.

Explanation: Duplication of invoice transactions can be recorded to generate a cheque and perpetrate a non-accomplice vendor scheme. Incorrect cash disbursement to vendors without manager or department head approval can enable an employee to perpetrate a non-accomplice vendor scheme. Also, if the same employee is handling various duties in an organization, then duplicate transactions can be recorded to perpetrate fraud.

Assertion(s) Tested: Occurrence and Authorization.

CAATT Expression: Duplicates.

Possible Red Flags:
- Same person handling the purchasing duties, accounting duties, invoice handling, and vendor payments.
- Organization not keeping a record of all bill payments to seller.
- Many cheques disbursed for the same invoice to different sellers.
- Manager or department head authorization not necessary before making cash disbursement to seller.

ACFE Fraud Tree Subcategory: Billing schemes.

Purpose: To detect schemes related to non-accomplice vendor.

Audit Test Procedure: Perform ratio analysis (max/max2) on payments to accounts.

Explanation: If a particular seller is receiving many cheque payments compared to other sellers, then it could be due to an employee purposely making changes in company records in order to perpetrate non-accomplice vendor scheme. Large variation indicates unusual payments made to perpetrate fraud and it could be due to improper segregation of duties in an organization. Wrong cash disbursement to vendors without the approval of manager or department head can enable an employee to perpetrate non-accomplice vendor scheme.

Assertion(s) Tested: Occurrence and Authorization.

CAATT Expression: Ratio analysis.

Possible Red Flags:
- Unusual payment to account ratio.
- Organization not keeping a record of all bill payments to seller.
- Manager or department head authorization not necessary before making cash disbursement to seller.

ACFE Fraud Tree Subcategory: Billing schemes.

Purpose: To detect schemes related to non-accomplice vendor.

Audit Test Procedure: Total cash disbursements by account, by bank, and by vendor.

Explanation: Summarizing the total cash disbursements made to a vendor can help to determine those vendors who received more payments compared to others. Employee could make wrong payments to vendors in order to perpetrate a non-accomplice vendor scheme. Fraud could happen due to no separation of duties in an organization or cash disbursements to sellers made without obtaining approval from manager or department head.

Assertion(s) Tested: Occurrence and Authorization.

CAATT Expression: Summarize.

Possible Red Flags:
- Same person handling the purchasing duties, accounting duties, invoice handling, and vendor payments.
- Organization not keeping a record of all bill payments to seller.
- Many cheques disbursed for the same invoice to different sellers.
- Manager or department head authorization not necessary before making cash disbursement to seller.

ACFE Fraud Tree Subcategory: Billing schemes.

Purpose: To detect schemes related to non-accomplice vendor.

Audit Test Procedure: Identify cheques paid to more than one payee at the same address.

Explanation: Many cheques paid to more than one vendor at the same address may indicate an error purposely made to intercept the cheque when it is returned by vendor. Wrong cash disbursement to vendors without manager or department head approval can enable an employee to perpetrate a non-accomplice vendor scheme. If duties are not segregated in an organization, a particular employee handling the accounts and cash disbursement duties manipulates company records to perpetrate a non-accomplice vendor scheme.

Assertion(s) Tested: Occurrence and Authorization.

CAATT Expression: Duplicates.

Possible Red Flags:
- Same person handling the purchasing duties, accounting duties, invoice handling, and vendor payments.
- Organization not keeping a record of all bill payments to seller.
- Multiple cheques disbursed for the same invoice.
- Manager or department head authorization not necessary before making cash disbursement to seller.

ACFE Fraud Tree Subcategory: Billing schemes.

Purpose: To detect schemes related to personal purchases.

Audit Test Procedure: Identify credits, receipts, and invoices not in proper sequence or range.

Explanation: If the employee completes purchases without manager or department head approval, then the purchases could be personal. Receipts or invoices not in the proper sequence or range may indicate an employee trying to conceal personal purchases fraud.

Assertion(s) Tested: Completeness and Authorization.

CAATT Expression: Sort/Index.

Possible Red Flags:
- Purchases done without obtaining approval from the manager or department head.
- Organization not keeping a record of all bill payments to seller.
- Missing credits, receipts, and invoices from organization records.

ACFE Fraud Tree Subcategory: Billing schemes.

Purpose: To detect schemes related to personal purchases.

Audit Test Procedure: Report on gaps in the sequencing of invoices generated.

Explanation: Gaps in invoices might be intentional to conceal personal purchases without manager or department head approval. Receipts or invoices not in the proper sequence or range may indicate an employee trying to conceal personal purchases fraud.

Assertion(s) Tested: Completeness and Authorization.

CAATT Expression: Gaps.

Possible Red Flags:
- Gaps in invoice numbers.
- Purchases done without obtaining approval from the manager or department head.
- Organization not keeping a record of all bill payments to seller.
- Missing credits, receipts, and invoices from organization records.

ACFE Fraud Tree Subcategory: Billing schemes.

Purpose: To detect schemes related to personal purchases.

Audit Test Procedure: Report on variances between delivery documents and invoices.

Explanation: If there are no adequate controls, then an employee working in purchasing could manipulate accounting records to conceal fraud. Variances in delivery documents and invoices may indicate personal purchases done by employees.

Assertion(s) Tested: Occurrence.

CAATT Expression: Expression/Equation and Filter/Display Criteria.

Possible Red Flags:
- Same person handling the purchasing duties, accounting duties, invoice handling, and vendor payments.
- Discrepancy between invoices and delivery documents in organization records.
- Employee making many purchases from a seller who does not sell business-related merchandise.

ACFE Fraud Tree Subcategory: Billing schemes.

Purpose: To detect schemes related to personal purchases.

Audit Test Procedure: Match stock receipts with vendor ledger and report variances.

Explanation: If there are no adequate controls, then an employee working in purchasing could manipulate accounting records to conceal fraud.
Variation in stock receipts and vendor ledger indicates personal purchases done by employees.

Assertion(s) Tested: Occurrence.

CAATT Expression: Join/Relate and Expression/Equation.

Possible Red Flags:
- Same person handling the purchasing duties, accounting duties, invoice handling, and vendor payments.
- Employee making many purchases from a seller who does not sell business-related merchandises.
- Discrepancy between invoices and delivery documents in organization records.

ACFE Fraud Tree Subcategory: Billing schemes.

Purpose: To detect schemes related to personal purchases.

Audit Test Procedure: Identify unusual delivery addresses.

Explanation: Unusual delivery addresses in company records may indicate that an employee is making personal purchases and having them delivered to non-business-related addresses.

Assertion(s) Tested: Occurrence.

CAATT Expression: Summarize and Filter/Display Criteria.

Possible Red Flags:
- Same person handling the purchasing duties, accounting duties, invoice handling, and vendor payments.
- Employee making many purchases from a seller who does not sell business-related merchandises.
- Discrepancy between invoices and delivery documents in organization records.

ACFE Fraud Tree Subcategory: Billing schemes.

Purpose: To detect schemes related to personal purchases.

Audit Test Procedure: Match delivery addresses with employee addresses.

Explanation: Similarity in delivery and employee addresses may indicate personal employee purchases not related to business.

Assertion(s) Tested: Occurrence.

CAATT Expression: Join/Relate.

Possible Red Flags:
- Same person handling the purchasing duties, accounting duties, invoice handling, and vendor payments.
- Employee making many purchases from a seller who does not sell business-related merchandises.
- Discrepancy between invoices and delivery documents in organization records.

ACFE Fraud Tree Subcategory: Billing schemes.

Purpose: To detect schemes related to personal purchases.

Audit Test Procedure: Identify orders received without purchase order or contract.

Explanation: Goods received without any purchase order or contract may indicate purchases done without proper authorization from manager or department head for personal purchases.

Assertion(s) Tested: Occurrence and Authorization.

CAATT Expression: Join/Relate.

Possible Red Flags:
- Same person handling the purchasing duties, accounting duties, invoice handling, and vendor payments.
- Employee making many purchases from a seller who does not sell business-related merchandises.
- Purchases completed without obtaining approval from the manager or department head.

ACFE Fraud Tree Subcategory: Billing schemes.

Purpose: To detect schemes related to personal purchases.

Audit Test Procedure: Identify vendor records where address changes are frequent.

Explanation: Address can be changed by an employee frequently in order to make personal purchases and have the items delivered to different places.

Assertion(s) Tested: Occurrence.

CAATT Expression: Summarize.

Possible Red Flags:
- Same person handling the purchasing duties, accounting duties, invoice handling, and vendor payments.
- Employee making many purchases from a seller who does not sell business-related merchandises.
- Discrepancy between invoices and delivery documents in the organization's records.

ACFE Fraud Tree Subcategory: Billing schemes.

Purpose: To detect schemes related to personal purchases.

Audit Test Procedure: Check for purchasing more than required:

- Project requirements to contract.
- Inventory remaining at end of project.
- Order greater than quantity received.

Explanation: More purchases completed than are beneficial to business may indicate personal purchases done without obtaining proper authorization from manager or department head. If there is no separation of duties in organization, perpetrator can make changes for personal purchases in company records.

Assertion(s) Tested: Occurrence and Authorization.

CAATT Expression: Join/Relate and Expression/Equation.

Possible Red Flags:

- Same person handling the purchasing duties, accounting duties, invoice handling, and vendor payments.
- Purchases done without obtaining approval from the manager or department head.

ACFE Fraud Tree Subcategory: Billing schemes.

Purpose: To detect schemes related to personal purchases.

Audit Test Procedure: Identify items (labour, materials) charged to jobs not on master job list.

Explanation: Items not in the master job list charged to jobs indicate no proper approval by manager or department head before purchases by employee. If there is no separation of duties in organization, perpetrator can make changes for personal purchases in company records.

Assertion(s) Tested: Occurrence and Authorization.

CAATT Expression: Join/Relate.

Possible Red Flags:

- Same person handling the purchasing duties, accounting duties, invoice handling, and vendor payments.
- Employee making many purchases from a seller who does not sell business-related merchandises.
- Purchases done without obtaining approval from the manager or department head.

ACFE Fraud Tree Subcategory: Billing schemes.

Purpose: To detect schemes related to personal purchases.

Audit Test Procedure: Compare completed work order quantities to materials ordered for the project.

Explanation: Difference in completed work order quantity and materials ordered may indicate items not required for the project purchased by employee without proper approval from manager or department head. If there is no separation of duties in organization, perpetrator can make changes for personal purchases in company records.

Assertion(s) Tested: Occurrence and Authorization.

CAATT Expression: Filter/Display Criteria and Expression/Equation.

Possible Red Flags:

- Same person handling the purchasing duties, accounting duties, invoice handling, and vendor payments.
- Employee making many purchases from a seller who does not sell business-related merchandises.
- Purchases done without obtaining approval from the manager or department head.

ACFE Fraud Tree Subcategory: Expense Reimbursement schemes.

Purpose: To detect schemes related to mischaracterized expense.

Audit Test Procedure: Travel claims for time when employee was on vacation or sick leave.

Explanation: Matching of employee travel claims to vacation and sick leave periods may indicate that the claim is not related to business and it is a personal expense. Employees with same travel claim days as vacation or sick leave days may indicate a mischaracterized expense.

Assertion(s) Tested: Occurrence.

CAATT Expression: Join/Relate.

Possible Red Flags:
- Employee expense claim days or hours identical to the employee vacation or sick leave or day off days.

ACFE Fraud Tree Subcategory: Expense Reimbursement schemes.

Purpose: To detect schemes related to mischaracterized expense.

Audit Test Procedure: Identify travel claims to exotic locations.

Explanation: Travel claims to exotic locations not related to business may indicate the expense is mischaracterized. Employee travel claim days not matching with the working days or hours may indicate that the claim is not related to business and it is a personal expense.

Assertion(s) Tested: Occurrence.

CAATT Expression: Filter/Display Criteria.

Possible Red Flags:
- Travel claims to locations where company has no corporate events.
- Employee expense claim days or hours identical to the employee vacation or sick leave or day off days.

ACFE Fraud Tree Subcategory: Expense Reimbursement schemes.

Purpose: To detect schemes related to mischaracterized expense.

Audit Test Procedure: Identify business travel with departure on Friday or Saturday and return on Sunday.

Explanation: Comparing employee travel schedule to the work schedule calendar can reveal if the travel made was genuine. Employee travel claim not matching with the work days or hours may indicate that the claim is not related to business and is a mischaracterized expense.

Assertion(s) Tested: Occurrence.

CAATT Expression: Filter/Display Criteria and Expression/Equation.

Possible Red Flags:
- Employee expense claim days or hours identical to the employee vacation or sick leave or day off days.

ACFE Fraud Tree Subcategory: Expense Reimbursement schemes.

Purpose: To detect schemes related to mischaracterized expenses.

Audit Test Procedure: Match expense claims items to items on corporate credit card.

Explanation: In order to perpetrate mischaracterized expenses, employees can buy personal items not related to business and make a claim for reimbursement. If a match is done between the expense claim and corporate credit card, an analysis can be done to determine personal items purchased by employee and fraud can be detected.

Assertion(s) Tested: Occurrence.

CAATT Expression: Join/Relate.

Possible Red Flags:
- Using personal credit card instead of organization credit card for business expense.
- Employee not submitting the section of the credit statement which explains what items were purchased.
- Employees not submitting the original copy of bills when making a reimbursement claim.
- Employees not providing any explanation about the time, place, and total money spent when making a reimbursement claim.

ACFE Fraud Tree Subcategory: Expense Reimbursement schemes.

Purpose: To detect schemes related to mischaracterized expense.

Audit Test Procedure: Accommodation, meals, and miscellaneous expense claims for time when employee was on vacation or sick leave.

Explanation: Matching of employee accommodation, meals, and miscellaneous expense claims to vacation and sick leave periods may indicate that the claim is not related to business. Employees could incur expenses such as accommodation, meals, or other miscellaneous expenses with their friends or family during vacation, sick leave, or days off and submit reimbursement claims in order to perpetrate mischaracterized expense scheme.

Assertion(s) Tested: Occurrence.

CAATT Expression: Join/Relate.

Possible Red Flags:
- Employee expense claim days or hours are identical to the employee was on vacation, sick leave, or other days off.

ACFE Fraud Tree Subcategory: Expense Reimbursement schemes.

Purpose: To detect schemes related to overstated expense.

Audit Test Procedure: Identify high-dollar cheque requests.

Explanation: Higher dollar cheque request by a particular employee compared to others indicate fraud. Expense more than actual may indicate overstating the expense to perpetrate fraud.

Assertion(s) Tested: Occurrence.

CAATT Expression: Filter/Display Criteria.

Possible Red Flags:
- Employee expense reimbursement schemes more than the budgeted expense or previous year expense.
- Employee expense reimbursement schemes more than other employees who perform the same duties in an organization.
- Employee making reimbursement claim above the permissible limit.

ACFE Fraud Tree Subcategory: Expense Reimbursement schemes.

Purpose: To detect schemes related to overstated expense.

Audit Test Procedure: Match expense claims amounts to amounts on corporate credit card.

Explanation: In order to perpetrate an overstated expense scheme, employees can overstate the expense incurred for business and make a claim for reimbursement. If a match is done between the expense claim amounts and the amounts on the corporate credit card, an analysis can be done for the purchases made by employee and fraud can be detected.

Assertion(s) Tested: Accuracy and Occurrence.

CAATT Expression: Join/Relate.

Possible Red Flags:
- Using personal credit card instead of organization credit card for business expense.
- Employee not submitting the section of the credit statement which explains what items were purchased.
- Employees not submitting the original copy of bills when making a reimbursement claim.
- Employees not providing any explanation about the time, place, and total money spent when making a reimbursement claim.

ACFE Fraud Tree Subcategory: Expense Reimbursement schemes.

Purpose: To detect schemes related to overstated expense.

Audit Test Procedure: Summarization by expense type by employee.

Explanation: Summarizing by expense type incurred by employee helps to detect more reimbursement claims made by a particular employee compared to others for the same expense type. Expenses more than actual may indicate overstating the expense to perpetrate fraud.

Assertion(s) Tested: Occurrence.

CAATT Expression: Summarize and Sort.

Possible Red Flags:
- Employee expense reimbursement schemes more than the budgeted expense or previous year expense.
- Employee expense reimbursement schemes more than other employees who perform the same duties in an organization.
- Employee making reimbursement claim above the permissible limit.

ACFE Fraud Tree Subcategory: Expense Reimbursement schemes.

Purpose: To detect schemes related to overstated expense.

Audit Test Procedure: Identify employees with expenses above the approved limit.

Explanation: Employees with expenses above the permitted level set by an organization may indicate fraud. If the organization has set a limit on expense amount for employee, then in order to perpetrate fraud, the employee tries to exceed the limit by overstating the expenses.

Assertion(s) Tested: Occurrence.

CAATT Expression: Join/Relate.

Possible Red Flags:
- Employee expense reimbursement schemes more than the budgeted expense or previous year expense.
- Employee expense reimbursement schemes more than other employees who perform the same duties in an organization.
- Employee making reimbursement claim above the permissible limit.

ACFE Fraud Tree Subcategory: Expense Reimbursement schemes.

Purpose: To detect schemes related to overstated expense.

Audit Test Procedure: Identify employees with high expense reimbursement claims.

Explanation: Employees with high expense reimbursement schemes must be analyzed to check the validity of the reimbursement claims. Reimbursement claims which are much higher when compared to other employees may indicate manipulations by fraudsters to claim more money when compared to other employees.

Assertion(s) Tested: Occurrence.

CAATT Expression: Filter/Display Criteria.

Possible Red Flags:
- Employee reimbursement requests are significantly higher than the budgeted expenses, or previous year's expenditures.
- Employee expense reimbursement schemes more than other employees who perform the same duties in an organization.
- Employee making reimbursement claim above the permissible limit.

ACFE Fraud Tree Subcategory: Expense Reimbursement schemes.

Purpose: To detect schemes related to fictitious expenses.

Audit Test Procedure: Consecutively numbered hotel invoices or meal receipts.

Explanation: If receipts are sequentially ordered, then they are fictitious as all services cannot be given to a particular customer at the same time or same day. Receipts might be bought by the employee from the provider fraudulently or by requesting to perpetrate a fictitious expense scheme.

Assertion(s) Tested: Occurrence.

CAATT Expression: Gaps.

Possible Red Flags:
- Receipt numbers submitted from the same vendor are sequential even though purchases were made on different days
- Many bills belonging to the same service provider submitted by the employee for making a reimbursement claim.

ACFE Fraud Tree Subcategory: Expense Reimbursement schemes.

Purpose: To detect schemes related to fictitious expense.

Audit Test Procedure: Match expense claims amounts to amounts on corporate credit card.

Explanation: If the expense claim amounts do not show up on the corporate credit card, it may indicate that the expense is fictitious. Employees can submit fake documents to make a fictitious reimbursement claim. By matching the expense claim to the corporate card, the validity of the claim can be determined and fictitious expense scheme can be detected.

Assertion(s) Tested: Occurrence.

CAATT Expression: Join/Relate and Expression Equation.

Possible Red Flags:
- Using personal credit card instead of organization credit card for business expense.
- Employee not submitting the section of the credit statement which explains what items were purchased.
- Employees not submitting the original copy of bills when making a reimbursement claim.
- Employees not providing any explanation about the time, place, and total money spent when making a reimbursement claim.

ACFE Fraud Tree Subcategory: Expense Reimbursement schemes.

Purpose: To detect schemes related to fictitious expense.

Audit Test Procedure: Identify claims for even amounts.

Explanation: After adding taxes to a bill, the chances of it being an even amount are less, so many even amounts claims made by an employee may indicate fraud. Employee could obtain the receipts fraudulently and make claims for expenses never incurred to perpetrate fictitious expense scheme.

Assertion(s) Tested: Occurrence.

CAATT Expression: Filter/Display Criteria.

Possible Red Flags:
- Employee makes numerous reimbursement claims for the identical amount.
- Employees not submitting the original copy of bills when making a reimbursement claim.
- Employees not providing any explanation about the time, place, and total money spent when making a reimbursement claim.
- Many bills belonging to the same service provider submitted by the employee for making a reimbursement claim.

ACFE Fraud Tree Subcategory: Expense Reimbursement schemes.

Purpose: To detect schemes related to fictitious expense.

Audit Test Procedure: Digital analysis of reimbursement claim record for employees.

Explanation: Benford's law states that in a table of statistics or in a listing of various data such as an invoice amount, cost, and worked hours, each digit has a certain probability of occurrence. If the reimbursement claims do not follow Benford's law, then it may indicate fictitious receipts generated to make a reimbursement claim by the employee.

Assertion(s) Tested: Occurrence.

CAATT Expression: Benford's Law.

Possible Red Flags:
- Employee makes numerous reimbursement claims for the identical amount.
- Employees not submitting the original copy of bills when making a reimbursement claim.
- Employees not providing any explanation about the time, place, and total money spent when making a reimbursement claim.
- Many bills belonging to the same service provider submitted by the employee for making a reimbursement claim.

ACFE Fraud Tree Subcategory: Expense Reimbursement schemes.

Purpose: To detect schemes related to multiple reimbursements.

Audit Test Procedure: Duplicate claims for same period.

Explanation: Employee can use the same expense to make multiple reimbursements and perpetrate fraud. Dual reimbursement claims made by an employee for the same period may indicate fraud.

Assertion(s) Tested: Occurrence.

CAATT Expression: Duplicates.

Possible Red Flags:
- Employee makes numerous reimbursement claims for the identical amount.
- Employees not submitting the original copy of bills when making a reimbursement claim.
- Employees not providing any explanation about the time, place, and total money spent when making a reimbursement claim.

ACFE Fraud Tree Subcategory: Expense Reimbursement schemes.

Purpose: To detect schemes related to multiple reimbursements.

Audit Test Procedure: Claims for use of personal vehicle and rental car for same period.

Explanation: Dual claims made for expenses incurred during the same period may indicate fraud. Personal vehicle and rental car cannot be used during the same period by any employee as it is an overlap of two expenses.

Assertion(s) Tested: Occurrence.

CAATT Expression: Join/Relate.

Possible Red Flags:
- Employee makes numerous reimbursement claims for the identical amount.
- Employees not submitting the original copy of bills when making a reimbursement claim.
- Employees not providing any explanation about the time, place, and total money spent when making a reimbursement claim.

ACFE Fraud Tree Subcategory: Expense Reimbursement schemes.

Purpose: To detect schemes related to multiple reimbursements.

Audit Test Procedure: Identify overlapping travel claims.

Explanation: Travel claim expenses made in the same period for two different places at the same time may indicate fabrication.

Assertion(s) Tested: Occurrence.

CAATT Expression: Filter/Display Criteria.

Possible Red Flags:
- Employee makes numerous reimbursement claims for the identical amount.
- Organization not using purchase cards to make payments to employees through cheque to avoid chance of dual payment.
- Employees not submitting the original copy of bills when making a reimbursement claim.
- Employees not providing any explanation about the time, place, and total money spent when making a reimbursement claim.

ACFE Fraud Tree Subcategory: Expense Reimbursement schemes.

Purpose: To detect schemes related to multiple reimbursements.

Audit Test Procedure: Analysis of travel expenses by employee for duplicates, high values, and frequency.

Explanation: Employee can submit the same expense multiple times to perpetrate a multiple reimbursement scheme. Duplication of claims, higher value, and frequency of reimbursement claim compared to other employees may signal multiple reimbursements done by employees.

Assertion(s) Tested: Occurrence.

CAATT Expression: Duplicates, Summarize, and Filter/Display Criteria.

Possible Red Flags:
- Employee makes numerous reimbursement claims for the identical amount.
- Organization not using purchase cards to make payments to employees through cheque to avoid chance of dual payment.
- Employees not submitting the original copy of bills when making a reimbursement claim.
- Employees not providing any explanation about the time, place, and total money spent when making a reimbursement claim.

ACFE Fraud Tree Subcategory: Payroll schemes.

Purpose: To detect schemes related to ghost employee.

Audit Test Procedure: Identify cheques paid to more than one payee at same address.

Explanation: Many cheques paid to more than one payee at the same address may indicate a ghost employee scheme. If there is no proper separation of duties between payroll generation, time sheet preparation, payment, and paycheque delivery functions, ghost employee schemes can be perpetrated.

Assertion(s) Tested: Occurrence.

CAATT Expression: Duplicates.

Possible Red Flags:
- Same person handling payroll generation, time sheet preparation, payment, and paycheque delivery functions.
- One bank account having numerous direct payments for several employee names with same address.

ACFE Fraud Tree Subcategory: Payroll schemes.

Purpose: To detect schemes related to ghost employee.

Audit Test Procedure: Match payroll master to employee master and report variances.

Explanation: Employee can add ghost employee to payroll master in order to generate payment for ghost. Matching of payroll and employee master file can be done to determine if employees not in the employee master file are receiving a fictitious salary and not working for the company.

Assertion(s) Tested: Occurrence.

CAATT Expression: Join Relate and Filter/Display Criteria.

Possible Red Flags:
- Payroll records containing dual names, addresses, SIN, or missing information of employees in company records.
- Anomalies found in the payroll file when compared to employee master file in HR division.

ACFE Fraud Tree Subcategory: Payroll schemes.

Purpose: To detect schemes related to ghost employee.

Audit Test Procedure: Report entries against authorization records for new or terminated employees.

Explanation: Employee can make changes to the new or terminated employee list to perpetrate ghost employee scheme. If entries against authorization record is not done by the manager or department head but by an employee, then a ghost employee scheme can be perpetrated.

Assertion(s) Tested: Occurrence and Authorization.

CAATT Expression: Join Relate.

Possible Red Flags:
- Modifications to payroll made without the authorization of manager or department heads.
- Anomalies found in the payroll file when compared to employee master file in HR division.

ACFE Fraud Tree Subcategory: Payroll schemes.

Purpose: To detect schemes related to ghost employee.

Audit Test Procedure: Identify duplicate direct deposit numbers.

Explanation: Fraudster can add ghost employees to the payroll records and make the salary payment to the fraudster's account. Each employee must have a unique direct deposit number; a listing of duplicate direct deposits may indicate ghost employees. Also, if there is no proper separation of duties in an organization, then the employee can add ghost employee to payroll list to perpetrate fraud.

Assertion(s) Tested: Occurrence.

CAATT Expression: Duplicates.

Possible Red Flags:
- One bank account having numerous direct payments for several employee names with same address.
- Same person handling payroll generation, time sheet preparation, payment, and paycheque delivery functions.

ACFE Fraud Tree Subcategory: Payroll schemes.

Purpose: To detect schemes related to ghost employee.

Audit Test Procedure: Identify duplicate employee names, addresses, and phone numbers.

Explanation: Fraudster can add ghost employees to the company records with the same name, addresses, and phone numbers to perpetrate ghost employee scheme. Each employee must have a unique employee name, address, and phone number; a listing of duplicates may indicate ghost employees.

Assertion(s) Tested: Occurrence.

CAATT Expression: Duplicates.

Possible Red Flags:
- Payroll records containing dual names, addresses, SIN, or missing information of employees in company records.
- Anomalies found in the payroll file when compared to employee master file in HR division.

ACFE Fraud Tree Subcategory: Payroll schemes.

Purpose: To detect schemes related to ghost employee.

Audit Test Procedure: Identify blank, false, invalid, and duplicate Social Insurance numbers (SINs).

Explanation: Employee can add ghost employees with blank, false, invalid, and duplicate SINs to perpetrate ghost employee scheme. Each employee must have a unique SIN; a listing of blank, false, invalid, and duplicate SINs may indicate fraudster adding ghost employees to company records.

Assertion(s) Tested: Occurrence.

CAATT Expression: Duplicates and Filter/Display Criteria.

Possible Red Flags:
- Payroll records containing dual names, addresses, SIN, or missing information of employees in company records.
- Anomalies found in the payroll file when compared to employee master file in HR division.

ACFE Fraud Tree Subcategory: Payroll schemes.

Purpose: To detect schemes related to ghost employee.

Audit Test Procedure: Identify persons on payroll with no deductions for income tax, insurance, medical, pension, or benefits.

Explanation: Perpetrator can add ghost employee to the payroll list with missing employee details. Each employee working in an organization must have deductions for income tax, insurance, medical, pension, or benefits; an absence of details may indicate ghost employees.

Assertion(s) Tested: Occurrence.

CAATT Expression: Filter/Display Criteria.

Possible Red Flags:

- Employees with no documentation details about their work career, tax filing information, or any benefits-related deduction information present in the organization database.
- Anomalies found in the payroll file when compared to employee master file in HR division.

ACFE Fraud Tree Subcategory: Payroll schemes.

Purpose: To detect schemes related to ghost employee.

Audit Test Procedure: Identify persons on payroll with no home address or telephone.

Explanation: Each employee must have a home address or contact information present in the organization records. Missing of information could indicate phantom employees created by the fraudster to perpetrate ghost employee scheme.

Assertion(s) Tested: Occurrence.

CAATT Expression: Join/Relate and Filter/Display Criteria.

Possible Red Flags:

- Payroll records containing dual names, addresses, SIN, or missing information of employees in company records.
- Anomalies found in the payroll file when compared to employee master file in HR division.

ACFE Fraud Tree Subcategory: Payroll schemes.

Purpose: To detect schemes related to ghost employee.

Audit Test Procedure: Identify persons on payroll with no employment history and no performance evaluations.

Explanation: Employee can add ghost employee to the payroll list with no employment history and performance evaluations. Employee must have an employee history with performance evaluation done; presence of none may indicate ghost employees.

Assertion(s) Tested: Occurrence.

CAATT Expression: Join/Relate and Filter/Display Criteria.

Possible Red Flags:

- Employees with no documentation details about their work career, tax filing information, or any benefits-related deduction information present in the organization database.
- Anomalies found in the payroll file when compared to employee master file in HR division.

ACFE Fraud Tree Subcategory: Payroll schemes.

Purpose: To detect schemes related to ghost employee.

Audit Test Procedure: Compare payroll date with employee start and termination dates.

Explanation: Employee can add ghost employees to the payroll file with fictitious details to perpetrate ghost employee scheme. Payroll date for each employee must match with the start and termination dates in the employee master file; difference in either may indicate manipulation done for ghost employees.

Assertion(s) Tested: Accuracy and Occurrence.

CAATT Expression: Join/Relate and Expression/Equation.

Possible Red Flags:
- Anomalies found in the payroll file when compared to employee master file in HR division.

ACFE Fraud Tree Subcategory: Payroll schemes.

Purpose: To detect schemes related to falsified wages.

Audit Test Procedure: Analysis of pay adjustments and overtime by employee-frequency, rates, and high payments compared to similar positions.

Explanation: An analysis of pay adjustments and overtime by employee-frequency, rates, and high payments can determine if employees are being paid the correct salary. Any anomalies found may indicate falsified wages paid to employees to perpetrate fraud. If pay-related adjustments are not properly authorized by the manager or department head, employees can get higher payments compared to similar positions.

Assertion(s) Tested: Authorizations and Occurrence.

CAATT Expression: Join/Relate.

Possible Red Flags:
- Overtime-related payments done without verifying the source documents or obtaining approval from manager or department head.
- Large deviation in payroll payment and labor expense more than actual expense.
- More salary payments to a particular employee compared to others in a similar position.

ACFE Fraud Tree Subcategory: Payroll schemes.

Purpose: To detect schemes related to falsified wages.

Audit Test Procedure: Identify changes in exemption, gross pay, hourly rates, and salary amounts.

Explanation: Employee can perpetrate falsified wages scheme in order to make payment for duties not performed or to make overpayments. If changes in exemption, gross pay, hourly rates, and salary amounts are done without obtaining approval from manager or department head then falsified wages schemes can be perpetrated.

Assertion(s) Tested: Authorization and Occurrence.

CAATT Expression: Join Relate and Filter/Display Criteria.

Possible Red Flags:
- Modifications to payroll made without the authorization of manager or department heads.
- Large deviation in payroll payment and labor expense more than actual expense.
- More salary payments to a particular employee compared to others in a similar position.

ACFE Fraud Tree Subcategory: Payroll schemes.

Purpose: To detect schemes related to falsified wages.

Audit Test Procedure: Extract all payroll cheques where amount exceeds set amount (by category of employee).

Explanation: A particular employee drawing more salary in a category compared to others could be due to fraudulent wages scheme. If higher salary payments are done without obtaining approval from manager or department head, then falsified wages schemes can be perpetrated.

Assertion(s) Tested: Occurrence and Authorization.

CAATT Expression: Filter/Display Criteria.

Possible Red Flags:
- Overtime-related payments without verifying the source documents or obtaining approval from manager or department head.
- Large deviation in payroll payment and labor expense more than actual expense.
- More salary payments to a particular employee compared to others in a similar position.

ACFE Fraud Tree Subcategory: Payroll schemes.

Purpose: To detect schemes related to falsified wages.

Audit Test Procedure: Review special pay, overtime, premium pay, bonuses, and commissions.

Explanation: By analyzing special pay, overtime, premium pay, bonuses, etc. for employees, falsified wages scheme can be detected. If overtime-related authorizations are not done by managers or department heads, but by the payroll department for employees before issuing the check falsified wages, a falsified wage scheme can be perpetrated.

Assertion(s) Tested: Authorization and Occurrence.

CAATT Expression: Filter/Display Criteria and Sample.

Possible Red Flags:
- Overtime-related payments done without verifying the source documents or obtaining approval from manager or department head.
- Large deviation in payroll payment and labor expense more than actual expense.
- More salary payments to a particular employee compared to others in a similar position.

ACFE Fraud Tree Subcategory: Payroll schemes.

Purpose: To detect schemes related to falsified wages.

Audit Test Procedure: Summarize payroll distributions and reconcile to general ledger (G/L) file.

Explanation: The sum total of payroll expense in the payroll file must match with the G/L. Any deviation in the actual and budgeted payroll may indicate falsified wages scheme perpetrated by employees.

Assertion(s) Tested: Accuracy and Occurrence.

CAATT Expression: Summarize and Join/Relate.

Possible Red Flags: Large deviation in payroll payment and labor expense more than actual expense.

ACFE Fraud Tree Subcategory: Payroll schemes.

Purpose: To detect schemes related to falsified wages.

Audit Test Procedure: Compare time card rates and pay rates to payroll and report variances.

Explanation: Employee can manipulate time cards by adding fictitious work details for falsified wages scheme. Time card rates and pay rates on payroll must be matching; any variation may indicate intentional changes made to perpetrate fraud.

Assertion(s) Tested: Accuracy and Occurrence.

CAATT Expression: Join/Relate and Expression Equation.

Possible Red Flags:

- Variations found in the time card rates when compared to the payroll file.
- Large deviation in payroll payment and labor expense more than actual expense.
- More salary payments to a particular employee compared to others in a similar position.

ACFE Fraud Tree Subcategory: Payroll schemes.

Purpose: To detect schemes related to falsified wages.

Audit Test Procedure: Reconcile salaries by job or project.

Explanation: Employees can sanction more salaries for a job or a project in order to perpetrate fraud. Variation(s) found while reconciling salaries by job or project may indicate falsified wages scheme perpetrated by employee to draw more salaries.

Assertion(s) Tested: Accuracy and Occurrence.

CAATT Expression: Join/Relate.

Possible Red Flags:

- Large deviation in payroll payment and labor expense more than actual expense.
- More salary payments to a particular employee compared to others in a similar position.

ACFE Fraud Tree Subcategory: Payroll schemes.

Purpose: To detect schemes related to falsified wages.

Audit Test Procedure: Compare pay rate with ranges for employee classification.

Explanation: Employee working in a particular category must receive the same pay rate as other employees. Employees can sanction more pay rates compared to other employees in the group in order to perpetrate fraud. Variation in pay rates may indicate that one employee in a particular group is drawing more salary due to fictitious wages scheme.

Assertion(s) Tested: Accuracy and Occurrence.

CAATT Expression: Stratify.

Possible Red Flags:

- Large deviation in payroll payment and labor expense more than actual expense.
- More salary payments to a particular employee compared to others in a similar position.

ACFE Fraud Tree Subcategory: Payroll schemes.

Purpose: To detect schemes related to falsified wages.

Audit Test Procedure: Perform ratio analysis of payroll (max/max2) by employee classification.

Explanation: Employee belonging to a particular category must not have large variation in their salaries. Employees can sanction more salaries compared to other employees in the group to perpetrate fraud. Large deviation in ratio analysis may indicate a particular employee in a category drawing more salary due to falsified wages scheme.

Assertion(s) Tested: Occurrence.

CAATT Expression: Ratio Analysis.

Possible Red Flags:
- Large deviation in payroll payment and labor expense more than actual expense.
- More salary payments to a particular employee compared to others in a similar position.

ACFE Fraud Tree Subcategory: Payroll schemes.

Purpose: To detect schemes related to falsified wages.

Audit Test Procedure: Compare trends in payroll amounts by G/L (and by year).

Explanation: Comparing yearly trends helps to identify variation compared to previous years and detect fraud. Large variation in trends indicates abnormal salaries being paid to employees due to falsified wages scheme.

Assertion(s) Tested: Occurrence.

CAATT Expression: Summarize and Join/Relate.

Possible Red Flags: Large deviation in payroll payment and labor expense more than actual expense.

ACFE Fraud Tree Subcategory: Payroll schemes.

Purpose: To detect schemes related to falsified wages.

Audit Test Procedure: Reconcile time cards to payroll.

Explanation: Employee can manipulate time card by adding fictitious work details for falsified wages scheme. Time card rates and pay rates on payroll must be matching; any variation may indicate intentional changes made to perpetrate fraud.

Assertion(s) Tested: Accuracy and Occurrence.

CAATT Expression: Join/Relate and Expression Equation.

Possible Red Flags:
- Variations found in the time card rates when compared to the payroll file.
- Large deviation in payroll payment and labor expense more than actual expense.
- More salary payments to a particular employee compared to others in a similar position.

ACFE Fraud Tree Subcategory: Payroll schemes.   **Assigned Code**: WIP-17

Purpose: To detect schemes related to falsified wages.

Audit Test Procedure: Identify duplicate time card or employee costs.

Explanation: Employee can manipulate time card or employee costs with fictitious work details to perpetrate fraud. Duplication of time cards or employee costs may indicate that dual payments are made to employee for falsified wages scheme.

Assertion(s) Tested: Occurrence.

CAATT Expression: Duplicates.

Possible Red Flags:
- Large deviation in payroll payment and labor expense more than actual expense.
- More salary payments to a particular employee compared to others in a similar position.

ACFE Fraud Tree Subcategory: Payroll schemes.

Purpose: To detect schemes related to falsified wages.

Audit Test Procedure: Compare reported service time to time card hours from payroll.

Explanation: Employee can manipulate time card by adding fictitious work details for falsified wages scheme. Time card rates and pay rates on payroll must be matching; any variation may indicate intentional changes made to perpetrate fraud.

Assertion(s) Tested: Accuracy and Occurrence.

CAATT Expression: Join/Relate.

Possible Red Flags:
- Variations found in the time card rates when compared to the payroll file.
- Large deviation in payroll payment and labor expense more than actual expense.
- More salary payments to a particular employee compared to others in a similar position.

ACFE Fraud Tree Subcategory: Payroll schemes.

Purpose: To detect schemes related to commission.

Audit Test Procedure: Calculate average sales amounts by product, sales representative, or region.

Explanation: Employee can create fictitious sales in order to get large commissions. By taking the average of sales amounts by various categories, summarizing it, and checking it for any deviation in trends, commission schemes can be detected.

Assertion(s) Tested: Occurrence.

CAATT Expression: Summarize and Expression/Equation.

Possible Red Flags:
- Variation in the current or actual sales pattern when compared to previous or budgeted sales.
- More commissions paid to a particular employee.
- When comparing the sales done by employee no linear relation between commission and sales.

ACFE Fraud Tree Subcategory: Payroll schemes.

Purpose: To detect schemes related to commission.

Audit Test Procedure: Review special pay, overtime, premium pay, bonuses, and commissions.

Explanation: Employee can perpetrate fraud by sanctioning more overtime pay, bonuses, or commissions. Large variation(s) from historical, normal trends may indicate fraud perpetrated by employee.

Assertion(s) Tested: Occurrence.

CAATT Expression: Filter/Display Criteria and Sample.

Possible Red Flags:
- Variation in the current or actual sales pattern when compared to previous or budgeted sales.
- More commissions paid to a particular employee.
- When comparing the sales done by employees, no linear relation between commission and sales.

ACFE Fraud Tree Subcategory: Payroll schemes.

Purpose: To detect schemes related to commission.

Audit Test Procedure: Generate sales and profitability reports by sales representative, product, and customer.

Explanation: Employee can create fictitious sales in order to get larger commissions. If sales and profitability by product, employee, and customers are summarized and checked for any deviation in trends, commission schemes can be detected.

Assertion(s) Tested: Occurrence.

CAATT Expression: Summarize.

Possible Red Flags:
- Variation in the current or actual sales pattern when compared to previous or budgeted sales.
- More commissions paid to a particular employee.
- When comparing the sales done by employee, there is no linear relationship between commission and sales.

ACFE Fraud Tree Subcategory: Payroll schemes.

Purpose: To detect schemes related to commission.

Audit Test Procedure: Calculate sales by region, customer, and category.

Explanation: Employee can create fictitious sales in order to get larger commissions. If sales by region, category, and customers are summarized and checked for any deviation in trends, commission schemes can be detected.

Assertion(s) Tested: Occurrence.

CAATT Expression: Summarize.

Possible Red Flags:
- Variation in the current or actual sales pattern when compared to previous or budgeted sales.
- More commissions paid to a particular employee.
- When comparing the sales done by employee, there is no linear relation between commission and sales.

ACFE Fraud Tree Subcategory: Payroll schemes.

Purpose: To detect schemes related to commission.

Audit Test Procedure: Compare current and previous periods to analyze sales trends.

Explanation: Employee can create fictitious sales in order to get larger commissions. If sales trends are matched to budgeted or previous years and checked for any deviation in trends, commission schemes can be detected.

Assertion(s) Tested: Occurrence.

CAATT Expression: Join/Relate.

Possible Red Flags:
- Variation in the current or actual sales pattern when compared to previous or budgeted sales.
- More commissions paid to a particular employee.
- When comparing the sales done by employee, there is no linear relation between commission and sales.

ACFE Fraud Tree Subcategory: Payroll schemes.

Purpose: To detect schemes related to commission.

Audit Test Procedure: Identify top-dollar products, customers, and sales representatives.

Explanation: Employee can create fictitious sales in order to get larger commission. If sales by top-dollar products, customers, and sales representatives are checked for any deviations in trends, then any variations due to fraud can be determined.

Assertion(s) Tested: Occurrence.

CAATT Expression: Index.

Possible Red Flags:
- Variation in the current or actual sales pattern when compared to previous or budgeted sales.
- More commissions paid to a particular employee.
- When comparing the sales done by employee, there is no linear relation between commission and sales.

ACFE Fraud Tree Subcategory: Payroll schemes.

Purpose: To detect schemes related to commission.

Audit Test Procedure: Summarize sales performance over time by product and sales representative.

Explanation: Employee can create fictitious sales in order to get larger commissions. Summarizing sales performance by product or sales representatives and checking for any deviation in trends, commission schemes can be detected.

Assertion(s) Tested: Occurrence.

CAATT Expression: Expression/Equation and Trend Analysis.

Possible Red Flags:
- Variation in the current or actual sales pattern when compared to previous or budgeted sales.
- More commissions paid to a particular employee.
- When comparing the sales done by employee, there is no linear relation between commission and sales.

ACFE Fraud Tree Subcategory: Payroll schemes.

Purpose: To detect schemes related to commission.

Audit Test Procedure: Calculate the number and value of sales by salesperson.

Explanation: Employee can create fictitious sales in order to get larger commissions. If the number and value of sales by salesperson are summarized and checked for any deviation in trends, commission schemes can be detected.

Assertion(s) Tested: Occurrence.

CAATT Expression: Summarize.

Possible Red Flags:
- Variation in the current or actual sales pattern when compared to previous or budgeted sales.
- More commissions paid to a particular employee.
- When comparing the sales done by employee, there is no linear relation between commission and sales.

ACFE Fraud Tree Subcategory: Payroll schemes.

Purpose: To detect schemes related to commission.

Audit Test Procedure: Calculate salesperson bonus amount compared to total sales for the year.

Explanation: Employee can get more bonus amounts for less sales done due to fraud. Calculating the salesperson bonus amounts and comparing to total sales and checking for any deviation in trends compared to previous years, commission/bonus schemes can be detected.

Assertion(s) Tested: Accuracy and Occurrence.

CAATT Expression: Expression/Equation and Summarize.

Possible Red Flags:
- Variation in the current or actual sales pattern when compared to previous or budgeted sales.
- More commissions paid to a particular employee.
- When comparing the sales done by employee, there is no linear relation between commission and sales.

ACFE Fraud Tree Subcategory: Register Disbursement schemes.

Purpose: To detect schemes related to false refund.

Audit Test Procedure: Compare physical stock count with computed stock counts.

Explanation: Comparing physical stock count and computed stock count helps to determine the accuracy of the inventory records. If the physical stock count and computed stock count totals are different, then it may indicate false refunds perpetrated by employees as one of the main reasons for this difference.

Assertion(s) Tested: Existence and Accuracy.

CAATT Expression: Summarize and Extract.

Possible Red Flags:
- Inventory account sharp decline or appearing manipulated.
- Same person handling the inventory counting and cash register handling functions.

ACFE Fraud Tree Subcategory: Register Disbursement schemes.

Purpose: To detect schemes related to false refund.

Audit Test Procedure: Reconcile physical stock levels to computed amounts.

Explanation: Comparing physical stock count and computed stock count helps to determine the accuracy of the inventory records. If the physical stock count and computed stock count totals are different, then it may indicate false refunds perpetrated by employee.

Assertion(s) Tested: Existence and Accuracy.

CAATT Expression: Sample.

Possible Red Flags:
- Inventory account sharp decline or appearing manipulated.
- Same person handling the inventory counting and cash register handling functions.

ACFE Fraud Tree Subcategory: Register Disbursement schemes.

Purpose: To detect schemes related to false refund.

Audit Test Procedure: Identify duplicate return transactions.

Explanation: If register refunds are done without recording proper documentation details, then there will be chances of duplications. Duplication in refunds can result in large amounts of refunds by fraudster compared to other employees, which may indicate a false refund scheme.

Assertion(s) Tested: Occurrence.

CAATT Expression: Duplicates.

Possible Red Flags:
- Refund paper appearing bogus or lost.
- Numerous refunds within tolerated threshold range.
- Large number of refunds by a particular employee compared to others.
- When matched to gross sales, a decline in net sales due to surge in refunds and discounts.
- Tampered register records and sales not recorded in proper order.

ACFE Fraud Tree Subcategory: Register Disbursement schemes.

Purpose: To detect schemes related to false refund.

Audit Test Procedure: Identify credit card purchase and refund to different credit card.

Explanation: A customer using one credit card to make purchase and using another credit card to claim refund may signal fraud.

Assertion(s) Tested: Occurrence.

CAATT Expression: Expression/Equation and Summarize.

Possible Red Flags:
- Reduction in cash transactions compared to credit transactions.
- Purchases and return transactions recorded on different credit card.

ACFE Fraud Tree Subcategory: Register Disbursement schemes.

Purpose: To detect schemes related to false refund.

Audit Test Procedure: Calculate the number and amount of refunds by clerk.

Explanation: Large number and amounts of refunds by a particular employee compared to other employees may indicate false refunds. Employee can use false documents or make changes to register records to perpetrate fraud.

Assertion(s) Tested: Occurrence.

CAATT Expression: Expression/Equation and Summarize.

Possible Red Flags:
- Refund paper appearing bogus or lost.
- Numerous refunds within tolerated threshold range.
- Large number of refund by a particular employee compared to others.
- When matched to gross sales, a decline in net sales due to surge in refunds and discounts.
- Tampered register records and sales not recorded in proper order.

ACFE Fraud Tree Subcategory: Register Disbursement schemes.

Purpose: To detect schemes related to false refund.

Audit Test Procedure: Calculate percentage of refunds by credit card.

Explanation: If a particular employee has more refunds to credit cards compared to cash (based on normal trends), or has more refunds compared to other employees, it may indicate fictitious refunds.

Assertion(s) Tested: Occurrence.

CAATT Expression: Expression/Equation and Summarize.

Possible Red Flags:
- Reduction in cash transactions compared to credit transactions.
- Large number of refunds by a particular employee compared to others.
- Purchase and return transactions recorded on different credit card.

ACFE Fraud Tree Subcategory: Register Disbursement schemes.

Purpose: To detect schemes related to false refund.

Audit Test Procedure: Identify refunds that are greater than selling price.

Explanation: Refund made to customer must be less than the selling price. If the refunds are not less, it may indicate false refund schemes perpetrated by employees. Employee could pocket the excess refund after paying the sale price as refund to customers.

Assertion(s) Tested: Occurrence.

CAATT Expression: Filter/Display Criteria.

Possible Red Flags:
- Large number of refunds by a particular employee compared to others.
- When matched to gross sales, a decline in net sales due to surge in refunds and discounts.
- Refunds more than the sale price given to customers.

ACFE Fraud Tree Subcategory: Register Disbursement schemes.

Purpose: To detect schemes related to false refund.

Audit Test Procedure: Compare amount of credit card payments by clerk.

Explanation: More credit card refunds compared to cash (based on typical trends) may indicate a false refund scheme. Summarizing the payments made by credit card and comparing it with other employees helps to detect fraud.

Assertion(s) Tested: Occurrence.

CAATT Expression: Summarize.

Possible Red Flags:
- Reduction in cash transactions compared to credit transactions.
- Large number of refunds by a particular employee compared to others.
- Purchase and return transactions recorded on different credit card.

ACFE Fraud Tree Subcategory: Register Disbursement schemes.

Purpose: To detect schemes related to false voids.

Audit Test Procedure: Compare physical stock count with perpetual (computed) stock counts.

Explanation: Comparing physical stock count and computed stock count helps to determine the accuracy of the inventory records. If the physical stock count and computed stock count totals are different, then it may indicate false voids perpetrated by employees, as one of the main causes of the shortage.

Assertion(s) Tested: Existence and Accuracy.

CAATT Expression: Summarize and Extract.

Possible Red Flags:
- Inventory account sharp decline or appearing manipulated.
- Same person handling the inventory counting and cash register handling functions.

ACFE Fraud Tree Subcategory: Register Disbursement schemes.

Purpose: To detect schemes related to false voids.

Audit Test Procedure: Calculate number and amount of voids by clerk.

Explanation: Large number and amounts of voids by a particular employee compared to other employees may indicate false voids. Register taps must be checked to determine the frequency and the amount of the voids.

Assertion(s) Tested: Occurrence.

CAATT Expression: Expression/Equation and Summarize.

Possible Red Flags:
- Void paperwork appearing bogus or lost.
- Numerous voids within tolerated threshold range.
- Large number of voids by a particular employee compared to others.
- Tampered register records and sales not recorded in proper order.

References

1. EisnerAmper. (2016). Fraudulent Disbursements – Billing Schemes. Retrieved from www.eisneramper.com/fraudulent-disbursements-billing-schemes-1116/
2. International Auditing and Assurance Standards Board (IAASB). (2010). International Standards of Auditing (ISA 240). Retrieved from www.ifac.org/system/files/downloads/a012-2010-iaasb-handbook-isa-240.pdf
3. Association of Certified Fraud Examiners. (2018). Report to the Nations on Occupational Fraud and Abuse. Retrieved from https://s3-us-west-2.amazonaws.com/acfepublic/2018-report-to-the-nations.pdf
4. Law 360. (2015). Philly Hotel Workers Ordered to Pay $3M for UPenn Fraud. Retrieved from www.law360.com/articles/726960/philly-hotel-workers-ordered-to-pay-3m-for-upenn-fraud
5. Federal Bureau of Investigation. (2014). Former Executives Admit to Defrauding Employer of $1 Million through Fraudulent Expense Claims. Retrieved from www.fbi.gov/baltimore/press-releases/2014/former-executives-admit-to-defrauding-employer-of-1-million-through-fraudulent-expense-claims

6. Chong, E. (2016). Ex-HR exec jailed for cheating employer of $1.2m. *The Straits Times*. Retrieved from www.straitstimes.com/singapore/courts-crime/ex-hr-exec-jailed-for-cheating-employer-of-12m

7. Milkovits, A. (2017). 5 arrested in check-fraud ring in Providence that netted hundreds of thousands, police say. *Providence Journal*. Retrieved from www.providencejournal.com/news/20171018/5-arrested-in-check-fraud-ring-in-providence-that-netted-hundreds-of-thousands-police-say

8. Fagan, M. (2018). Glen Rock market cashier stole $12,000 from register, police say. *Northjersey.com*. Retrieved from www.northjersey.com/story/news/bergen/glen-rock/2018/03/19/glen-rock-nj-cashier-accused-stealing-12-000-register/439113002/

9. Wells, J. T. (2011). *Corporate Fraud Handbook: Prevention and Detection*, Hoboken, NJ: John Wiley & Sons.

10. Association of Certified Fraud Examiners. (2012). Report to the Nations on Occupational Fraud and Abuse: 2012 Global Fraud Study. Retrieved from www.acfe.com/uploadedFiles/ACFE_Website/Content/rttn/2012-report-to-nations.pdf

11. Association of Certified Fraud Examiners. (2011). Introduction to Fraud Examination. Retrieved from www.acfe.com/uploadedFiles/Shared_Content/Products/Self-Study_CPE/intro-to-fraud-exam-2011-extract.pdf

12. Green, C. L., & McGovern & Greene LLP. Using the Right to Audit Clause to Detect Procurement Fraud. Retrieved from www.mcgovern-greene.com/archives/archive_articles/Craig_Greene_Archives/shell_comp_schemes.html

13. Gee, S. (2014). *Fraud and Fraud Detection: A Data Analytics Approach*, Hoboken, NJ: John Wiley & Sons.

14. Kramer, W. M. (2012). The most common procurement fraud schemes and their primary red flags. *International Anti-Corruption Resource Center, 3*, 2016.

15. Zweighaft, D. (2004). Slicing the salami: Small-dollar recurring fraud. *Journal of Investment Compliance, 5*(2), 138–142.

16. Wells, J. T. (2013). *Corporate Fraud Handbook: Prevention and Detection*, Hoboken, NJ: John Wiley & Sons.

17. Association of Certified Fraud Examiners. (2018). Unnamed Article. Retrieved from www.acfe.com/article.aspx?id=4294968370

18. Offit Kurman. (2015). The 4 Most Common Employee Theft Schemes and How to Protect Against Them. Retrieved from www.offitkurman.com/blog/2015/05/28/the-4-most-common-employee-theft-schemes-and-how-to-protect-against-them/

19. Marasco, J. (2007). Payroll fraud: How it's done, how to prevent it. *Stonebridge Business Partners, Fraud Matters, Summer 2007*. Retrieved from https://stonebridgebp.com/library/uncategorized/payroll-fraud-how-its-done-how-to-prevent-it/

20. Albrecht, W. S., Albrecht, C. O., Albrecht, C. C., & Zimbelman, M. F. (2012). *Fraud Examination*, Boston, MA: Cengage Learning.

21. Wells, J. T. (2002). Keep ghosts off the payroll. *Journal of Accountancy, 194*(6), 77–82.

4

Compendium of CAATT-Based Audit Tests for the Detection of Financial Statement Fraud

Introduction

Financial statement (F/S) fraud, also sometimes referred to as management fraud, refers to fraud schemes such as reporting fictitious revenues, improper asset valuations, and concealed liabilities and expenses, which may not be as common as bribery, forgery, or falsified wages (average of 10% of all frauds), but their impact is markedly significant with the median F/S fraud loss hitting $800,000 according to the 2018 Report to the Nations (RTTN). Even more notable, however, is how long fraud typically takes to detect. As such, F/S fraud requires quicker detection to mitigate losses and duration. Mapping F/S fraud schemes to applicable audit tests, testing management assertions and applicable Computer-Assisted Audit Tools and Techniques (CAATT) expressions, as well as internal controls and associated red flags, reveal more than 80 CAATT-based F/S audit tests and 50 recommended internal controls to improve F/S fraud detection and reduce the financial impact of these fraud schemes.

Occupational or internal fraud happens when an employee, manager, or owner of a company or organization commits fraud. The Association of Certified Fraud Examiners' (ACFE) Fraud Tree breaks occupational fraud down into three categories: corruption, asset misappropriation, and F/S fraud. F/S fraud is usually committed by a company's management to make the company "more profitable" through deceit and "cooking the books." Because a company's F/Ss are used to secure investors, obtain bank approvals, justify bonuses or expenses, or to demonstrate success to stakeholders, deliberate misrepresentation can have short-term and, given the length of detection time, even long-term benefits for those doing it. Since this type of fraud is typically performed at higher levels of management, F/S fraud often goes unnoticed with most instances being detected via whistleblowers rather than through internal or external audits; many within and outside of the organization are unaware of the fraud and take the enterprise's F/Ss at face value [1].

Case Histories

Since the late 1990s, many well-known companies have filed bankruptcy after being accused of F/S fraud, including Enron, WorldCom, Tyco, and HealthSouth. Often labeled financial irregularities, F/S fraud can fly under the radar, making the news only when it's made public [2].

Tesco

Britain's most popular supermarket/retail chain, Tesco, overstated its profit for the 2014 fiscal year to the tune of £250 million ($327 million). The former Chairman, Sir Richard Broadbent, subsequently resigned due to the accounting scandal. Dubbed "aggressive accounting," the F/S fraud stemmed from Tesco's first profit decline in 20 years; instead of working to resolve the company's profit issues, they inflated their numbers to make the company look more profitable than it was. A direct violation of revenue recognition rules, Tesco's F/S fiasco resulted in further financial decline even after Broadbent left: Tesco's market share consequently shrank from 30.1% to 28.4%. Tesco has since switched its external auditing firm from PwC to Deloitte auditors who maintain that Tesco's profits were overstated by £70 million ($109 million) in the 2013–2014 fiscal year [3–5].

Toshiba

Another more recent scandal involves the well-known Toshiba Corporation, a Japanese electronics firm, which overstated its profits by ¥152 billion ($1.2 billion) from 2008 to the third quarter of 2014's fiscal year [6] largely due to the company's demands that employees meet unreasonable and unachievable profit goals [7]. The 82-page, independent panel report highlights a corporate culture that prevents employees from contradicting or interfering with management's decisions. Toshiba's CEO, Hisao Tanaka, continually and deliberately pressured employees to meet the sales goals following the 2008 global recession. While Tanaka resigned in 2015 and accepted responsibility for the accounting irregularities, he claims that he didn't ask employees to falsify F/Ss. The investigation report also mentions other accounting irregularities such as postponing losses in later years, booking profits early, and improper valuation of inventory results in accounting irregularity [7–9].

Olympus

An example of a problematic and detrimental F/S fraud was best illustrated by the Olympus Corporation scandal in 2011. A Japanese electronics manufacturing giant known for its cameras and medical imaging equipment, Olympus hired a British CEO to bring in a fresh perspective and an executive who could deliver, but what Michael Woodford did was to commit a ¥117.7 billion ($1.5 billion) F/S fraud over 13 years. Considered one of the largest, longest, and most hidden financial scandals in Japan's corporate history, the discovery tanked Olympus's stock market valuation by nearly 80% in addition to resulting in subsequent resignations, investigations, arrests, and lawsuits [10–13].

Because F/S fraud has a greater financial impact than other types of fraud, and remains concealed longer, early detection is key to addressing the problem of low detection (15% by internal audit and 4% by external audit as per the ACFE's 2018 RTTN). Consequently, increasing CAATT can aid in exposing the various types of F/S fraud.

While the Tesco, Toshiba, and Olympus scandals are the biggest in recent history, F/S fraud has also plagued Penn West Petroleum Ltd. where $300 million of expenses were misclassified [14], at Mobily where "accounting errors" forced a restatement of 18 months' worth of earnings [15], and at Steinhoff where CEO Markus Jooste quit amid suspicion of inflated earnings, delayed financial results, and an audit by PwC [16].

Discussion

Mostly commonly, organizations across the world utilize external F/S audits (approx. 80%), codes of conduct (80%), and CEO/CFO certification requirements for F/Ss (72%) – but fraud still occurs even when these control tactics are performed. However, when active detection methods (e.g., surveillance and monitoring) were employed, both loss and duration were significantly minimized. Researching, analyzing, and testing detection methods using CAATT audit procedures for F/S fraud (internally, externally, and for forensic auditors), along with evaluating and assessing management assertions and red flags associated with this type of fraud, ultimately results in a comprehensive list of active detection methods and anti-fraud controls that will bolster the detection of F/S fraud [1].

Prevention

F/S fraud is defined as "the deliberate misrepresentation of the financial condition of an enterprise accomplished through the intentional misstatement or omission of amounts or disclosures in the financial statements to deceive financial statement users." [17] Because perpetrators of fraud doubt they'll get caught, prevention is essential to limiting occupational fraud. Employing fraud prevention techniques, then, is the first line of defense against fraud. While adopting prevention techniques isn't a guarantee against fraudulent activity, increased detection and vigilance on the organization's behalf discourages employees and management from acting on fraudulent impulses which are often triggered by pressure, rationalization, and opportunity [18]. In the case of F/S fraud, where F/Ss imply accuracy, fact, and integrity, corporate culture is often a contributing factor in the occurrence of fraud, and moving toward a more ethical corporate culture, together with internal anti-fraud controls, is a crucial component of fraud prevention [15].

Internal controls can prevent occupational fraud. Best described as "a process, effected by an entity's board of directors, management and other personnel, designed to provide reasonable assurance regarding the achievement of objectives relating to operations, reporting and compliance" [8], internal controls are valuable tools for fraud prevention, but on their own, they just aren't enough. These internal controls must be supplemented by tools and technology to either prevent fraud of limit its impact [19].

Fraud Detection

Prevention is not an exact science, so risk is always a factor. The key is in closing the gap between prevention and detection by strengthening anti-fraud controls. The most common detection method according to the ACFE were tips provided by other employees (40% of the cases). These whistleblowers are more often anonymous employees tipping via reporting hotlines, emails, or websites [1]. The next most common detection methods in 2018 were internal audits (15%), management review (13%), by accident (7%), and account reconciliation (5%). While tips are the most common method of detection, companies can't fully rely on just tips and whistleblowing as the main preventive control, and must, therefore, implement proactive fraud detection procedures based on CAATT data analysis. Automated fraud detection technology can analyze journal entries, looking for abnormal transactions (particularly those occurring at month or near year-end). CAATT can also assess revenues and expense accounts that can be falsified to increase net income to reach incentive targets [20]. Automated fraud detection technology can also be useful for noting abnormal transactions for future investigation, especially in purchasing and expense records (an organization's most risky areas for occupational fraud) [21].

F/S Fraud Schemes

The ACFE's Fraud Tree subdivides F/S fraud into two primary sections: Net Worth/Net Income Overstatements and Net Worth/Net Income Understatements (see Figure 4.1), but they share the same scheme categories:

Timing Differences Scheme: Recording revenues or expenses in incorrect periods which can be done by recording sales before they have earned or by posting expenses to the next accounting period – both of which boost income by shifting revenues

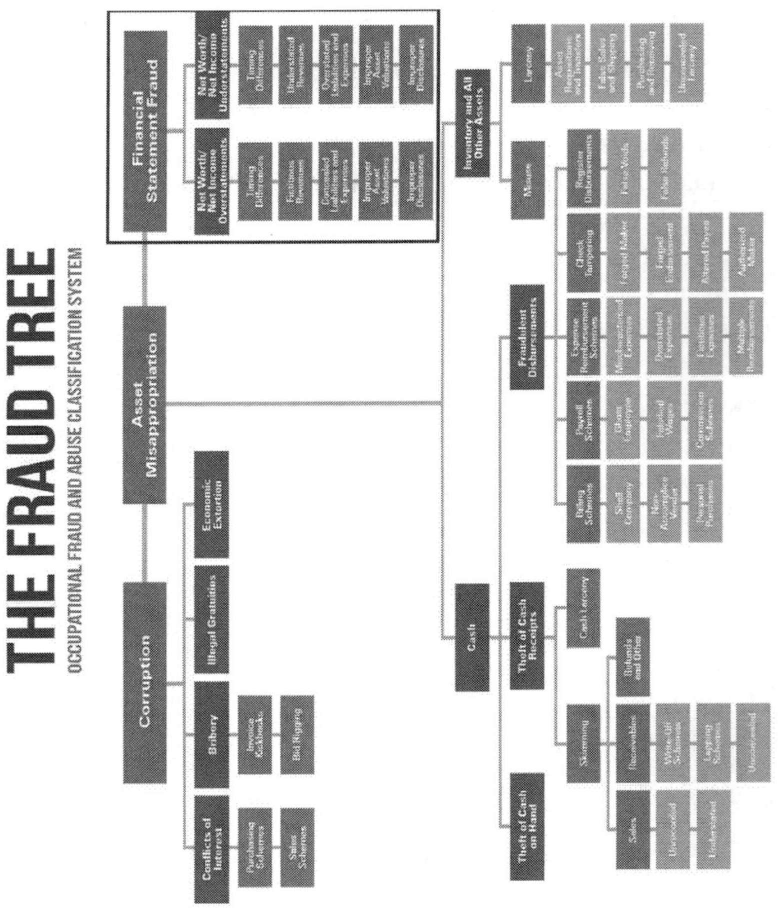

Figure 4.1 Occupational Fraud and Abuse classification system. (*Source:* www.acfe.com/rttn2016/schemes/occupational.aspx, 2016).

and expenses around to increase or decrease earnings. Red flags associated with timing differences include unusual profit growth, recurring negative cash flows, and unusual increases in a company's gross margins [22].

Fictitious Revenues Schemes: Where a company shows sales of goods or services that haven't happened. These fictitious transactions usually involve fake customers, but sometimes involve real customers by creating fictitious invoices for goods/services that never reached those customers. To hide this fraud, these sales are reversed back into the next accounting period. Red flags for fictitious revenues include complex transactions near year-end or period-end, sales to unknown ownership entities, and related party transactions [23].

Concealed Liabilities and Expenses Schemes: Hiding the liabilities or expenses of company to make it appear more profitable than it is. This kind of fraud can be committed by omitting liabilities or expenses, capitalizing on expenses, and failing to disclose warranty costs. Red flags associated with concealed liability and expenses include allowances for sales returns and warranty claims, unusual increases in gross margins, estimating assets, and providing revenues and liabilities based on subjective judgments.

Improper Asset Valuation Schemes: Showing more assets than a company has in order to look more stable to creditors and investors. Paying off a company's liabilities of a company depends on the use of its assets and earning profits; inventory, accounts receivable, business combinations, and fixed assets are the most improperly valued assets. Red flags associated with improper asset valuation include allowances for bad debts, unusual changes in fixed assets and depreciations, and unusual increases in assets compared to other competitors [1].

Improper Disclosure Schemes: Hiding material information like contingent liabilities, subsequent events, management fraud, or accounting changes to mislead those reviewing F/Ss. Red flags connected with improper disclosure include management dominated by a single person, significant related party transactions, and oversight by the board of directors on the financial reporting process [23].

Conclusion

The ACFE's Report on Occupational Fraud and Abuse (RTTN 2018) highlights two key issues of F/S fraud: the significant financial impact (over four times the loss due to corruption and over seven times the loss due to asset misappropriation in the same period) and the prolonged detection time (for F/S fraud schemes, it's an average for 2 years – 6 months longer than the median). Together, these issues present organizations with substantial fraud risk and potential loss. The organizations most vulnerable to fraud are those with less than 100 employees, where trust is often the preferred prevention choice (and the most unreliable since it's not an internal control). However, regardless of an organization's size, the biggest weakness in fraud prevention and detection is a lack of internal controls. Since the perpetrators of fraud tend to be executive and upper management, having active controls in place along with an objective and independent checks of processes and revenue/expenditure patterns is crucial to an effective financial fraud risk management strategy [1].

Recommended CAATT-Based Audit Tests

- F/S fraud audit tests address each of the seven categories of this fraud type: Timing Differences, Fictitious Revenues, Understated Revenues, Concealed Liabilities and Expenses, Overstated Liabilities and Expense, Concealed/Overstated Liabilities, and Expenses and Improper Asset Valuations.
- There are 87 CAATT-based audit tests identified for F/S fraud detection:
  - 7 for Timing Differences
  - 23 for Fictitious Revenues
  - 10 for Concealed Liabilities and Expenses
  - 10 for Improper Asset Valuations
  - 23 for Overstated Liabilities and Expenses
  - 9 for Concealed/Overstated Liabilities and Expenses
  - 5 for Understated Revenues
- There is a total of 50 recommended internal controls for F/S fraud:

- 6 for Timing Differences
- 20 for Fictitious/Understated Revenues
- 9 for Concealed/Overstated Liabilities and Expenses
- 9 for Improper Asset Valuations
- 6 for Improper Disclosures.

Recommended Controls for F/S Fraud Risk Mitigation

ACFE FRAUD SCHEME CATEGORY	INTERNAL CONTROLS BEST PRACTICES FOR F/S FRAUD PREVENTION
1. Timing Differences	1. The agreement of sale and purchase must be signed by authorized person.
	2. There should not be improper sales cutoffs in which the transactions are recorded beyond balance sheet date to enhance current period sales.
	3. Make sure shipments reach designated purchasers. Shipments must not go to seller's representatives or public warehouses.
	4. Shipment deliveries can only be considered complete if the installation, customer testing, and customer acceptance have occurred (depending on contractual conditions).
	5. Invoice review, delivery documents, and contracts determine if the portion of delivered services have been recognized in the right accounting period.
	6. Items with wrong specifications must not be shipped to customers.
2. Fictitious/ Understated Revenues	1. Processing sales orders, invoicing products, product returns, and processing cash receipts must be performed by different employees.
	2. Employee who enters cash receipts into accounting periods must be different from those who do bank reconciliations.
	3. Cheques must be prenumbered and in sequence.
	4. Documents (invoices, receipts) can only be approved by authorized employees.
	5. Goods returned for credit must be approved by supervisor of the sales department.
	6. Shipping documents must be reconciled with sales invoices.
	7. Sales summaries must be reconciled with invoice totals.
	8. Goods can only be released from warehouses after sale order approval by an authorized employee.
	9. Goods shipped to customers must agree with the goods ordered by customers.
	10. Customer cheques must not be misappropriated before/after being forwarded to cashier for deposit.
	11. Goods shipped to customers must be billed only once and authorized by sales manager.

(Continued)

ACFE FRAUD SCHEME CATEGORY	INTERNAL CONTROLS BEST PRACTICES FOR F/S FRAUD PREVENTION
	12. Sales invoices must be posted to correct customer accounts.
	13. All suppliers and customers must be approved and placed in the organization's approved supplier or client list prior to any purchased or sale transaction. Furthermore, these approved lists need to be reviewed and updated on a regular basis.
	14. Outstanding balance reports must be mailed to customers monthly.
	15. Cheques outstanding for more than 90 days must be investigated.
	16. Total invoice amounts must be compared with the accounts receivable ledger.
	17. Employee who approved the goods return must see the actual return of goods physically.
	18. Write offs for uncollectible receivables must be authorized by a designated employee.
	19. The internal audit function must audit quarterly F/Ss to help ensure their veracity.
	20. Accounting employees, especially those dealing with receivable responsibilities, must take mandatory vacations and their duties may be performed by other employees during vacations.
3. Concealed/ Overstated Liabilities and Expenses	1. There should be a system for the authorization and approval of expenses. For example, the department manager can approve up to $5,000 of expenses; anything above the limit requires a senior management approval.
	2. Separation of duties must be performed when purchasing goods. For example, employee who authorizes purchases must be different from one who receives goods and records transactions.
	3. The purchasing manager or an authorized employee must review and reconcile quantity of the goods on receipts, purchase orders, and purchase invoices.
	4. There should be system for accurately and completely recording all purchasing transactions by the responsible employees.
	5. Employees dealing with purchasing and accounts payable responsibilities must take mandatory vacations and their duties must be performed by other employees.
	6. The purchasing department may take quotations from different vendors and all purchases must be approved by the purchasing manager.
	7. Records of all current and long term liabilities should be approved by accountable personnel.
	8. Confirmation letters must be received from vendors to confirm liabilities.
	9. Capitalization of asset and repair/maintenance expenses must be reviewed by management.

(Continued)

ACFE FRAUD SCHEME CATEGORY	INTERNAL CONTROLS BEST PRACTICES FOR F/S FRAUD PREVENTION
4. Improper Asset Valuations	1. Inventories must be valued and recorded as per prevalent accounting standards.
	2. Capital asset addition, recording, and disposal must be approved by an authorized employee.
	3. Capital asset records must contain detailed information about assets. E.g. Description, date of purchase, fair value on date of acquisition, funding source.
	4. Equipment and inventory must be reconciled with records and must be done by an employee who does not have custody of assets (equipment/inventory).
	5. Only authorized employees can have inventory access.
	6. Inventories can only be released on basis of approved requisition.
	7. Employees dealing with inventory, shipping, and receiving must take mandatory vacations and their duties must be performed by other employees.
	8. Accounts receivables must be reported on net realizable value. E.g. Amounts which are not expected to be collected (bad debt) must be subtracted from total receivables.
	9. Write-offs for uncollectible receivables must be authorized by a designated employee.
5. Improper Disclosures	1. There should be proper disclosure of loan covenants and/or contingent liabilities.
	2. All subsequent events (including court judgments and regulatory decisions) that may affect a company's assets and liabilities must be disclosed.
	3. Frauds committed by executives/management must be disclosed in F/S and company notes.
	4. Related party transactions must be disclosed and approved by board of governance.
	5. Conflicts of interest and breaches in code of ethics must be disclosed.
	6. Changes in accounting policies related to reporting entities must also be disclosed.

Audit Tests Worksheet Section

ACFE Fraud Tree Subcategory: Timing Differences.

Purpose: To detect schemes related to timing differences.

Audit Test Procedure: Calculate the average days from delivery of goods or services to the billing date and receipt of payment (by clerk and by customer).

Explanation: To find out the average days required for the delivery of goods/services to receipt of payments.

Assertion(s) Tested: Cut-off.

CAATT Expression: Age and Summarize.

Possible Red Flag: Inappropriate revenue recognition for delivery of goods/services, usually near the end of an accounting period.

ACFE Fraud Tree Subcategory: Timing Differences.

Purpose: To detect schemes related to timing differences.

Audit Test Procedure: Calculate the days aged for receivables, by customer, to support contract negotiations.

Explanation: To compare the number of days a customer has taken to pay its account payables versus its agreed upon trade credit terms.

Assertion(s) Tested: Cut-off.

CAATT Expression: Age and Summarize.

Possible Red Flag: numerous payments received after due dates.

ACFE Fraud Tree Subcategory: Timing Differences.

Purpose: To detect schemes related to timing differences.

Audit Test Procedure: Identify orders received without purchase order or contract.

Explanation: Discover orders that are received without purchase orders.

Assertion(s) Tested: Cut-off.

CAATT Expression: Join/Relate.

Possible Red Flag: Shipment received without any singed contract or orders placed.

ACFE Fraud Tree Subcategory: Timing Differences.

Purpose: To detect schemes related to timing differences.

Audit Test Procedure: Analyze scheduled versus actual receipt dates.

Explanation: To determine whether the actual receipt dates and scheduled dates are in accordance with the signed contract.

Assertion(s) Tested: Cut-off.

CAATT Expression: Age.

Possible Red Flag: Difference between scheduled dates and actual receipts dates.

ACFE Fraud Tree Subcategory: Timing Differences.

Purpose: To detect schemes related to timing differences.

Audit Test Procedure: Calculate late shipment by vendor and analyze impact.

Explanation: To check the delivery and scheduled date of order posted and analyze its impact.

Assertion(s) Tested: Cut-off.

CAATT Expression: Age, Summarize, and Expression/Equation.

Possible Red Flag: Shipments received later than the scheduled date.

ACFE Fraud Tree Subcategory: Timing Differences.

Purpose: To detect schemes related to timing differences.

Audit Test Procedure: Calculate an average sale by customer for the first three quarters of the year and relate it to the last quarter of the year.

Explanation: To find out the inflated last quarter of the year sales by comparing average of last quarter with other three average quarters sales (if they exist).

Assertion(s) Tested: Accuracy/Existence.

CAATT Expression: Summarize.

Possible Red Flag: End of year sales entries made to inflate annual sales figures.

ACFE Fraud Tree Subcategory: Timing Differences.

Purpose: To detect schemes related to timing differences.

Audit Test Procedure: Calculate the total sales by customer for the first three quarters of the year and relate it to the last quarter of the year.

Explanation: To find out the inflated last quarter of the year sales by comparing the total of the last quarter's sales with the other three total quarters sales (if they exist).

Assertion(s) Tested: Accuracy/Existence.

CAATT Expression: Summarize.

Possible Red Flag: Year-end sales entries made to inflate annual sales figures.

ACFE Fraud Tree Subcategory: Fictitious Revenues.

Purpose: To detect schemes related to fictitious revenues.

Audit Test Procedure: Identify high-value credit notes, balances, and invoices by customer and by clerk.

Explanation: To make sure that fictitious revenues are not generated due to management's pressure to achieve targeted goals.

Assertion(s) Tested: Occurrence.

CAATT Expression: Filter/Display Criteria.

Possible Red Flag: High amount transactions in accounts receivables (credit notes, balances, and invoices).

ACFE Fraud Tree Subcategory: Fictitious Revenues.

Purpose: To detect schemes related to fictitious revenues.

Audit Test Procedure: Identify duplicate invoices, credits, and receipts.

Explanation: To check the duplicate transactions against account receivables for the same sales of goods or services to reveal fictitious revenues.

Assertion(s) Tested: Occurrence.

CAATT Expression: Duplicates.

Possible Red Flag: Multiple transactions with the same invoice numbers or receipts numbers.

ACFE Fraud Tree Subcategory: Fictitious Revenues.

Purpose: To detect schemes related to fictitious revenues.

Audit Test Procedure: Credits, receipts, and invoices are not in proper sequence or range.

Explanation: To check the transactions recorded (credits, receipts, and invoices) have actually occurred and are in proper sequence and range.

Assertion(s) Tested: Completeness.

CAATT Expression: Gaps or Sort.

Possible Red Flag: Transactions which are not in proper sequencing and range. For example, invoice number must be in between 1 and 1,000, but a transaction has an invoice number of 1,050.

ACFE Fraud Tree Subcategory: Fictitious Revenues.

Purpose: To detect schemes related to fictitious revenues.

Audit Test Procedure: Generate invoice summaries by customer or invoice amount.

Explanation: To check that customers have paid only once for a bill.

Assertion(s) Tested: Occurrence.

CAATT Expression: Summarize.

Possible Red Flag: Multiple payments for the same bill.

ACFE Fraud Tree Subcategory: Fictitious Revenues.

Purpose: To detect schemes related to fictitious revenues.

Audit Test Procedure: Identify high-value credit notes, balances, and invoices.

Explanation: To check that all transactions recorded have actually occurred.

Assertion(s) Tested: Occurrence.

CAATT Expression: Filter/Display Criteria.

Possible Red Flag: High-value invoices recorded near the end of an accounting period.

ACFE Fraud Tree Subcategory: Fictitious Revenues.

Purpose: To detect schemes related to fictitious revenues.

Audit Test Procedure: Identify customer accounts with no address or telephone information.

Explanation: To check the customer accounts without telephone numbers or addresses.

Assertion(s) Tested: Existence.

CAATT Expression: Expression/Equation.

Possible Red Flag: High-value receivables without customer contact information.

ACFE Fraud Tree Subcategory: Fictitious Revenues.

Purpose: To detect schemes related to fictitious revenues.

Audit Test Procedure: Identify credits and debits to dormant or unused accounts.

Explanation: To check the accounts where there has been no financial activity for an extended period but where payments have suddenly started.

Assertion(s) Tested: Occurrence.

CAATT Expression: Age and Expression/Equation.

Possible Red Flag: High-dollar transactions from unused accounts.

ACFE Fraud Tree Subcategory: Fictitious Revenues.

Purpose: To detect schemes related to fictitious revenues.

Audit Test Procedure: Generate confirmation letters to confirm customer payments.

Explanation: Generate confirmation letters to confirm customer payments.

Assertion(s) Tested: Existence.

CAATT Expression: Export and Mail Merge.

Possible Red Flag: Customers who have to pay high-value amounts to company and also the difference between customer confirmation and company account balances.

ACFE Fraud Tree Subcategory: Fictitious Revenues.

Purpose: To detect schemes related to fictitious revenues.

Audit Test Procedure: Identify accounts with even balances.

Explanation: To identify different accounts which contains even amounts balances to inflate revenues.

Assertion(s) Tested: Existence.

CAATT Expression: Filter/Display Criteria.

Possible Red Flag: Even account balances.

ACFE Fraud Tree Subcategory: Fictitious Revenues.

Purpose: To detect schemes related to fictitious revenues.

Audit Test Procedure: Track year-to-date activity for large operating accounts.

Explanation: To examine how business is generating profits from operating accounts from beginning of the year to present.

Assertion(s) Tested: Occurrence.

CAATT Expression: Summarize.

Possible Red Flag: High-value changes in sales.

ACFE Fraud Tree Subcategory: Fictitious Revenues.

Purpose: To detect schemes related to fictitious revenues.

Audit Test Procedure: Identify large adjustment transactions.

Explanation: To check the occurrence of adjustment transactions.

Assertion(s) Tested: Occurrence.

CAATT Expression: Filter/Display Criteria.

Possible Red Flag: Many adjustment entries.

ACFE Fraud Tree Subcategory: Fictitious Revenues.

Purpose: To detect schemes related to fictitious revenues.

Audit Test Procedure: Identify large adjustment transactions.

Explanation: To isolate high balance inventory accounts that are overdue.

Assertion(s) Tested: Existence.

CAATT Expression: Age and Filter/Display Criteria.

Possible Red Flag: High-value items.

ACFE Fraud Tree Subcategory: Fictitious Revenues.

Purpose: To detect schemes related to fictitious revenues.

Audit Test Procedure: Identify duplicate items or serial numbers.

Explanation: To check for duplicate items and serial numbers.

Assertion(s) Tested: Occurrence.

CAATT Expression: Duplicates.

Possible Red Flag: Duplicate serial numbers for different items.

ACFE Fraud Tree Subcategory: Fictitious Revenues.
Purpose: To detect schemes related to fictitious revenues.
Audit Test Procedure: Report high value items purchased by buyers.
Explanation: To check items purchased by buyers that contain high-dollar values.
Assertion(s) Tested: Occurrence.
CAATT Expression: Duplicates.
Possible Red Flag: Unexplained sales of high-value items.

ACFE Fraud Tree Subcategory: Fictitious Revenues.
Purpose: To detect schemes related to fictitious revenues.
Audit Test Procedure: Compare historical standard to sales prices to identify unrealized
profits.
Explanation: To check the value of purchased items and the current market value of same
items for determination of unrealized profits.
Assertion(s) Tested: Accuracy.
CAATT Expression: Join/Relate.
Possible Red Flag: Higher market value allocation for an item.

ACFE Fraud Tree Subcategory: Fictitious Revenues.
Purpose: To detect schemes related to fictitious revenues.
Audit Test Procedure: Calculate turnover to determine usage and ordering efficiency.
Explanation: To determine the turnover ratio of customer orders.
Assertion(s) Tested: Occurrence.
CAATT Expression: Age.
Possible Red Flag: Excessive reordering of items by a customer or a group of customers.

ACFE Fraud Tree Subcategory: Fictitious Revenues.
Purpose: To detect schemes related to fictitious revenues.
Audit Test Procedure: Highlight high-value balances.
Explanation: To verify that the high-value balances really exist.
Assertion(s) Tested: Existence.
CAATT Expression: Filter/Display Criteria.
Possible Red Flag: Abnormally high-value transactions.

ACFE Fraud Tree Subcategory: Fictitious Revenues.
Purpose: To detect schemes related to fictitious revenues.
Audit Test Procedure: Identify unusual delivery addresses.
Explanation: To figure out abnormal delivery addresses.
Assertion(s) Tested: Existence.
CAATT Expression: Summarize and Filter/Display Criteria.
Possible Red Flag: High-value sales with delivery addresses that does not exist.

ACFE Fraud Tree Subcategory: Fictitious Revenues.

Purpose: To detect schemes related to fictitious revenues.

Audit Test Procedure: Identify items with high merchandise returns or discount allowance rates.

Explanation: To check the items which have higher returns and allowance rates (sales returns and allowance rate is contra-revenue account).

Assertion(s) Tested: Existence.

CAATT Expression: Summarize and Filter/Display Criteria.

Possible Red Flag: Account(s) with high return rates, or accounts that have been assessed large allowance (discount) rates.

ACFE Fraud Tree Subcategory: Fictitious Revenues.

Purpose: To detect schemes related to fictitious revenues.

Audit Test Procedure: Identify vendors with names spelled or sounding similar to well-known vendors.

Explanation: To identify sales related to vendors with names that resemble well-known vendors.

Assertion(s) Tested: Occurrence.

CAATT Expression: Soundslike(), and Filter/Display Criteria.

Possible Red Flag: Different vendors having names that sounds like each other's.

ACFE Fraud Tree Subcategory: Fictitious Revenues.

Purpose: To detect schemes related to fictitious revenues.

Audit Test Procedure: Calculate sales by region, customer, and category.

Explanation: To determine overall sales with respect to regions, customers, and categories that might result in fictitious revenues.

Assertion(s) Tested: Occurrence.

CAATT Expression: Summarize.

Possible Red Flag: Regions with lower populations that have more revenue generation than those with high populations.

ACFE Fraud Tree Subcategory: Fictitious Revenues.

Purpose: To detect schemes related to fictitious revenues.

Audit Test Procedure: Compare current and previous periods to analyze sales trends.

Explanation: To analyze the sales trends among different periods.

Assertion(s) Tested: Occurrence.

CAATT Expression: Join/Relate.

Possible Red Flag: Unexplained surge in sales during period(s), compared to historical trends.

ACFE Fraud Tree Subcategory: Fictitious Revenues.

Purpose: To detect schemes related to fictitious revenues.

Audit Test Procedure: Calculate current sales ratio to open receivables (high to low).

Explanation: To check the ratio between current sales and open receivables (money due for services or supplies).

Assertion(s) Tested: Occurrence.

CAATT Expression: Expression/Equation and Trend Analysis.

Possible Red Flag: Unusual increase in the ratio of sales versus receivables during period(s).

ACFE Fraud Tree Subcategory: Concealed Liabilities and Expenses.

Purpose: To detect schemes related to concealed liabilities and expenses.

Audit Test Procedure: Report on gaps in the sequencing of invoices generated.

Explanation: To check that all invoices are in proper sequencing order.

Assertion(s) Tested: Existence.

CAATT Expression: Gaps.

Possible Red Flag: Gaps in invoice(s) suggesting concealed purchases.

ACFE Fraud Tree Subcategory: Concealed Liabilities and Expenses.

Purpose: To detect schemes related to concealed liabilities and expenses.

Audit Test Procedure: Identify instances where one clerk has processed all the invoices for the account.

Explanation: To check the instances where one clerk processed all the invoices for a specific account.

Assertion(s) Tested: Accuracy.

CAATT Expression: Cross Tab/Pivot Table.

Possible Red Flag: No invoices for an account processed by other clerks.

ACFE Fraud Tree Subcategory: Concealed Liabilities and Expenses.

Purpose: To detect schemes related to concealed liabilities and expenses.

Audit Test Procedure: Calculate and compare variances in accounts between periods.

Explanation: To check the variances in liabilities and expense accounts in different accounting periods.

Assertion(s) Tested: Accuracy.

CAATT Expression: Summarize and Join/Relate.

Possible Red Flag: Unexplained trends in liabilities and expenses.

ACFE Fraud Tree Subcategory: Concealed Liabilities and Expenses.

Purpose: To detect schemes related to concealed liabilities and expenses.

Audit Test Procedure: Total purchases by ordering clerk and by vendor.

Explanation: To segregate all purchases by ordering clerk and vendor to detect unusual trends.

Assertion(s) Tested: Accuracy.

CAATT Expression: Summarize.

Possible Red Flag: Unusually high-dollar value of purchases are ordered by the same clerk and through the same vendor.

ACFE Fraud Tree Subcategory: Concealed Liabilities and Expenses.

Purpose: To detect schemes related to concealed liabilities and expenses.

Audit Test Procedure: Match contract price to invoice and report on variances.

Explanation: To figure out the variances between contract price and invoices.

Assertion(s) Tested: Accuracy.

CAATT Expression: Join/Relate and Expression/Equation.

Possible Red Flag: A match of invoice price(s) indicates larger charges than those stipulated in the supporting contract.

ACFE Fraud Tree Subcategory: Concealed Liabilities and Expenses.

Purpose: To detect schemes related to concealed liabilities and expenses.

Audit Test Procedure: Calculate profit variances by item.

Explanation: To analyze the cost variances of different purchased items compared to previous period(s).

Assertion(s) Tested: Accuracy.

CAATT Expression: Join/Relate and Expression/Equation.

Possible Red Flag: The cost of some purchased items is up significantly without any explanations.

ACFE Fraud Tree Subcategory: Concealed Liabilities and Expenses.

Purpose: To detect schemes related to concealed liabilities and expenses.

Audit Test Procedure: Calculate an average purchase by vendor for the first three quarters of the year and relate it to the last quarter of the year.

Explanation: To compare the first three average quarter purchases by vendor and average last quarter purchases to discover any concealed expenses.

Assertion(s) Tested: Accuracy/Existence.

CAATT Expression: Summarize.

Possible Red Flag: Significantly lower value for last quarter purchases.

ACFE Fraud Tree Subcategory: Concealed Liabilities and Expenses.

Purpose: To detect schemes related to concealed liabilities and expenses.

Audit Test Procedure: Aged outstanding purchase orders with no invoices charged.

Explanation: To discover purchase orders without any invoices – may represent unrecorded purchases.

Assertion(s) Tested: Occurrence.

CAATT Expression: Age.

Possible Red Flag: Purchases without invoices.

ACFE Fraud Tree Subcategory: Concealed Liabilities and Expenses.

Purpose: To detect schemes related to concealed liabilities and expenses.

Audit Test Procedure: Stratify fixed asset additions.

Explanation: To discover capitalized high-dollar fixed assets that should be expensed.

Assertion(s) Tested: Classification.

CAATT Expression: Stratify.

Possible Red Flag: High-dollar values of capitalized fixed assets.

ACFE Fraud Tree Subcategory: Concealed Liabilities and Expenses.

Purpose: To detect schemes related to concealed liabilities and expenses.

Audit Test Procedure: Stratify fixed asset additions by month.

Explanation: To analyze the addition of high-dollar value fixed assets by month.

Assertion(s) Tested: Classification.

CAATT Expression: Age.

Possible Red Flag: Capitalizing asset(s) instead of expensing them.

ACFE Fraud Tree Subcategory: Improper Asset Valuations.

Purpose: To detect schemes related to improper asset valuations.

Audit Test Procedure: Identify surplus or obsolete inventory.

Explanation: To check asset valuation of obsolete inventory and surplus inventory.

Assertion(s) Tested: Accuracy and Valuation.

CAATT Expression: Join/Relate.

Possible Red Flag: Incorrect asset valuation of obsolete inventory.

ACFE Fraud Tree Subcategory: Improper Asset Valuations.

Purpose: To detect schemes related to improper asset valuations.

Audit Test Procedure: Show items depreciated to cost in order to highlight assets greater than cost.

Explanation: To find the assets that are not depreciated.

Assertion(s) Tested: Accuracy and Valuation.

CAATT Expression: Expression/Equation and Sort.

Possible Red Flag: Net carrying value of the asset is not changing on a yearly basis.

ACFE Fraud Tree Subcategory: Improper Asset Valuations.

Purpose: To detect schemes related to improper asset valuations.

Audit Test Procedure: Recalculate expense and reserve amounts using replacement costs.

Explanation: To find the replacement cost of inventory.

Assertion(s) Tested: Accuracy.

CAATT Expression: Expression/Equation.

Possible Red Flag: Gross profit ratio is increasing without an increase in sales price.

ACFE Fraud Tree Subcategory: Improper Asset Valuations.

Purpose: To detect schemes related to improper asset valuations.

Audit Test Procedure: Compare the value of physical inventory to general ledger amounts.

Explanation: To find the variance between value of inventory physically present and inventory recorded in general ledger.

Assertion(s) Tested: Completeness/Accuracy.

CAATT Expression: Join/Relate.

Possible Red Flag: Recording of obsolete inventory in general ledgers.

ACFE Fraud Tree Subcategory: Improper Asset Valuations.

Purpose: To detect schemes related to improper asset valuations.

Audit Test Procedure: Calculate the age and the value of receivables by range of days (30, 60, 90, 120).

Explanation: To check the schedule of account receivables under 30, 60, 90, 120 days (also useful for determination of potential bad debts).

Assertion(s) Tested: Valuation.

CAATT Expression: Age.

Possible Red Flag: Unpaid receivables that are older than 90 days.

ACFE Fraud Tree Subcategory: Improper Asset Valuations.

Purpose: To detect schemes related to improper asset valuations.

Audit Test Procedure: Duplicate inventory listings by amount and description, as well as quantity and amount.

Explanation: To check for duplicate inventory listings by amount and description and amount and quantities to inflate period end balances.

Assertion(s) Tested: Valuation and Allocation.

CAATT Expression: Duplicates.

Possible Red Flag: Duplicate inventory with the same descriptions, amounts, and quantities.

ACFE Fraud Tree Subcategory: Improper Asset Valuations.

Purpose: To detect schemes related to improper asset valuations.

Audit Test Procedure: Inventory price greater than retail price.

Explanation: To check for inventory prices that are greater than retail prices.

Assertion(s) Tested: Valuation and Allocation.

CAATT Expression: Expression/Equation.

Possible Red Flag: Goods with inventory prices greater than retail prices.

ACFE Fraud Tree Subcategory: Improper Asset Valuations.

Purpose: To detect schemes related to improper asset valuations.

Audit Test Procedure: Compares actual unit price to standard unit price (on a part-by-part basis).

Explanation: To compare actual unit price to standard unit price which results in improper asset valuation.

Assertion(s) Tested: Accuracy/Valuation and Allocation.

CAATT Expression: Expression/Equation.

Possible Red Flag: An inflated actual unit price as compared to the standard price.

ACFE Fraud Tree Subcategory: Improper Asset Valuations.

Purpose: To detect schemes related to improper asset valuations.

Audit Test Procedure: Extract inventory items without descriptions.

Explanation: To check for inventory items without descriptions which are more prone to be fictitiously added.

Assertion(s) Tested: Existence/Valuation and Allocation.

CAATT Expression: Filter/Display Criteria.

Possible Red Flag: Inventory items without descriptions.

ACFE Fraud Tree Subcategory: Improper Asset Valuations.

Purpose: To detect schemes related to improper asset valuations.

Audit Test Procedure: Duplicate fixed asset listing by amount and description.

Explanation: To find out the duplicates fixed assets with respective amounts and descriptions which can inflate period end balances.

Assertion(s) Tested: Existence/Valuation and Allocation.

CAATT Expression: Duplicates.

Possible Red Flag: Duplicated entries of fixed assets.

ACFE Fraud Tree Subcategory: Overstated Liabilities and Expenses.

Purpose: To detect schemes related to overstated liabilities and expenses.

Audit Test Procedure: Calculate age and value of payables by range of days (30, 60, 90, 120).

Explanation: To check the schedule of account receivables under 30, 60, 90, 120 days, which is also useful for determination of potential bad debts.

Assertion(s) Tested: Existence.

CAATT Expression: Age.

Possible Red Flag: Large accounts payables carrying balances from last accounting periods.

ACFE Fraud Tree Subcategory: Overstated Liabilities and Expenses.

Purpose: To detect schemes related to overstated liabilities and expenses.

Audit Test Procedure: Summarize large invoices without purchase orders.

Explanation: To discover the large purchase invoices without purchasing orders.

Assertion(s) Tested: Completeness.

CAATT Expression: Filter/Display Criteria and Expression/Equation.

Possible Red Flag: Large (high amount) invoices that do not have corresponding purchase orders.

ACFE Fraud Tree Subcategory: Overstated Liabilities and Expenses.

Purpose: To detect schemes related to overstated liabilities and expenses.

Audit Test Procedure: Identify freight and tax overcharges.

Explanation: To identify the values in accounts payables which might be overstated in amounts.

Assertion(s) Tested: Accuracy.

CAATT Expression: Expression/Equation and Filter/Display Criteria.

Possible Red Flag: High values of freight and tax overcharges.

ACFE Fraud Tree Subcategory: Overstated Liabilities and Expenses.

Purpose: To detect schemes related to overstated liabilities and expenses.

Audit Test Procedure: Identify charges to dormant or unused accounts.

Explanation: To check the charges related to dormant or unused accounts (legitimate account holders may not be monitoring the account).

Assertion(s) Tested: Existence.

CAATT Expression: Summarize and Filter/Display Criteria.

Possible Red Flag: Abnormal debit entries from dormant accounts.

ACFE Fraud Tree Subcategory: Overstated Liabilities and Expenses.

Purpose: To detect schemes related to overstated liabilities and expenses.

Audit Test Procedure: Identify checks issued to vendors with names that sound like known vendors.

Explanation: To discover checks issued under the vendor name that resemble known vendors.

Assertion(s) Tested: Existence.

CAATT Expression: Soundslike().

Possible Red Flag: High value (or a significant number of low-value checks) issued to vendors with similar names to well-known vendors or service providers.

ACFE Fraud Tree Subcategory: Overstated Liabilities and Expenses.

Purpose: To detect schemes related to overstated liabilities and expenses.

Audit Test Procedure: Identify high-value credit notes, balances, and invoices.

Explanation: To check unusually high-value payment transactions that result in an overstatement of expenses.

Assertion(s) Tested: Accuracy.

CAATT Expression: Filter/Display Criteria.

Possible Red Flag: High-value invoices recorded near the end of an accounting period.

ACFE Fraud Tree Subcategory: Overstated Liabilities and Expenses.

Purpose: To detect schemes related to overstated liabilities and expenses.

Audit Test Procedure: Compute weighted and average interest rates across periods.

Explanation: To check that the applied interest rates are accurate for different periods. Usually, the weighted average interest rate is between the lowest and highest interest rates.

Assertion(s) Tested: Accuracy.

CAATT Expression: Join/Relate and Expression/Equation.

Possible Red Flag: Interest rates below the lowest or above the highest interest rate.

ACFE Fraud Tree Subcategory: Overstated Liabilities and Expenses.

Purpose: To detect schemes related to overstated liabilities and expenses.

Audit Test Procedure: Prepare trail balances and account reconciliations.

Explanation: To see if a company's account ledger balance can be reconciled to bank statements.

Assertion(s) Tested: Existence.

CAATT Expression: Summarize.

Possible Red Flag: Unbalanced journal entries in expense or liability accounts.

ACFE Fraud Tree Subcategory: Overstated Liabilities and Expenses.

Purpose: To detect schemes related to overstated liabilities and expenses.

Audit Test Procedure: Calculate the difference between actual and standard costs.

Explanation: To check for differences between actual and standard costs if items (may result in overstated liabilities and expenses).

Assertion(s) Tested: Accuracy.

CAATT Expression: Join and Expression/Equation.

Possible Red Flag: High allocation of cost to items.

ACFE Fraud Tree Subcategory: Overstated Liabilities and Expenses.

Purpose: To detect schemes related to overstated liabilities and expenses.

Audit Test Procedure: Identify duplicate purchase order numbers.

Explanation: To discover duplicate purchases according to order numbers (may overstate expenses).

Assertion(s) Tested: Existence.

CAATT Expression: Duplicates.

Possible Red Flag: Same quantities ordered many times in a short period.

ACFE Fraud Tree Subcategory: Overstated Liabilities and Expenses.

Purpose: To detect schemes related to overstated liabilities and expenses.

Audit Test Procedure: Identify older purchase orders or purchase orders with only partial quantities received.

Explanation: To discover old purchase orders or those where only partial quantities were received (may lead to overstatement of expenses).

Assertion(s) Tested: Accuracy.

CAATT Expression: Age and Filter/Display Criteria.

Possible Red Flag: Variances between purchase orders and orders received.

ACFE Fraud Tree Subcategory: Overstated Liabilities and Expenses.

Purpose: To detect schemes related to overstated liabilities and expenses.

Audit Test Procedure: Analyze travel expenses by employee-duplicates, high values, and frequency.

Explanation: To check if there are any travel expense duplications for employees that result in an overstatement of expenses.

Assertion(s) Tested: Occurrence.

CAATT Expression: Duplicates, Summarize, and Filter/Display Criteria.

Possible Red Flag: More than one travel expense claim for same time period.

ACFE Fraud Tree Subcategory: Overstated Liabilities and Expenses.

Purpose: To detect schemes related to overstated liabilities and expenses.

Audit Test Procedure: Analyze education and training expenses by employee for duplicates, high values, and frequency.

Explanation: To check for duplication of educational and training expenses for employees that result in overstatement of expenses.

Assertion(s) Tested: Occurrence.

CAATT Expression: Duplicates, Summarize, and Filter/Display Criteria.

Possible Red Flag: More than one educational and training expense claim for the same time period.

ACFE Fraud Tree Subcategory: Overstated Liabilities and Expenses.

Purpose: To detect schemes related to overstated liabilities and expenses.

Audit Test Procedure: Identify duplicate vendor numbers on vendor master file.

Explanation: To identify vendor number duplications in the vendor master file which may result in an overstatement of expenses.

Assertion(s) Tested: Occurrence.

CAATT Expression: Duplicates.

Possible Red Flag: A particular vendor holding more than one vendor number in the vendor master file.

ACFE Fraud Tree Subcategory: Overstated Liabilities and Expenses.

Purpose: To detect schemes related to overstated liabilities and expenses.

Audit Test Procedure: Match vendor and employee names, addresses, and phone numbers.

Explanation: To discover instances where the vendor and employee name, address, and phone numbers are the same.

Assertion(s) Tested: Occurrence.

CAATT Expression: Join/Relate.

Possible Red Flag: An employee and a vendor having the same contact information.

ACFE Fraud Tree Subcategory: Overstated Liabilities and Expenses.

Purpose: To detect schemes related to overstated liabilities and expenses.

Audit Test Procedure: Duplicate claims for the same period.

Explanation: To find expenses recorded more than once.

Assertion(s) Tested: Occurrence.

CAATT Expression: Duplicates.

Possible Red Flag: The same expense records occurring more than once.

ACFE Fraud Tree Subcategory: Overstated Liabilities and Expenses.

Purpose: To detect schemes related to overstated liabilities and expenses.

Audit Test Procedure: Claims for use of personal vehicle and rental car for the same period.

Explanation: To check rental and personal car claims during a specific period of time.

Assertion(s) Tested: Occurrence.

CAATT Expression: Join/Relate.

Possible Red Flag: Discovering the same dates from an employee for more than one car claim (i.e. a rental and personal claim on the same day).

ACFE Fraud Tree Subcategory: Overstated Liabilities and Expenses.

Purpose: To detect schemes related to overstated liabilities and expenses.

Audit Test Procedure: Consecutively numbered hotel invoices or meal receipts faked to show more expenses.

Explanation: To ensure that receipts are consecutive in number and are not faked to show more expenses.

Assertion(s) Tested: Occurrence.

CAATT Expression: Gaps.

Possible Red Flag: Missed series or gaps in sequence.

ACFE Fraud Tree Subcategory: Overstated Liabilities and Expenses.

Purpose: To detect schemes related to overstated liabilities and expenses.

Audit Test Procedure: Travel claim for time when employee was on vacation or sick leave.

Explanation: To ensure that travel claims do not occur while employees are off sick or on vacation.

Assertion(s) Tested: Occurrence.

CAATT Expression: Join/Relate.

Possible Red Flag: Travel claim that coincides with an employee's sick time or vacation.

ACFE Fraud Tree Subcategory: Overstated Liabilities and Expenses.

Purpose: To detect schemes related to overstated liabilities and expenses.

Audit Test Procedure: Match expense claim amounts to amounts on corporate credit card.

Explanation: To make sure that the same expense does not occur on corporate credit card and employee credit/debit card at same time.

Assertion(s) Tested: Occurrence.

CAATT Expression: Join/Relate.

Possible Red Flag: Time, place, and date on corporate credit card receipts and personal claim receipts are exactly the same.

ACFE Fraud Tree Subcategory: Overstated Liabilities and Expenses.

Purpose: To detect schemes related to overstated liabilities and expenses.

Audit Test Procedure: Identify travel claims to exotic locations.

Explanation: To check whether travels to these locations were business related or whether the exotic location really exists.

Assertion(s) Tested: Occurrence.

CAATT Expression: Filter/Display Criteria.

Possible Red Flag: Fake location details (names and addresses), or travel was for personal reasons.

ACFE Fraud Tree Subcategory: Overstated Liabilities and Expenses.

Purpose: To detect schemes related to overstated liabilities and expenses.

Audit Test Procedure: Identify business travel with departures on Friday or Saturday and return on Sunday.

Explanation: To check the records of business travel where employees travel over weekends only.

Assertion(s) Tested: Occurrence.

CAATT Expression: Filter/Display Criteria and Expression/Equation.

Possible Red Flag: Weekend traveling of employees.

ACFE Fraud Tree Subcategory: Overstated Liabilities and Expenses.

Purpose: To detect schemes related to overstated liabilities and expenses.

Audit Test Procedure: Identify overlapping travel claims.

Explanation: To check that travel expense claims don't overlap with each other (e.g., one expense claim must not cover another expense claim – there should be two distinct claims).

Assertion(s) Tested: Occurrence.

CAATT Expression: Filter/Display Criteria.

Possible Red Flag: High-value expense claims.

ACFE Fraud Tree Subcategory: Concealed/Overstated Liabilities and Expenses.

Purpose: To detect schemes related to concealed/overstated liabilities and expenses.

Audit Test Procedure: Identify items with yearly volumes over/under total quantity ordered.

Explanation: To identify ordered items that run over or fall under the total volume in a year.

Assertion(s) Tested: Occurrence.

CAATT Expression: Expression/Equation.

Possible Red Flag: Unusual ordering of items.

ACFE Fraud Tree Subcategory: Concealed/Overstated Liabilities and Expenses.

Purpose: To detect schemes related to concealed/overstated liabilities and expenses.

Audit Test Procedure: Compare book and tax depreciation values and report variances.

Explanation: To discover variances between book and tax depreciation.

Assertion(s) Tested: Accuracy.

CAATT Expression: Join/Relate and Expression/Equation.

Possible Red Flag: Large variances between book and tax depreciation where the depreciation amount has been increasing without any purchase of fixed assets.

ACFE Fraud Tree Subcategory: Concealed/Overstated Liabilities and Expenses.

Purpose: To detect schemes related to concealed/overstated liabilities and expenses.

Audit Test Procedure: Calculate variance from standard pricing.

Explanation: To check items that contain prices over or under the standard prices (may result in overstated/concealed liability and expenses).

Assertion(s) Tested: Accuracy.

CAATT Expression: Expression/Equations.

Possible Red Flag: Very high or very low prices of items.

ACFE Fraud Tree Subcategory: Concealed/Overstated Liabilities and Expenses.

Purpose: To detect schemes related to concealed/overstated liabilities and expenses.

Audit Test Procedure: Compare recurring monthly expenses to posted/paid invoices.

Explanation: To check that monthly expenses have been paid with the same (correct) amounts and there are no overstatement/understatements of expenses in F/Ss.

Assertion(s) Tested: Completeness.

CAATT Expression: Join/Relate.

Possible Red Flag: Differences between the actual and posted/paid expenses.

ACFE Fraud Tree Subcategory: Concealed/Overstated Liabilities and Expenses.

Purpose: To detect schemes related to concealed/overstated liabilities and expenses.

Audit Test Procedure: Compare voucher or invoice amounts to purchase order or contract amounts.

Explanation: To check the accuracy of both invoice amounts and contract amounts to make sure that there is no overstatement/understatement of expenses.

Assertion(s) Tested: Completeness/Accuracy.

CAATT Expression: Join/Relate.

Possible Red Flag: Difference between invoice receipts and contract amounts.

ACFE Fraud Tree Subcategory: Concealed/Overstated Liabilities and Expenses.

Purpose: To detect schemes related to concealed/overstated liabilities and expenses.

Audit Test Procedure: Generate confirmation letters to verify customer balances.

Explanation: To check that declared accounts payables actually exist and that the appropriate amounts were or are being paid.

Assertion(s) Tested: Existence.

CAATT Expression: Export and Mail Merge.

Possible Red Flag: Differences between the account balances and customer confirmations.

ACFE Fraud Tree Subcategory: Concealed/Overstated Liabilities and Expenses.

Purpose: To detect schemes related to concealed/overstated liabilities and expenses.

Audit Test Procedure: Report on variances between delivery documents and invoices.

Explanation: To ensure that delivery documents and invoices have the same recorded amounts.

Assertion(s) Tested: Accuracy.

CAATT Expression: Expression/Equation and Filter/Display Criteria.

Possible Red Flag: Differences between the amounts on invoices and delivery documents.

ACFE Fraud Tree Subcategory: Concealed/Overstated Liabilities and Expenses.

Purpose: To detect schemes related to concealed/overstated liabilities and expenses.

Audit Test Procedure: Compare purchase quantities and pricing to contract.

Explanation: To verify that there are no variances between purchase quantities and pricing and the contract.

Assertion(s) Tested: Accuracy.

CAATT Expression: Join/Relate.

Possible Red Flag: Very high and/or very low prices.

ACFE Fraud Tree Subcategory: Concealed/Overstated Liabilities and Expenses.

Purpose: To detect schemes related to concealed/overstated liabilities and expenses.

Audit Test Procedure: Analyze open orders and open invoices.

Explanation: To check for variances between open orders and open invoices (may be concealed liabilities and expenses).

Assertion(s) Tested: Accuracy.

CAATT Expression: Filter/Display Criteria and Summarize.

Possible Red Flag: Very high and/or very low invoice prices and/or quantities.

ACFE Fraud Tree Subcategory: Understated Revenues.

Purpose: To detect schemes related to understated revenues.

Audit Test Procedure: Report on gaps in the sequencing of invoices generated.

Explanation: To check that accounts receivable invoices are in proper sequencing for lower chances of declaration of understated revenues.

Assertion(s) Tested: Cut-off.

CAATT Expression: Age and Summarize.

Possible Red Flag: Abnormal transactions at year end.

ACFE Fraud Tree Subcategory: Understated Revenues.
Purpose: To detect schemes related to understated revenues.
Audit Test Procedure: Identify items below the standard margin.
Explanation: Identify all those items that fall under a standard margin (may result in understated revenues).
Assertion(s) Tested: Accuracy.
CAATT Expression: Filter/Display Criteria and Expression/Equation.
Possible Red Flag: Deliberately false calculation of sales or cost of goods sold.

ACFE Fraud Tree Subcategory: Understated Revenues.
Purpose: To detect schemes related to understated revenues.
Audit Test Procedure: Stratify customer sales orders, shipments, and sales invoices.
Explanation: To stratify customer sales orders by shipments and invoices.
Assertion(s) Tested: Occurrence.
CAATT Expression: Stratify.
Possible Red Flag: Abnormal count of invoices under the normal stratification range.

ACFE Fraud Tree Subcategory: Understated Revenues.
Purpose: To detect schemes related to understated revenues.
Audit Test Procedure: Complete a trend analysis of sales invoices by customer.
Explanation: To carry out trend analysis of sales customers by invoices.
Assertion(s) Tested: Accuracy.
CAATT Expression: Trend Analysis.
Possible Red Flag: Abnormal decrease percentage change in sales amount of a particular customer.

ACFE Fraud Tree Subcategory: Understated Revenues.
Purpose: To detect schemes related to understated revenues.
Audit Test Procedure: Confirmation of customer receivable balances.
Explanation: To confirm the accounts receivables from customers.
Assertion(s) Tested: Existence.
CAATT Expression: Export and Mail Merge.
Possible Red Flag: Differences between customers' recorded and confirmed account balances.

References

1. Association of Certified Fraud Examiners. (2018). Report to the Nations on Occupational Fraud and Abuse. Retrieved from https://s3-us-west-2.amazonaws.com/acfepublic/2018-report-to-the-nations.pdf
2. Patsuris, P. (2002, July 25). The corporate scandal sheet. *Forbes*. Retrieved from www.forbes.com/2002/07/25/accountingtracker.html

3. Miller, A. (2015). Tesco Scandal. *Association of Chartered Certified Accountants*. Retrieved from www.accaglobal.com/zm/en/student/sa/features/tesco-scandal.html

4. Tadeo, M. (2014). Tesco chairman Sir Richard Broadbent resigns following accounting scandal. *Independent*. Retrieved from www.independent.co.uk/news/business/news/tesco-chairman-sir-richard-broadbent-resigns-following-accounting-scandal-9812877.html

5. Brinded, L. (2015). Tesco is really unsure about the accounting probe outcome but it knows it's going to be BAD. *Business Insider UK*. Retrieved from http://uk.businessinsider.com/tesco-accounting-overstatement-scandal-investigation-update-2015-5

6. Smith, G. (2015). Toshiba just lost its CEO to a huge accounting scandal. *Fortune*. Retrieved from http://fortune.com/2015/07/21/toshiba-just-lost-its-ceo-to-a-huge-accounting-scandal/

7. Mochizuki, T. (2015). Toshiba must adjust operating profit down by $1.2 billion. *The Wall Street Journal*. Retrieved from www.wsj.com/articles/toshiba-must-adjust-operating-profit-down-by-151-8-billion-1437400355

8. Linder, B. (2015). Toshiba CEO resigns after overstating profits by $1.2 billion. *Liliputing*. Retrieved from https://liliputing.com/2015/07/toshiba-ceo-resigns-after-overstating-profits-by-1-2-billion.html

9. Du, L. (2015). 5 Things to know about Toshiba's accounting scandal. *The Wall Street Journal*. Retrieved from http://blogs.wsj.com/briefly2015/07/21/5-things-to-know-about-toshibas-accounting-scandal-2/

10. Lubin, G. (2012). Michael Woodford: Olympus never would have hired me if they weren't desperate. *Business Insider*. Retrieved from www.businessinsider.com/olympus-hired-woodford-out-of-desperation-2012-3

11. Langeland, T. (2014). Olympus sued for $273 million after 13-year fraud. *Bloomberg*. Retrieved from www.bloomberg.com/news/articles/2014-04-09/olympus-sued-for-273-million-after-13-year-fraud

12. Inagaki, K., & Dvorak, P. (2011). Olympus admits to hiding losses. *The Wall Street Journal*. Retrieved from www.wsj.com/articles/SB10001424052970204190704577024680506345936

13. Voigt, K. (2011). Board members in Olympus cover-up resign. *CNN*. Retrieved from www.cnn.com/2011/11/24/business/japan-olympus-scandal/index.html

14. Cattaneo, C. (2014). Rocked by accounting scandal, Penn West has now turned the corner, CEO says. *Financial Post*. Retrieved from http://business.financialpost.com/commodities/energy/rocked-by-accounting-scandal-penn-west-has-now-turned-the-corner-ceo-says

15. Martin, M. (2014). Saudi Arabia's Mobily suspends CEO after accounting error. *Bloomberg*. Retrieved from www.bloomberg.com/news/articles/2014-11-23/saudi-arabia-s-mobily-suspends-ceo-after-accounting-error

16. Cotterill, J., Vandevelde, M., Storbeck, O., & Marriage, M. (2017). Prosecutors probe for 'inflated revenue' at deal-hungry Steinhoff. *Financial Times*. Retrieved from www.ft.com/content/ea50383c-da64-11e7-a039-c64b1c09b482

17. Association of Certified Fraud Examiners. (2015). *Fraud Examiner Manual*.

18. Wells, J. (2001). Why employees commit fraud. *Journal of Accountancy*. Retrieved from www.journalofaccountancy.com/issues/2001/feb/whyemployeescommitfraud.html

19. Jans, M., Lybaert, N., & Vanhoof, K. (2009). A framework for internal fraud risk reduction at IT integrating business processes: The IFR^2 framework. *The International Journal of Digital Accounting Research*, *9*, 1–29.

20. The Institute of Internal Auditors, The American Institute of Certified Public Accountants, & The Association of Certified Fraud Examiners. (2008). Managing the Business Risk of Fraud: A Practical Guide. Retrieved from www.acfe.com/uploadedfiles/acfe_website/content/documents/managing-business-risk.pdf

21. Price Waterhouse Coopers Australia. (2008). Fraud: A Guide to Its Prevention, Detection and Investigation. Retrieved from www.pwc.com.au/consulting/assets/risk-controls/fraud-control-jul08.pdf

22. Rivest, D. (2006). Detecting Occupational Fraud in Canada: A Study of its Victim and Perpetrator. Retrieved from www.acfe.com/uploadedfiles/acfe_website/content/documents/rttn-canadian.pdf

23. Wells, J. (2011). *Corporate Fraud Handbook: Prevention and Detection*, Hoboken, NJ: John Wiley & Sons.

5

Compendium of CAATT-Based Audit Tests for the Detection of Corruption

Introduction

According to the 2018 Report to the Nations (RTTN), corruption represents one of the most significant fraud risk for enterprises across the globe. In the United States, over 30% of the cases reported in the 2018 RTTN involved corruption. These figures increase to 40% for Canada, 51% for the Latin America and the Caribbean, 60% for Eastern Europe and Central Asia region, and a whopping 62% for the Southern Asian countries. Industries affected with the highest proportion of corruption cases are the energy sector (53%), manufacturing (51%), and government/public administration (50%). Corruption fraud schemes tend to last, on average, about 22 months before being detected and are often concealed using fraudulent documents. Interestingly, while most organizations susceptible to occupational fraud schemes such as asset misappropriation tend to lack internal controls, with corruption schemes, existing internal controls are overridden by perpetrators [1].

Case Histories

Walmart

In 2012, Walmart was exposed in a massive bribery scandal that involved some of the company's top executives. Even worse, senior management knew about it and tried to cover it up. The bribery scheme involved Walmart de Mexico "systematically bribing" Mexican government authorities for years, which was concealed with a billing scheme, by creating false invoices to disguise the bribes as normal legal bills [2]. Alerted by a whistleblower (a former executive) in 2005, Walmart became aware that their Mexican subsidiary "orchestrated a campaign of bribery to win market dominance. In its rush to build stores, he said, the company had paid bribes to obtain permits in virtually every corner of the country". The whistleblower provided details, dates, names, and amounts that launched an investigation that revealed more than $24 million in bribes – but instead of expanding the investigation, Walmart shut it down [3]. Jump forward to 2017, and Walmart was still dealing with the aftermath, preparing to pay around $300 million to settle the bribery probe. This corruption case cost Walmart more than $800 million in legal fees and internal investigations [4].

Odebrecht

Odebrecht is a Latin American construction giant with its headquarters in Brazil and subsidiaries in engineering, construction, chemicals, and petrochemicals. Founded in 1944, the company even built notable projects in the United States, including the Florida International University Stadium and the Adrienne Arsht Center for the Performing Arts in Miami, Florida. In 2017, Odebrecht's reputation took a turn for the worse when it confessed to corruption and paid $2.6 billion in fines, in addition to 77 executives agreeing to plea bargains and/or jail time [5].

State of Missouri Transportation

In 2017, the Missouri State Auditor, Nicole Galloway, launched an investigation into conflicts of interest in the state transportation department, finding that three former employees violated conflict of interest laws. These employees gave preferential treatment to a vendor, HELP, Inc., favoring the company at competitors' expense. The conflict of interest was initially overlooked, with action only taken after the department's audit was completed [6].

Horizon Power

In 2018, Western Australia's Corruption and Crime Commission began investigating a Horizon Power employee who allegedly used his position to hire his own company to provide exclusive services to his employer. The conflict of interest scheme involved Paul Thomas, Horizon Power employee and director of Trusted Solutions (a private IT company), contracting Trusted Solutions to provide IT services to Horizon Power without declaring the potential conflict. Thomas allegedly concealed his involvement with Trusted Solutions, which billed Horizon Power for more than $1.6 million in services from 2013 to 2017. Thomas is also being investigated for using his position to hire his wife as a contractor in 2017 without declaring the relationship [7].

U.S. Army

In 2010, a retired U.S. Army colonel, Kevin Davis, pleaded guilty to three counts of accepting illegal gratuities. In 2004, Col. Davis was in a position of authority to source Department of Defense contracts for warehouse construction in Iraq and accepted two plane tickets and $50,000 in cash from the contractor whose bid for the projects were successful. The Department of Justice and the U.S. Army Criminal Investigation Command used this case to highlight their efforts to minimize procurement fraud in overseas operations [8].

Discussion

Corruption is a type of occupational fraud where an individual or groups of individuals wrongly use their position or power for personal gain and includes schemes like kickbacks, bid rigging, illegal gratuities, and economic extortion. While corruption fraud can and does occur in every industry, worldwide, it's particularly a problem in the public sector, resulting in the creation of anti-corruption organizations and laws like the United Nations' Anti-Fraud and Anti-Corruption Framework and national anti-corruption legislation like Canada's Foreign Bribery Act, United States of America's Foreign Corrupt Practices Act 1977, United Kingdom's Corruption Acts 1889–1916, Bribery Act 2010 and Nigeria's Corrupt practices and other related offences Act 2000. Despite legislation, corruption still runs rampant in the global economy [9].

Preventing bribery is a global pursuit warranting anti-bribery laws in 46 jurisdictions and introducing criminal liability for individuals involved in bribery. In the private sector, companies are adopting anti-corruption compliance programs and focusing on how external environments affect corporate responses to corruption – most just succumb to it. In low-integrity environments, the argument for not operating ethically often devolves into "that's-just-the-way-they-do-business-over-there." The possibility of actual prosecution or punishment in these environments is low, so business leaders tend to go with the flow, refusing to rock the boat and seeing themselves as victims in an unjust system. However, research in Egypt, Zimbabwe, and India reveal that building a reputation for ethical operations is an opportunity few are taking advantage of. Furthermore, rather than performing audits or implementing strong internal controls for corruption, most organizations turn to surveillance software to prevent or mitigate corruption schemes – which is an element of an anti-corruption program, but not as a standalone solution [9,10].

Unfortunately, there is far less focus on the organizational system – how groups and teams behave when they might have a corruption problem; a significant omission because the influence of group norms and culture on individual behavior is paramount. In fact, reviews of corruption litigation reveal that the greatest influences encouraging employees to commit fraud are an organization's culture, structures, and incentives [11].

The Impact of Organizational Corruption

Even though most people picture hardened bad guys committing crimes, corporate criminal activities more often involve respected professionals. In fact, the FBI and the Association of Certified Fraud Examiners (ACFE) estimate that "white collar crime" like occupational corruption costs "between $300 and $600 billion a year." In fact, the U.S. Department of Justice estimates that corporate crime costs seven to 25 times more than street crime. An even more troubling trend in white-collar crime is that these crimes are increasingly perpetrated by multiple insiders rather than a single misguided individual [12,13].

Corruption is a major hindrance to sustainable economic, political, and social development, for emerging, developing, and developed economies as it decreases efficiency and increases inequality [14]. On average, corruption increases total business expenses by up to 10%. Furthermore, corruption results in inefficient use or waste of public funds: corrupt politicians and business people don't allocate resources to appropriate sectors and projects, rather they re-allocate resources for their own personal benefit [15].

The Three Pillars of Normalization

The key component of occupational corruption is how seemingly ethical people engage in unethical and criminal activity. To explain this phenomenon, Ashforth and Anand argue that three factors lead to normalized corruption: institutionalization, rationalization, and socialization (Figure 5.1) [14].

> *Institutionalization:* In institutionalized corruption, the corrupt behaviors are repetitive and ongoing, becoming a routine part of most enterprise structures and processes.
>
> *Rationalization:* Perpetrators don't see themselves as criminals, rather they acknowledge their corruption by rationalizing the actions and denying criminality. They cope with their wrongdoing by reframing their behavior to suit their self-image.
>
> *Socialization:* A necessary tool for maintain corruption schemes, newcomers are essential trained to enact and work within the existing corrupt structures and practices.

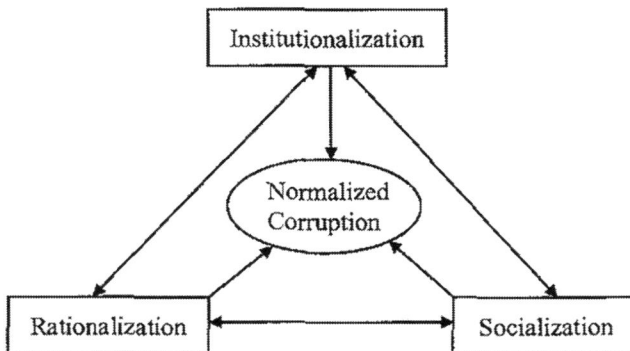

Figure 5.1 The three pillars of normalization. (*Source:* Ashforth and Anand, 2003.)

ISO 37001 as an Anti-Corruption Management Systems

The World Bank estimates that both businesses and people pay approximately \$1.5 trillion in bribes annually (that's 2% of the global GDP). As a result, corruption causes significant harm to development and economic growth. On a global level, corruption is a significant barrier to international trade, while within an organization it has a highly negative impact on employee morale [16].

ISO (International Organization for Standardization) is a non-governmental, independent international organization that includes a member of 161 national standard bodies. ISO works to share knowledge and experience while also creating innovative solutions to global problems. Because bribery is such a destructive challenge, ISO 37001 – Anti-bribery management systems was designed to instill an anti-corruption culture within organizations in addition to implementing appropriate controls. A management system that specifies internal controls and organizational measure to prevent, detect, and deal with bribery, ISO 37001 covers corruption in the private, not-for-profit, and public sectors, including bribes paid or received through or by a third party and bribery by and against an organization or its staff [17].

The measures outlined and detailed in ISO 37001 are designed for integration into existing management processes and control and can be easily integrated into other existing management systems such as quality, environmental, and safety. An effective internal control system, ISO 37001 provides minimal requirements and detailed supporting guidance for executing or benchmarking an anti-corruption/bribery management system and assurance to customers, management, investors, employees and other stakeholders that participating organizations are taking reasonable steps to prevent bribery. Using a system like ISO 37001 isn't a guarantee against bribery, but it can help organizations implement robust and proportionate measures to substantially reduce the risk of bribery and address bribery where it does occur [17].

Corruption Schemes

Corruption is any form of wrongdoing executed to gain an unfair advantage over others [18] and its schemes include undisclosed conflicts of interest (purchasing and sales schemes), bribery (invoice kickbacks and bid rigging), illegal gratuity, and economic extortion (Figure 5.2) [18].

Bribery Schemes

Bribery involves employees or executives offering, giving, accepting, or requesting anything of value in exchange for influence or advantage [11]. In business, bribery is mostly carried out to win contract over other bidders. Bribery schemes are divided into public sector, official bribery, and private sector, commercial bribery. Essentially, official bribery involves public or government officials, whereas commercial bribery involves private individuals in business. Although bribery schemes are not as rampant as asset misappropriation schemes, it's very difficult to detect and costly to rectify [19]. There are two types of bribery schemes: invoice kickbacks and bid rigging.

Kickback Schemes   An arranged bribery, kickbacks involve both parties meeting privately in advance to negotiate and agree upon the value of the kickback in exchange for the favor – it's basically an overpayment for goods and services where the overpayment is given to the perpetrator. Typically enacted by employees in purchasing, those in a position to award contracts or purchase products and services are at high risk for participating in kickback schemes [20]. In all situations, kickbacks involve an exchange of value (money or assets) to manipulate decision-making. Unlike asset misappropriation billing schemes, which also involve fictitious or inflated invoices, kickbacks involve collaboration between insiders and outsiders. For example, a supplier and a purchasing employee agree to a value and the supplier provides a fraudulent or inflated invoice to purchasing employee, who obtains necessary approval and ensure the invoice is paid. The supplier then pays the employee a kickback in exchange for facilitating the payment. Most kickback schemes are carried out by employees with purchasing roles and responsibilities because they tend to have one-on-one contact with the suppliers, enabling them to establish collusive relationships [1].

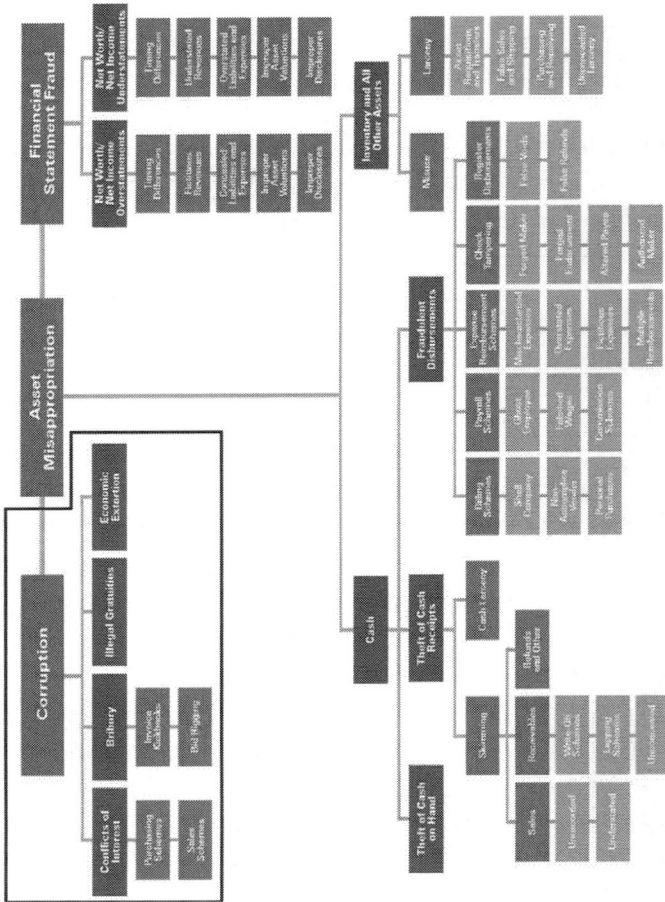

Figure 5.2   Corruption arm of the ACFE. (*Source:* Fraud Auditing and Forensic Accounting, 2015.)

Bid Rigging   When public calls for bids are made, the expectation is that companies respond to and compete for the bid fairly. Bid rigging can occur in two separate ways: (1) the individual in charge of awarding a commercial contract promises to award the contract to a company even though it's a public bid; (2) bidders collude to manipulate the bid results. In the second form of bid rigging, there are several types: complementary bidding (bidders agree to submit bids that will be unsuccessful), bid suppression (potential bidders agree not to submit a bid to allow another company to win), change order abuse (a contractor, in collusion with procurement official, can submit a low bid to insure winning a contract, and then increase its price and profits by submitting change order requests after the contract is awarded), phantom bids (false bids to encourage higher bids), and bid rotation (bidders alternate which companies are the successful bidders). These types of bid rigging can occur independently, or several can occur simultaneously. In most countries, include the United States, Canada, and the United Kingdom, bid rigging is an illegal practice that can be criminally prosecuted; however, it's common in auto sale auctions, foreclosed home auctions, and the construction industry [19].

Conflict of Interest Schemes

A conflict of interest (COI) happens when people or companies (both public and private) are able to exploit their position for personal or corporate gain – it happens when people can abuse their positions for private benefit. However, COI only becomes corruption when people *do* abuse their power for private gain [21]; essentially, they have a personal interest in a transaction but keep it hidden. COI schemes are either purchasing schemes or sales schemes:

Purchasing Schemes: Vendors overbilling goods or services (or provide inferior goods and services) where an employee has an undisclosed financial interest or ownership in the vendor company, hindering efficiency and good will (though not necessarily resulting in monetary loss).

Sales Schemes: Employees discount goods or services to companies they have an undisclosed interest in, creating a loss of revenue for the employer.

COI schemes don't always result in monetary loss, but they do degrade an organization's ethics and reputation. Some common forms of COI include self-dealing, outside, nepotism, and pump and dump schemes.

Self-Dealing: Where an employee in a managerial position uses his or her position to enter the company in business dealings with companies he or she has a personal interest in.

Outside Employment: Where an employee works for competing organizations and doesn't disclose it.

Nepotism: Where friends, spouses, children, or other close relatives are favored for employment over other qualified candidates.

Pump and Dump: Where a stock broker artificially inflates (or attempts to inflate) the value of a stock through hyperbolic recommendations to increase the price and then selling their stocks at the higher price.

Illegal Gratuity Scheme

Illegal gratuities are valuable items given, offered, or promised to reward a decision after it's been made rather than before. Unlike bribery, which influences the decision, an illegal gratuity or an unlawful tip is offered as a "thank you." While often perceived as harmless, illegal gratuities often lead to bribery schemes: rewarded employees are likely to act in the gift-givers' favor in future in hopes of being compensated [22].

Economic Extortion Schemes

Economic extortion is the opposite of bribery. Where bribery is used to sway favor with reward, extortion uses actual or threatened force to procure payment for decisions. That is, economic extortion cases are the "Pay up or else" corruption schemes.

Conclusion

Corruption is a massive, global issue. Not only does it often result in direct financial loss to organizations, but it also damages reputations, discourages shareholders and investors, jeopardizes efficiency, and weakens development [23]. On a societal level, corruption distorts the market, compromises ethics, undermines institutions, and promotes inequality [24]. Corruption taints organizations of all types, sizes, regions, and industries – it knows no bounds. Not unlike other types of fraud, organizations with weak or nonexistent internal controls are most susceptible to corruption schemes, but Computer-Assisted Audit Tools and Techniques (CAATT) auditing, combined with an ethical work culture and effective internal controls, can mitigate these losses.

In this section, we present a total of eight CAATT-based audit tests to help detect various corruption schemes, along with a total of 32 recommended corruption-related controls and/or best practices, as presented next.

Recommended CAATT-Based Audit Tests

- Corruption audit tests address five categories of this fraud type: Purchasing Schemes, Bid Rigging, Sales Schemes, Kickback Schemes, and Conflict of Interest Schemes.
- There are eight CAATT-based audit tests identified for corruption:
  - 3 for Purchasing Schemes
  - 1 for Bid Rigging
  - 2 for Sales Schemes
  - 1 for Kickback Schemes
  - 1 for Conflict of Interest Schemes
- There is a total of 32 recommended internal controls for corruption:
  - 9 for Purchasing Schemes
  - 4 for Sales Schemes
  - 9 for Kickback Schemes
  - 10 for Bid Rigging

ACFE FRAUD TREE SUBCATEGORY	INTERNAL CONTROLS/GOOD CONCEPTS AND PRACTICES FOR CORRUPTION-RELATED FRAUD PREVENTION OR DETECTION
(A) COIS	
1. Purchasing Schemes	1. The frequency of purchases and amount of vendor spend particularly with new vendors should/must not sharply increase from previous periods without reason.
	2. Vendor used consistently in the past should not be suddenly changed without any significant reason or error on the part of the vendor.

(Continued)

ACFE FRAUD TREE SUBCATEGORY	INTERNAL CONTROLS/GOOD CONCEPTS AND PRACTICES FOR CORRUPTION-RELATED FRAUD PREVENTION OR DETECTION
	3. The use of vague descriptions provided on invoices (e.g., materials purchased or services rendered) should be avoided.
	4. Internal auditors should check for unusual number of purchases below approval threshold level (i.e., look for purchases broken into smaller pieces).
	5. Internal auditors should look for unexplainable discrepancies where one client receives substantial, on-going discounts while other similar clients pay the full invoice.
	6. The volume of purchases must be supported by a rational need.
	7. Business dealings must be conducted only with valid (approved) sellers.
	8. Larger purchases must be made only after obtaining approval from manager or department head.
	9. Purchase orders must include detailed explanations about the goods purchased, date, time, quantity, price, etc.
2. Sales schemes	1. Sales trends out of line with industry norms should be investigated.
	2. Commissions or bonuses paid to sales personnel must be correctly calculated, based on actual quantities sold during a period. Also, look for commissions due but not paid to sales representatives.
	3. There should be no excessive returns after a period end.
	4. Unusual increases in the number of day sales in receivables should be investigated.
(B) BRIBERY	
1. Kickback Schemes	1. Order quantities exceeding the optimal reorder quantity should be red flagged by the inventory management system.
	2. Periodic reports comparing the total business volume by both agent and vendor should be analyzed every period.
	3. Internal auditors should look for a lack of competitive bidding procedures.
	4. Quantities ordered should be matched with quantities received.
	5. Purchases of more expensive items than required should be flagged and investigated.
	6. Approval procedures to include a vendor on the approved vendor list should include cheques to determine of if the vendor is facing legal or regulatory problems.
	7. The organization should have a written, formal, and enforced policy regarding the acceptance of gifts or favors from various vendors.
	8. Internal auditors should look for instances where management is applying pressure on its purchasing agents to use a particular vendor.

(Continued)

ACFE FRAUD TREE SUBCATEGORY	INTERNAL CONTROLS/GOOD CONCEPTS AND PRACTICES FOR CORRUPTION-RELATED FRAUD PREVENTION OR DETECTION
	9. Vendors in highly competitive industries where kickbacks and bribery are commonplace should be further scrutinized.
2. Bid Rigging	1. Internal auditors should check for contractors with an unusually high number of approved bids to ensure that the bidding process and procedures were correctly followed.
	2. Internal auditors should check for patterns of low-ball bids from contractors that are followed by subsequent significant changes to increase the price of the contract.
	3. Management must ensure that there is always a reasonable period of time to respond to requests for bids and that these requests for bids are well advertised.
	4. Internal auditors should check for splitting purchases so that procured amounts are below the bidding limit (to allow non-competitive or sole source awards).
	5. The organization should have a formal and enforced policy aimed at preventing bidder intimidation or threats aimed at discouraging some bidders from submitting their bids.
	6. Management should implement a second review procedure to ensure that bidders are not improperly disqualifying bidders due to immaterial or easily correctable errors.
	7. Bid due dates should never be extended or changed without a valid and defensible reason.
	8. Unauthorized individuals should not be allowed to influence the bid evaluation process.
	9. Interference in the bid selection process by senior officials without a valid and defensible reason should not be allowed.
	10. Relevant information related to each bid, such as the ranking of bidders and bid prices, should be documented in a periodic bidding report and made available to internal and external auditors.

Audit Tests Worksheet Section

ACFE Fraud Tree Subcategory: Purchasing Schemes.

Purpose: To detect schemes related to purchasing schemes.

Audit Test Procedure: Compare rates for similar products from other vendors. Ratio analysis on unit price by product (check high-ratio details).

Explanation: Employee might divert the company's business to their own personally owned company.

Assertion(s) Tested: Occurrence and Authorization.

CAATT Expression: Ratio Analysis and Expression/Equation.

Possible Red Flags: Purchases done without obtaining approval from the manager or department head. Presence of invoices without any purchase orders in organization's records.

ACFE Fraud Tree Subcategory: Purchasing Schemes.

Purpose: To detect schemes related to purchasing schemes.

Audit Test Procedure: Total purchases by ordering clerk, by vendor.

Explanation: Check the total purchases made by the ordering clerk and vendor to find out if there were purchases made from suppliers that are not on the company's supplier's list.

Assertion(s) Tested: Occurrence and Authorization.

CAATT Expression: Summarize.

Possible Red Flags: Purchases made from unknown suppliers. Presence of invoices without any purchase orders in organization records.

ACFE Fraud Tree Subcategory: Purchasing Schemes.

Purpose: To detect schemes related to purchasing schemes.

Audit Test Procedure: Match contract price to invoice and report on variances.

Explanation: The Employee in charge of procurement might inflate the price submitted by the vendor on the invoice thereby making a gain from the company purchases.

Assertion(s) Tested: Occurrence and Authorization.

CAATT Expression: Join/Relate and Expression/Equation.

Possible Red Flags: Same person handling the purchasing duties, accounting duties, invoice handling, and payment to vendor. Organization makes frequent buying from a single supplier compared to others.

ACFE Fraud Tree Subcategory: Bid Rigging.

Purpose: To detect schemes related to fictitious bids.

Audit Test Procedure: Verify bidders and prices.

Explanation: Employee in charge of procurement might inflate the price submitted by the vendor or divert the difference to a personal account.

Assertion(s) Tested: Occurrence and Authorization.

CAATT Expression: Join/Relate and Expression/Equation.

Possible Red Flags: Same person handling the purchasing duties, accounting duties, invoice handling, and payment to vendor.

ACFE Fraud Tree Subcategory: Sales Schemes.

Purpose: To detect schemes related to false sales and shipping.

Audit Test Procedure: Match delivery addresses with employees' addresses.

Explanation: Employee in charge of sales might have manipulated sales delivery to his personal address and adjusted the sales figure on the company's records This test aims at checking the criteria where employee's address is the same as vendor's address.

Assertion(s) Tested: Occurrence and Validity.

CAATT Expression: Join/Relate and Expression/Equation.

Possible Red Flags: Same person handling the purchasing duties, accounting duties, invoice handling, and payment to vendor. The address of an employee is the same as the Vendor's address.

ACFE Fraud Tree Subcategory: Sales Schemes.

Purpose: To check for purchases of more expensive items than required.

Audit Test Procedure: Analyze and compare the various data in the account payable and supplier records to see if there are figures that are unnecessarily higher than what is required.

Explanation: Check for any irregular and inconsistent payment made on behalf of the company. The employee in charge of approving contract and the one in charge of payment authorization may collide to inflate the contract price.

Assertion(s) Tested: Accuracy, Validity, and Existence.

CAATT Expression: Ratio Analysis.

Possible Red Flags: A pattern of substantial purchases in terms of volume and/or frequency coupled with higher prices for items paid than necessary.

ACFE Fraud Tree Subcategory: Kickback Schemes.

Purpose: To check for purchase of excess inventory and to determine if the excess inventory is being purchased from a specific vendor.

Audit Test Procedure: Compare inventory order quantity to optimal reorder quantity.

Explanation: Excess inventory purchases from a specific vendor could be indicative of the fact that the purchasing agent may be receiving a kickback from a vendor based on larger quantities purchased.

Assertion(s) Tested: Occurrence.

CAATT Expression: Join/Relate and Expression/Equation.

Possible Red Flags: Inventory purchases above the optimal reorder quantity without a reasonable explanation.

ACFE Fraud Tree Subcategory: Conflict of Interest Schemes.

Purpose: To identify any unusual trends and to determine the high-value payment amounts.

Audit Test Procedure: Match contract price to invoice and report on variances.

Explanation: Check for any irregular and inconsistent payment made on behalf of the company. The employee in charge of approving contract and the one in charge of payment authorization may collide to inflate the contract price.

Assertion(s) Tested: Existence, Occurrence, Authorization, and Validity.

CAATT Expression: Summarize.

Possible Red Flags: Unusual payment to vendor. Unjustified high prices or price increases for common goods or services. Vendor(s) with known inadequate quality products or services are continually awarded contracts.

References

1. Association of Certified Fraud Examiners. (2018). Report to the Nations on Occupational Fraud and Abuse. Retrieved from https://s3-us-west-2.amazonaws.com/acfepublic/2018-report-to-the-nations.pdf
2. Henry, B. (2012, April 22). BUSTED: Walmart caught in huge bribery scandal – Senior management knew about it and tried to cover it up. *Business Insider*. Retrieved from www.businessinsider.com/walmart-bribery-scandal-2012-4

3. Barstow, D. (2012, April 12). Wal-Mart hushed up a vast Mexican bribery case. *The New York Times*. Retrieved from www.nytimes.com/2012/04/22/business/at-wal-mart-in-mexico-a-bribe-inquiry-silenced.html

4. Reuters. (2017, May 10). Walmart is reportedly getting ready to settle a bribery probe for $300 million. *Fortune*. Retrieved from http://fortune.com/2017/05/10/walmart-bribery-investigation-settlement/

5. Gallas, D. (2017, March 7). Brazil's Odebrecht corruption scandal. *BBC*. Retrieved from www.bbc.com/news/business-39194395

6. Havranek, A. (2018, April 26). State auditor finds conflicts-of-interest in state transportation 'Weigh in Motion' contracts. *KY3*. Retrieved from www.ky3.com/content/news/State-Auditor-finds-conflicts-of-interest-in-state-transportation-Weigh-in-Motion-contracts-481011071.html

7. Farcic, E. (2018, May 6). Corruption watchdog probes horizon power misconduct claims. *Perth Now: Sunday Times*. Retrieved from www.perthnow.com.au/news/crime/corruption-watchdog-probes-horizon-power-misconduct-claims-ng-b88828401z

8. The United States Department of Justice. Former U.S. Army Colonel Pleads Guilty to Accepting Illegal Gratuities Related to Contracting in Support of Iraq War. Retrieved from www.justice.gov/opa/pr/former-us-army-colonel-pleads-guilty-accepting-illegal-gratuities-related-contracting-support

9. Global Compliance News. (2017). Anti-Corruption Laws Around the World. Retrieved from https://globalcompliancenews.com/anti-corruption/anti-corruption-laws-around-the-world/

10. Velamuri, S. R., Harvey, W. S., & Venkataraman, S. (2017, March 23). Being an ethical business in a corrupt environment. *Harvard Business Review*. Retrieved from https://hbr.org/2017/03/being-an-ethical-business-in-a-corrupt-environment

11. ACFE. (2018). Bribery and corruption: Anti-corruption programs. *ACFE*. Retrieved from www.acfe.com/uploadedFiles/ACFE_Website/Content/review/bc/06-Anti-Corruption-Programs.pdf

12. Deehan, S. (2015, July 9). White-collar crime costs between $300 to $600 billion a year. *Comprehensive Financial Investigative Solution*. Retrieved from www.aitcfis.com/2015/07/09/white-collar-crime-costs-between-300-to-600-billion-a-year/

13. Imana, M. (2010, August 25). Street crime vs corporate crime - which is more damaging to the country? *Ezine Articles*. Retrieved from http://ezinearticles.com/?Street-Crime-Vs-Corporate-Crime---Which-is-MoreDamaging-to-the-Country?&id=4928011

14. Ashfort, B. E., & Anand, V. (2003). The normalization of corruption in organizations. *Research in Organizational Behavior, 25*, 1–52.

15. OECD. (2014). *OECD Foreign Bribery Report: An Analysis of the Crime of Bribery of Foreign Public Officials*, OECD Publishing. Retrieved from https://read.oecd-ilibrary.org/governance/oecd-foreign-bribery-report_9789264226616-en#page4

16. The World Bank. (2017, September 26). Combating Corruption. Retrieved from www.worldbank.org/en/topic/governance/brief/anti-corruption

17. ISO. (2018). Standards: ISO 37001 – Anti-Bribery Management Systems. Retrieved from www.iso.org/iso-37001-anti-bribery-management.html

18. ACFE. (2016). The fraud tree: Occupational fraud and abuse classification system. *Association of Certified Fraud Examiners*. Retrieved from www.acfe.com/rttn2016/docs/2016-report-to-the-nations.pdf

19. ACFE. (2015). *Fraud Examiners Manual (International)*. Austin, TX: Association of Certified Fraud Examiners.

20. Coenen, T. (2009). Investigation of corruption schemes. *Expert Fraud Investigation: A Step-by-Step Guide*. Retrieved from www.expertfraud.com/investigation-of-corruption-schemes/

21. Catchick, P. (2014). Conflict of interest: Gateway to corruption. *ACFE*. Retrieved from www.acfe.com/article.aspx?id=4294980862

22. Mounir, A. (2016). What does gratuity mean, and in what context is it used? *Fraud Protection*. Retrieved from www.fraud-scam.com/2016/07/what-does-gratuity-mean-and-in-what.html

23. Ray, L. The effects of corruption on business. *Chron*. Retrieved from http://smallbusiness.chron.com/effects-corruption-business-52808.html

24. Corruption Watch. (2018). Corruption Affects Us All. Retrieved from www.corruptionwatch.org.za/learn-about-corruption/what-is-corruption/we-are-all-affected/

6

CAATT IN FRAUD AUDITING

Introduction

Computer-Assisted Audit Tools and Techniques (CAATT) are specialized software that use artificial intelligence to perform and automate different functions in auditing – they're used to "simplify or automate the data analysis process" [1]. Whereas auditors traditionally reviewed limited samples to perform audits and determine risks, advanced CAATT analyze comprehensive data, searching for anomalies – effectively reviewing all digital data in a business unit. At its most basic level, CAATT include basic computer software such as Excel spreadsheets, but advanced CAATT offer statistical analysis, specific risk testing, data queries and stratification, calculations, cross tabulation, and even business intelligence. CAATT offer increased speed and accuracy as well as computer-generated models and simulations. Because CAATT are cost-effective, they have the capacity to payback audit investment as well as the ability to continuously and autonomously monitor business processes and transactions. As with any technology, CAATT are only as good as the user: if data isn't entered, software isn't updated or customized, and the auditors aren't choosing the appropriate audit tests, CAATT can't reach their full potential. Data analysis is a challenging job. Auditors, fraud examiners, accountants, and finance professionals are compiling data from various sources with different formats and with different experience levels – no matter what, there's a high risk for error [2].

But despite the risks for error, the need for effective fraud auditing is crucial. The Association of Certified Fraud Examiners (ACFE) Shows that the magnitude of fraud detected by internal and external audit activities in 2018 was 15% and 4%, respectively [3]. PwC's research indicates that economic crime is experienced by 36% of organizations but only 8% of those organizations are using data analytics tools to detect fraud [4]. Increasing instances of fraud and unsatisfactory detection by internal and external audit activities are alarming. The effective implementation and use of CAATT can help auditors in exercising not only a greater level of due diligence and due professional care, but more importantly, greater fraud detection during various audit activities.

Case Studies

According to the 2018 Report to the Nations (RTTN) published by the ACFE, total loss due to occupational fraud exceeded $7 billion in 125 countries across the globe, with the typical loss of 5% of organizational revenues each year. The most common methods of detecting frauds are tips and complaints and internal audit.

There are a number of CAATT technologies available on the market. Interestingly, most of these technologies have been developed in Canada. While Audit Command Language (ACL) is currently the market leader, other CAATT developers include ActiveData, Arbutus, and CaseWare Analytics, a firm that's been continually creating and innovating technological solutions for finance and accounting, governance, and risk and audit professionals since 1988. Their CAATT software, Interactive Data Extraction and Analysis (IDEA), is used by over 400,000 professionals in 130 countries. CaseWare Analytics details their clients' success stories on their website, keeping some company names confidential. What follows is a sample of case studies directly from CaseWare Analytics [5].

Petroleum and Natural Gas Company

A $10 billion petroleum and natural gas exploration and production company faced small breaches in their internal control system which failed to address or track policy breaches or comprehensively monitor data and transactions, including accounts payable. As a result, the company was leaking revenues. To address their weak internal controls, the enterprise implemented CaseWare Monitor, a CAATT program configured to catch "revenue leakage, strengthen internal controls, and find opportunities to increase compliance." Four risk areas were found by CaseWare Analytics' Professional Services team: vendor management, accounts payable, audit automation, and purchase card. Within accounts payable, duplicate invoices added up to more than $147 million; over $614 million was lost in unapplied vendor discounts; and over $1.2 million payments exceeded the approved limits. Over $1.6 million purchases – involving more than 10,000 transactions – were flagged as personal purchases. In vendor management, almost 400 bank accounts matched between vendor and employees. There were also over 2,000 duplicate vendors (names or addresses) with 80 employees whose addresses matched vendor addresses [6].

Tate and Tryon

A fraud prevention and consulting firm, Tate & Tryon, services the United States' non-profit organizations. Using IDEA Data Analysis software on a client's accounts payable data, their testing uncovered a match between a vendor and employee address, as well as a high number of expense reimbursements by the same employee. A review of these findings revealed that the employee's expense reimbursements totaled $18,000 for the prior year. Consequently, a thorough investigation ensued to examine "financial documents accounting records, expense reports, check requests, cancelled checks, invoices and receipts" which ultimately unveiled an asset misappropriation: the employee listed his landlord as a vendor to use employer funds to pay his rent; the employee submitted fake invoices and receipts for over 120 reimbursements (including using colleagues' credit cards to support them). Ultimately, using IDEA Data Analysis software, Tate & Tryon discovered that the employee had misappropriated $150,000 from the client [7].

Banco de Costa Rica

A leading financial service provider in Latin America, Banco de Costa Rica's (BCR) internal audit department was only using "a data analysis tool to test controls and monitor compliance" at its 150 branches – but the practice couldn't control responses to exceptions. To further explain, BCR couldn't adequately manage the volume of reports, the internal control system responses, or the daily monitoring load in their internal auditing process. By successfully implementing CaseWare Monitor, BCR's internal auditing department was able to remotely monitor all branch activities and reconcile internal accounts [8].

Discussion

As discussed in previous chapters, *asset misappropriation* is the most common type of fraud (89% of reported cases) and *financial statement fraud* causes the biggest median losses ($800,000). Despite these incredible losses and startling statistics, however, the most common fraud detection method is tips (40% of cases) – which isn't a planned detection method or a formal type of internal control. While organizations with hotlines for whistleblowing are more likely to detect fraud, when fraud is revealed through intentional detection methods (e.g., surveillance, monitoring, account reconciliation), both losses and durations are lower. Consequently, anti-fraud controls result in quicker detection and lower losses, making an anti-fraud control like CAATT an invaluable method of preventing and detecting fraud [3].

Computer-Assisted Audit Tools and Techniques

The dramatic changes in processing, reporting, storing, and publishing accounting information and increased reliance on information technology have created more challenges and risks for internal and external auditors in terms of collecting client data, loading that data into audit software, and performing audit tests. A commissioned study conducted by Forrester shows that by employing ACL, a U.S. state government administration agency achieves 702% ROI (return on investment) over 3 years. Furthermore, the study indicates that continuous monitoring helps to generate more efficient audit reviews, saving 3,900 h annually, recovering $2.9 million from incorrect vendor pricing and reducing purchasing card fraud losses of $250,000 while reviewing 100,000 purchasing card transactions monthly [9].

Traditionally, audits were performed manually, but with advancements in IT and information systems, particularly for white-collar financial crimes, audit function is currently using standardized audit software to detect fraud. This means that transparent financial statement reviews and business operations are the most critical and important steps in building confidence among the stakeholders and decreasing instances of fraud. With companies like Enron, dubbed as "America's most innovative company" by *Fortune* magazine cooking their books and collapsing [10], audit trails can provide a high level of assurance that financial statements are fairly presented. CAATT allow auditors and fraud investigators to access and analyze a large volume of data to uncover fraudulent activities while also obtaining a quick overview of business operations [11]. When CAATT are in place, auditor can better improve the effectiveness and efficiency of the audit process [12].

Using artificial intelligence to perform sophisticated manipulations, CAATT enable auditors to obtain relevant, sufficient audit evidence to predict financial failure and detect fraudulent activity [13]. As specialized software that performs different audit functions [14], information technology can be used in four different types of audits: computer-assisted audit techniques, audit with computers, audits around computers, and audits through the computers. In information technology, auditing of these four stages can be done via substantive testing, a test of control, and audit planning [15].

A critical factor in the adoption of CAATT is to obtain the right data and understand what that data means. Companies have hundreds of thousands of transactions; CAATT enable auditors to quickly analyze those transactions individually and look for the anomalies. Therefore, CAATT such as IDEA help auditors to focus and put their efforts in high-risk areas that have a higher probability of misrepresentation, rather than focusing on low-risk transactions. Since manual processes lead auditors to dig through a mountain of paper, CAATT increase the efficiency of the audit process. However, CAATT can only modify the audit methodology; they do not change the objective. Because of the increased volume of business transactions and complexities in accounting information systems, CAATT are quickly replacing more traditional auditing methods [16,17].

Techniques, Challenges, and Considerations in Using CAATT

CAATT use several techniques to analyze data, including join/create, duplicates, gaps, sort/index, filter, stratify, Benford's law, regression analysis, and summarization. A combination of techniques can also be applied while performing audits [1].

The following table illustrates different CAATT and their comparisons to each other based on different data analysis tasks [18,19].

DATA ANALYSIS TASKS	EXPLANATION	IDEA	ACL	EXCEL	ACTIVEDATA
Benford's law	Finds abnormal duplication of a specific number, digits, and or round numbers in company data.	YES	YES	NO	YES
Duplicates	Identifies duplicate transactions and values or duplicate items.	YES	YES	NO	YES
Aging	Determines the age summary of the transaction.	YES	YES	NO	YES
Merge/Append	Joins two files having identical fields into a signal database or file.	YES	YES	YES	YES
Gaps	Identifies missing items, series, or sequence.	YES	YES	NO	YES
Join/Relate	Joins two different files into a single field.	YES	YES	NO	YES
Sample	Creates a random sample of the statistical population.	YES	YES	NO	NO
Statistics	Calculates statistical parameters: minimum, maximum, standard deviation, variance, and also averages positive and negative records.	YES	YES	YES	YES
Stratify	Identifies unexpected combinations of numbers and digits and categorizes them into different ranges, numeric fields, or strata.	YES	YES	NO	YES
Summarize	Categorizes records and counts number of records having unique categories and also accumulates numerical values.	YES	YES	YES	YES
Sort	Sorts data into ascending or descending order.	YES	YES	YES	YES
Export	Exports files to other file formats (e.g., Excel sheet to Access file).	YES	YES	YES	YES
Cross Tabulate	Sets data in rows and columns in order to analyze character fields.	YES	YES	YES	NO

The challenges and considerations of using CAATT could arise from any of the following:

a. *Silo Systems*: Data stored in silos are at times difficult to use because it may not reveal definite patterns due to its restricted flow of information, giving rise to inconsistencies.
b. *Large Volume Data*: Carrying out varying types of analysis on extremely large volume of data consisting of hundreds of thousands or even millions of transactions can prove to be a challenging task.
c. *Inadequate Access to Data*: Lack of information regarding data, hindrance in data availability due to policies, and limited access to sensitive data due to data protection laws.

Ultimately, CAATT allow auditors to test an entire population, which is both effective and efficient, saving time and increasing accuracy [20,21].

Prevalence and Popularity among Auditors

Auditors use CAATT to improve the effectiveness and efficiency of audit procedures and to select transaction samples with clearly defined criteria (to enable the auditor to gather evidence regarding the effectiveness of controls being tested) [22]. But despite its effectiveness, CAATT tend to be more popular among auditors that work for larger organizations, as well as the big auditing firms [23]. This popularity stems from the fact that these audit service providers have clients with elaborate data. Furthermore, whether or not auditors use CAATT is impacted by user expectations regarding system performance, the amount of data entry work required, and whether audit clients have the technical and organizational infrastructure in place to facilitate the use of such tools [24]. Therefore, auditors' use of CAATT may be inhibited by the lack of in-depth knowledge of the technology, hence the continued use of traditional, non-CAATT methods [25].

Benefits and Limitations

The benefits of CAATT include programmed test controls, reduced human error, ability to test larger data volumes, speed and accuracy, ability to test on data source location, cost-effectiveness, and increased efficiency and effectiveness. Fraud detection is more effective when CAATT are utilized because auditors are able to evaluate 100% of the data in all transactions [11]. Additionally, more data can be stored in a computer program, which enables auditors to track audit trails, monitor trends, and detect red flags. The primary limitation of CAATT lies with auditors' unwillingness to use CAATT due to inadequate technical abilities [24]; however, CAATT are becoming increasingly easier to learn and use. Below is a table illustrating the several types of CAATT including their functions, advantages, and disadvantages.

TYPES OF CAATT	FUNCTIONS	ADVANTAGES	DISADVANTAGES
Test data packs	Used to determine the accuracy of program processing procedures and effectiveness of program controls.	Low cost of design and running of the program.	Detailed knowledge of the accounting application is required.
Computer audit programs	Used to retrieve information and perform tests on transactions and balances.	Enables the auditor to examine large volumes while minimizing human error.	The cost of development is high.
Flowcharting	Use of software to generate a flowchart variant of the client's application program.	Enables the auditor to see trends in the data.	Requires computer knowledge and accurate use of the computer application.
System program data analysis	Used to examine system logs for follow-up actions.	Enables auditor to verify that program amendment was properly authorized before implementation.	In-depth computer knowledge is required.

An auditor's professional experience with CAATT inevitably leads to increased efficiency and effectiveness. Continual technological improvements in CAATT (e.g., the ability of CAATT to read and parse PDF documents) indicate that auditors must keep up with the changing technology [26]. Since auditors must avoid pre-audit assumptions, CAATT are designed to align with the nature, timing, and extent of further audit procedures. As such, auditors must rely on persuasiveness and articulation to convince audit partners and managers to invest in CAATT audit solutions, rather than the common use of Excel [22].

CAATT-Based Related Frameworks

While management is primarily responsible for fraud detection and prevention, the International Standard on Auditing (ISA) states that the auditor is responsible for gaining reasonable assurance that financial statements are fairly presented and free from error or fraud. Since the objective of the audit is to develop stakeholder confidence in the financial statements, the purpose of a financial statements audit is to obtain reasonable assurance that there is no material misstatement in financial statement. The factor that differentiates error and fraud is whether or not the misstatement is caused intentionally or unintentionally. Risk assessment procedures should be performed by auditors to provide a premise that recognizes and assesses the risk of material misstatement at the assertion and financial statement level. The auditor can revise risk assessments if additional evidence is gained. ISA contends that CAATT can aid in empowering testing of accounting files and electronic transaction and may be valuable in recognizing unexpected transaction relationships or revenues [27].

Because internal auditors are required to have sufficient skills, knowledge, and competencies to perform their professional responsibilities while dealing with fraud, the Institute of Internal Auditors' (IIA) *International Standards for the Professional Practice of Internal Auditing* require that auditors have the adequate skills to assess fraud risk. Furthermore, the standards indicate that internal auditors must consider the likelihood of noncompliance, fraud occurrence, or errors managing of fraud risk while exercising due professional care. The IIA encourages the use of CAATT: "In exercising due professional care internal auditors must consider the use of technology-based audit and other data analysis techniques" [28].

ISACA (Information Systems Audit and Control Association) recommends using CAATT to perform various audit procedures such as tests of details of transactions and balances, analytical review procedures, compliance tests of IS general controls, compliance tests of IS application controls, and penetration testing [29].

Fraud Auditing Process

Fraud auditing may require more advanced tools, and techniques to unveil fraud schemes, because in this type of audits, auditors must be able to precisely find the suspicious transactions among thousands or hundreds of thousands of transactions. As such, CAATT can help auditors focus their efforts, reducing time pressures and ensuring a comprehensive reach. CAATT allow auditors to perform their desired operations on the data; while doing so, auditors must ensure that the data's integrity isn't compromised [30]. The figure below summarizes the typical fraud auditing cycle (Figure 6.1).

With CAATT, the fraud investigation process begins with the fraud allegation or expected fraud events identified in fraud auditing process. Once fraud is reported and referred for further investigation to a

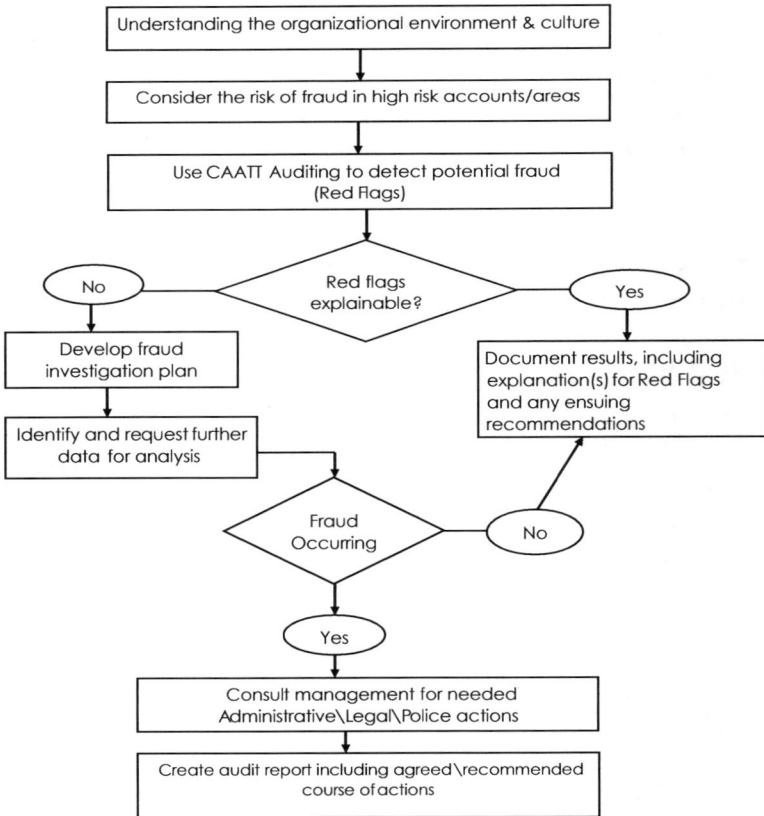

Figure 6.1   Fraud investigation using CAATT.

fraud examiner, a pre-investigation is done regarding the existence of fraud symptoms. If a fraud investigator finds red flags, a formal fraud investigation plan is developed. The primary objective of the fraud investigation plan is to discover the truth of whether fraud has been committed or the red flag is due to an unintentional error. A fraud investigation plan also defines the use of CAATT, the objective of the investigation, and the investigation team. Once the use of CAATT is identified, the fraud investigator will need a source to extract data from and will then convert the extracted data into a common format [30]. By performing CAATT testing on the data and collecting documentary evidence, the fraud investigator will generate a report of the CAATT findings. If the findings show that fraud is committed by perpetrators, management needs to be consulted in terms of administrative and/or legal action should be taken against the perpetrator. Important considerations should also be part of the fraud investigation process. For example, the team should determine why the fraud was committed, the reasons for the fraud occurrence, and preventive measures to implement for future prevention.

The presence of fraud risk can be tracked by meeting one or more conditions identified in the fraud triangle (i.e., perceived pressure, opportunity, and rationalization). The fraud auditing process begins by understanding the organizational culture and business environment in order to identify high-risk areas (one of the important and most critical steps in fraud detection). Once the area is defined and fraud symptoms are identified, CAATT should be used in the investigation and analysis of fraud symptoms. If a fraud examiner finds anything suspicious, a proper fraud investigation process should be developed in dealing with the fraud.

The Fraud Investigation Procedure Using CAATT

The use of CAATT does not change the objective of the audit; rather, it strengthens the fraud investigation process. The fundamental reason for adopting CAATT in fraud investigation is to improve the effectiveness and efficiency of the audit process. Thus, increasing the auditor's ability to review data, convert data into valuable results, and provide findings-based recommendations.

While searching for unintentional errors or anomalies, the traditional method of auditing uses random sampling and stratification to determine errors in population (since errors and anomalies occur at regular intervals and are caused by weak internal controls). On the other side, fraud is committed intentionally. Sampling techniques, in this case, are not an effective way to detect fraud because a sample collected may not be representative of the entire population that contains fraudulent data [31]. As it pertains to fraud auditing, CAATT assist auditors in analyzing the entire population (every single transaction) in order to reveal anomalies, suggestive of potential fraud [31].

The development of data analytics tools in fraud investigation plays a vital role in the improvement of audit quality. Audit quality should focus on meeting stakeholder needs while also complying with auditing standards, and/or legally-compliant fraud investigation procedures [32]. There are two categories of a fraud investigation: specific allegation and exception reporting [33,34].

1. *Specific Allegation*: The fraud investigator should prove or disprove identified specific allegation or risk. For example, specific allegation received regarding the use of inventory for personal use.
2. *Exception Reporting*: The fraud investigator should report on inconsistencies, patterns, or red flags that can cause fraud. For example, in the specific allegation, an employee is using company card for personal use. However in the exception reporting fraud investigation category, irregularities or atypical trends are analyzed. The figure below outlines the typical steps and procedures related to exception reporting.

The essential factors to consider in exception reporting are understanding the business and its environment, understanding the business' data, and asking the right questions. Without these criteria, the auditor or fraud investigator is unable to build an appropriate audit strategy or obtain the right data. CAATT allow fraud investigators to gain a better understanding of the data, enabling the auditor to catch irregularities (Figure 6.2).

Adoption of CAATT for Fraud Auditing

The traditional audit is an engagement that starts by establishing a contract between auditee and auditor [36]. First, an audit plan

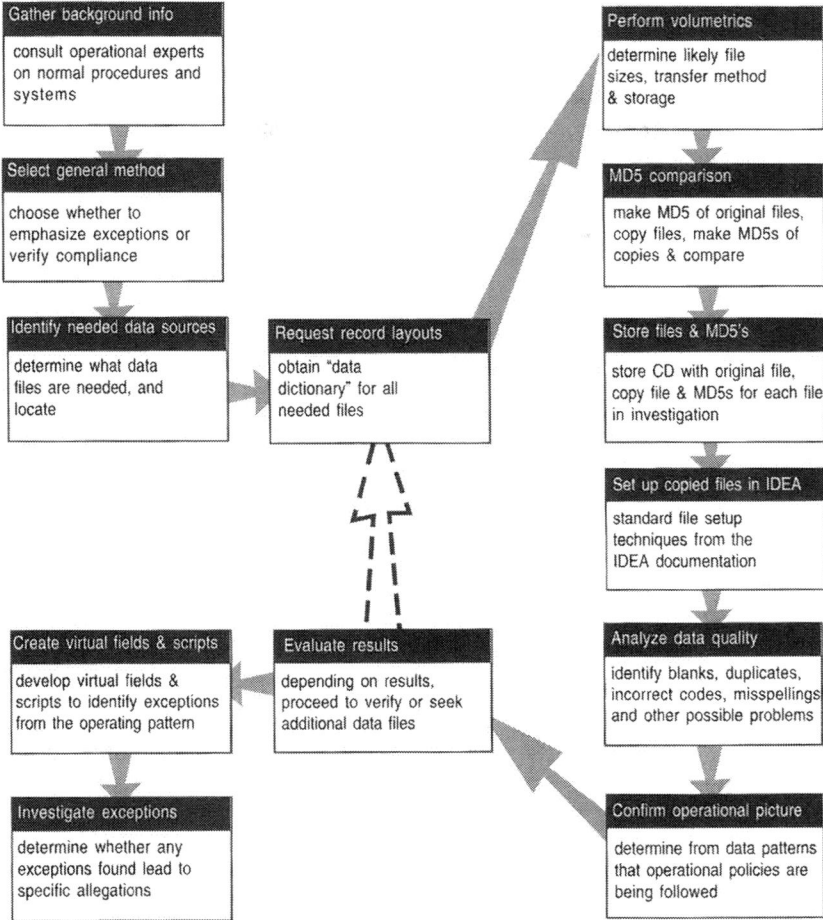

Figure 6.2 Exception reporting flowchart [34,35].

is designed, defining the audit's objective and scope as well as risk assessment. Furthermore, in the traditional audit, the auditor collects and analyzes evidence to form an audit opinion. At the end of the audit engagement, the auditor presents the audit report containing findings and opinions to management. However, the auditor and client relationship can be biased, and unconscious human behavior can result in key evidence being overlooked. Further, the collection, processing, and reporting of findings is both time-consuming and costly. In fast-paced business environments, stakeholders require immediate feedback; CAATT, then, allows auditors to obtain a better understanding of the business and to complete the audit quicker, thus increasing the chances of success [30].

With the use of digital devices in committing various financial frauds, auditors are being challenged to detect frauds in the digital environment. When using CAATT, auditors tend to be aware of its benefits but can still lack confidence in adoption. Therefore, the main challenges to a successful CAATT implementation are the compatibility of CAATT to the organizational system, the auditor's attitude and approach, the auditor's level of technical knowledge and expertise, and the client's willingness to provide confidential data and access to a live database for auditing. Small- and medium-sized organizations that don't implement CAATT in auditing tend to refrain because the costs associated with CAATT implementation, training, development are viewed as not worth the costs of implementation. Thus, comparing the advantages of adopting data analytics and costs may be much smaller or sometimes even negligible for smaller organizations [37].

The Unified Theory of Acceptance and Use of Technology (UTAUT) may also apply to the reluctance to employ CAATT in fraud auditing. UTAUT posits that four independent variables play a motivational role in the successful adoption of technology: facilitating conditions, performance expectancy, social influence, and effort expectancy [38].

> *Performance Expectancy*: Performance expectancy refers to an individual's beliefs that consideration and use of technology will help in getting the desired results in job performance. While an auditor may see CAATT as the means to improve job performance, some may feel intimidated by the technology and believe that trying to use it will actually decrease job performance.
>
> *Effort Expectancy*: Effort expectancy is the degree of ease associated with the adoption of technology. CAATT play an important role in the automation of audit process; it reduces legwork and effort. Again, CAATT are proven to increase productivity, but if the auditor believes too much effort is required to learn how to use it, he or she may be reluctant. The best way to counter this fear is to ensure auditors receive proper training.

Social Influence: Social influence stems from an individual's perception on who believes the technology is worthwhile. This means that CAATT adoptions absolutely require buy-in from entire teams to be successfully implemented – when everyone is on board, social influence is an advantage.

Facilitating Conditions: Facilitating conditions refers to an individual's belief that the organization is equipped with the technical infrastructure to support implementation and use. Here, the information systems must be proven to align with the CAATT being implemented (Figure 6.3) [37].

When clients' businesses are using accounting software, audit firms are more likely to adopt CAATT. Companies that use a computer for accounting and maintain electronic transaction records of transactions allow for a more effective, productive, and useful CAATT adoption [39]. IIA standards state that

> Auditors should use CAATTs if the controls activities are performed by a computer (automated). Furthermore, they also assert that in responding to fraud risk, CAATTs are a more effective method for testing accounts files and transactions [28].

Importance of Red Flags in Fraud Detection

Fraud perpetrators are often savvy enough to hide their tracks from auditors aiming to detect the existence of fraud. As such, auditors must watch for fraud symptoms or red flags in the fraud identification process. Red flags increase the probability of fraud identification in the auditing process [31]. The most common red flags are divided into the following categories [3,35]:

RED FLAGS/FRAUD SYMPTOMS	EXAMPLE
Accounting anomalies	Incorrect ledger balance
	Balances are not reconciled
	Unusual relationship between journal entries
Control symptoms	Lack of segregation of duties
	Weak internal controls
Behavioral symptoms	Work habits unexpectedly change (e.g., staying late and coming in early)

(Continued)

IMPLEMENTATION BEST PRACTICE

- CAATTs Champion and expert user
- Support from the management
- Enthusiasm and commitment
- Cooperation from other departments
- Ability to demonstrate the benefits
- Good understanding of the host system
- Ability to download data
- Training
- User Manual
- Regular Usage

CHALLENGES

- Technical Complexity
- Attitude of the auditors

Implementation phase

CAATTs ADOPTION

Post adoption

PERFORMANCE MEASUREMENT

- Improvement in Audit Coverage
- Feedback from stakeholder
- Resource savings

Pre-adoption

MOTIVATION

- Performance Expectancy
- Effect of Externalities
- Facilitating Conditions

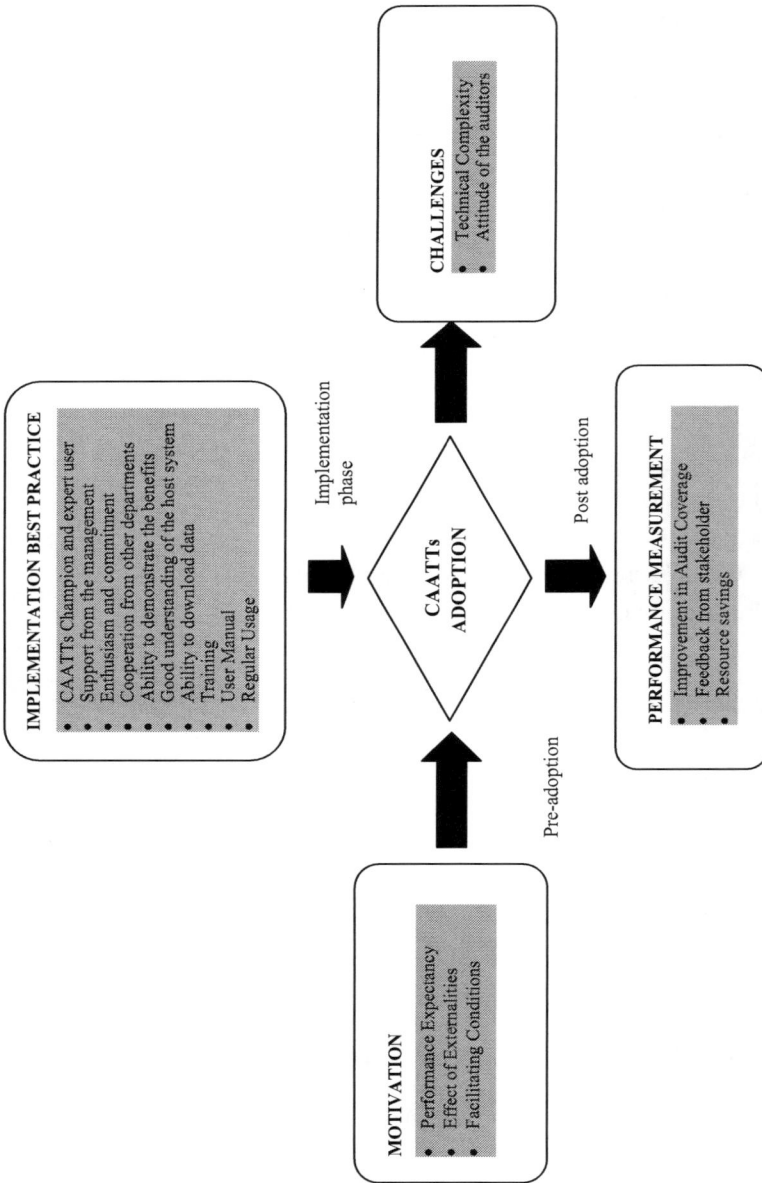

Figure 6.3   CAATT adoption model [37].

RED FLAGS/FRAUD SYMPTOMS	EXAMPLE
Analytical symptoms	Product prices increase
	Quality decreases
	Bulk purchases from favorite vendors
Lifestyle symptoms	Extravagant lifestyle
	Spending on luxuries and expensive products
	Expenses more than income
Tips and complaints	Quality complaints
	Product complaints
	Anonymous complaints

Anti-Fraud Policy and Strategy

The anti-fraud policy begins with upper management. To incorporate an anti-fraud policy, a mechanism must be developed to deal with fraud identification and prevention and to execute the policy with the aim to achieve the objectives set by upper management. Despite the fact that management is responsible for the successful implementation of the anti-fraud policy, everyone in the organization must know their role in fraud prevention and detection. The aim of an anti-fraud strategy is to prevent and detect fraud occurring in an organization. Components include fraud prevention, fraud detection, fraud deterrence, and fraud response (Figure 6.4) [40,41].

Each component of anti-fraud strategy is essential in dealing with fraud, since all the components are interlinked. The preventive controls are in place to limit, restrict, and reduce opportunities for potential fraud to be committed, but a fraud prevention strategy cannot 100% guarantee that fraud will be prevented [41]. Fraud detection uses analytics to look for anomalies, but it also serves to warn fraudsters since it indicates that the organization is actively dealing with fraud and proper procedures are in place. Consistently responding to fraud events is also important because it shows that organization is seriously dealing with fraud and legal action will be taken against fraudsters [42].

Familiarization with File and Business Environment

Once the data is obtained and the objectives of the investigation are identified, fraud examiners should assess the data's completeness and

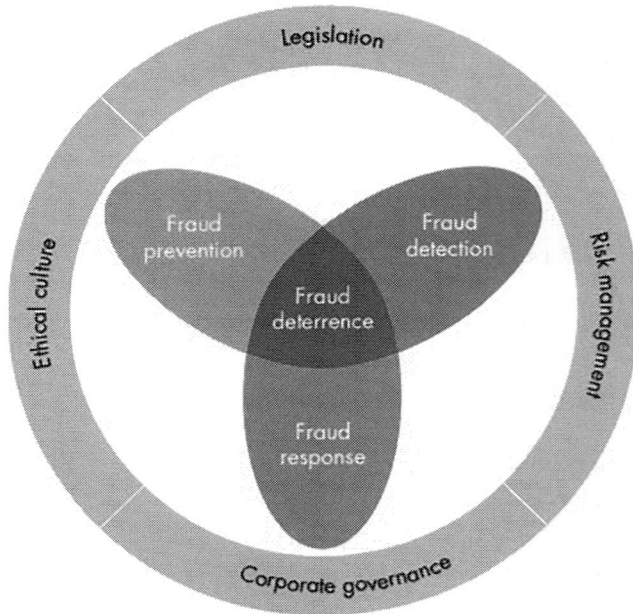

Figure 6.4   Anti-fraud strategy [41].

integrity. Examiners must become familiar with the data in terms of its format, range, and what the data conveys. Understanding the business environment helps to understand the operational and control environments so that auditors can identify weaknesses and high-risk areas. As mentioned before, the goal is to identify any patterns and discrepancies indicative of fraud.

Fraud detection professionals commonly apply the following CAATT functions and commands in the course of their audit activities.

Gap Detection

The gap detection test allows auditors to find records that have any missing items, series, or sequences. Gap detection techniques quickly find the transaction that is not in proper sequence, allowing investigators to focus on those transactions and determine fraudulent nature. For example, IDEA allows three types of gap detection: date, numeric, and character gap detection.

Identifying Fields with Blanks and Incorrect Lengths

A blank function allows auditors to find records with blanks. If the blank function is applied on a Social Security (SIN in Canada) Number (SSN), for example, it will retrieve all the records with blank SSN or SIN fields. The length function checks whether transactions or records have the correct length or are suspiciously added to accounting records.

Field Manipulation/Append

Field manipulation/append functions allow investigators to create virtual fields in the active database. Virtual fields do not alter the original data but create a calculated new field in the active database (including a parameter, description, calculations, criteria, removing spaces, and conditions). For an effective investigation, fraud examiners can use virtual fields and compare those fields to the native or original fields.

Duplicate Key

The duplicate key test allows auditors to highlight records with duplicate transactions, words, or values. IDEA allows three types of duplicate key: detection, exclusion, and fuzzy duplicate detection.

Field Statistics

Field statistics are important because they are used for statistical parameters calculations (e.g., minimum, maximum, standard deviation, variance, averages, and also positive and negative records). Field statistics enable fraud investigators to become familiar with data to find fraudulent activities.

Summarization and Stratification

Summarization categorizes records and counts the number of records with unique categories. It also calculates the sum of the data, sorts information by indicated fields, and gives detailed views of the transaction. The stratification function identifies the unexpected combination of numbers, digits, or unexpected occurrences.

Join

The join function combines multiple fields from different database or data files to find unusual transactions. There are different ways to join databases; for example, records with no secondary match, records with no primary match, matches only, all records in the primary file, and all records in both files. The join function can also join databases on predefined criteria.

Aging Analysis

The aging analysis function analyzes the number of days for various transaction in order to reveal age-related transaction anomalies.

Comparing Files

In the fraud investigation process, comparing files plays an important role in fraud detection. Comparing files allows fraud investigators to find whether the source file, document, or data have been altered or tampered.

Benford's Law

Benford's law allows auditors to find irregularities in the numerical data by analyzing the digits. The primary objective of using the Benford's law function is to enable auditors to turn raw facts and figures into information and to develop a better understanding of the data to perform subsequent actions. CAATT allows fraud investigators to analyze data, form and test hypotheses, and obtain results quickly [35].

Conclusion

The primary objective for using CAATT is to enhance the fraud auditing process, allowing auditors to analyze fraud symptoms and abnormal transactions to detect organizational fraud with effectiveness and efficiency. CAATT adoption in the fraud domain is not only significant for businesses, but also a fundamental part of audit methodologies. CAATT implementation in fraud auditing provides a high level of assurance that can lead to increased confidence among stakeholders in an organization's financial reporting system, ultimately reducing the duration and total loss of organizational fraud schemes. While there are a number of high quality CAATT solutions in the marketplace for most needs and organizational budgets, in the following section, we have utilized IDEA (V.9) to provide an almost step-by-step demonstration of some of the more common CAATT audit tests. Auditors and fraud examiners can use the next audit test demo section to practice some of these tests in order to gain additional confidence in utilizing CAATT software solutions.

References

1. Bourke, J. (2010). Computer assisted audit techniques or CAATS: What's so great about it? *AICPA*. Retrieved from www.aicpastore. com/Content/media/PRODUCER_CONTENT/Newsletters/ Articles_2010/CPA/Jan/CAATS.jsp
2. Lacoma, T. (n.d.). Advantages and disadvantages to an assisted audit. *Chron*. Retrieved from http://smallbusiness.chron.com/advantages-disadvantages-assisted-audit-20298.html
3. Association of Certified Fraud Examiners. (2018). Report to the Nations on Occupational Fraud and Abuse. Retrieved from https://s3-us-west-2. amazonaws.com/acfepublic/2018-report-to-the-nations.pdf
4. PWC. (2016). Global economic crime survey 2016. *Price Waterhouse Cooper*. Retrieved from www.pwc.com/gx/en/economic-crime-survey/ pdf/GlobalEconomicCrimeSurvey2016.pdf
5. Caseware Analytics. (2018). About Us. Retrieved from www. casewareanalytics.com/about-us
6. Caseware Analytics. (n.d.). Petroleum and Natural Gas Company. Retrieved from www.casewareanalytics.com/success-stories/ petroleum-and-natural-gas-company
7. Caseware Analytics. (n.d.). Tate and Tryon. Retrieved from www. casewareanalytics.com/success-stories/tate-and-tryon
8. Caseware Analytics. (n.d.). BCR. Retrieved from www.casewareana-lytics.com/success-stories/bcr
9. Owens, S. (2017, June). The Total Economic Impact™ Of ACL. Retrieved from www.acl.com/pdfs/forrester-tei-study-acl-platform-summer-2017.pdf
10. Obringer, L. A. (2005). How cooking the books works. *How Stuff Works*. Retrieved from https://money.howstuffworks.com/cooking-books7.htm

11. Olasanmi, O. O. (2013). Computer aided audit techniques and fraud detection. *Research Journal of Finance and Accounting.* Retrieved from www.iiste.org/Journals/index.php/RJFA/article/view/5084/5455

12. Mansour, E. (2016). Factor affecting the adoption of computer assisted audit tools and techniques in audit process: Finding from Jordan. *Business and Economic Research,* 6(1), 248.

13. Debreceny, R., Lee, S. L., Neo, W., & Shuling, J. T. (2004). Employing Generalized Audit Software in the Financial Services Sector: Challenges and Opportunities. Retrieved from http://raw.rutgers.edu/docs/wcars/8wcars/contassurronaldjdaigle_files/DebrecenyCAATSBanks_paper.pdf)

14. Pedrosa, I., & Costa, C. J. (2012). Financial Auditing and Surveys: How are financial auditors using information technology? An approach using expert interviews. *Proceedings of the Workshop on Information Systems and Design of Communication,* Lisbon, Portugal: ISDOC '12, (pp. 37–43).

15. Akbar, M. S., & Suraida, I. (2017). Competence and professional care of external auditor on information technology audit. *Trikonomika.* Retrieved from http://journal.unpas.ac.id/index.php/trikonomika/article/view/418/234

16. Coderre, D. (2013). *Computer-Aided Fraud Prevention and Detection* (1st Edition, pp. 41–43, 71–73). Hoboken, NJ: John Wiley & Sons.

17. Coman, M. D., Coman, D. M., & Horga, M. (2014). Information technology for fraud detection. *Valahian Journal of Economic Studies,* 85–92. Retrieved from http://search.proquest.com/docview/1685869576/fulltextPDF/995A5D501AF848CBPQ/1?accountid=10243

18. Caseware Analytics (n.d.). 5 Reasons to Use a Professional Data Analytics Tool. Retrieved from www.casewareanalytics.com/sites/default/files/whitepapers/5_reasons_to_swap_spreadsheets_2015_final.pdf

19. Lanza, R. (n.d.). Fraud data interrogation tools: Comparing best software for fraud examinations. *Fraud Magazine.* Retrieved from www.informationactive.com/data/attachments/fraudsoftware.PDF

20. ACFE. (2014). *Fighting Fraud in the Government.* Austin, TX: Association of Certified Fraud Examiners.

21. Bierstaker, J., Janvrin, D., & Lowe, D. J. (2014). What factors influence auditors' use of computer-assisted audit techniques? *Advances in Accounting,* 30(1), 67–74. DOI: 10.1016/j.adiac.2013.12.005

22. Moroney, R., Campbell, F., Hamilton, J., & Warren, V. (2012). *Auditing: A Practical Approach* (Canadian Edition). Mississauga, ON: John Wiley & Sons Canada Ltd.

23. Pedrosa, I., & Costa, J. C. (2012). Computer assisted audit tools in real world: Idea applications and approaches in real context. *International Journal of Computer Information Systems and Industrial Management Applications.* Retrieved from www.academia.edu/12774281/COMPUTER_ASSISTED_AUDIT_TOOLS_IN_REAL_WORLD_IDEA_APPLICATIONS_AND_APPROACHES_IN_REAL_CONTEXT

24. Bierstaker, J., Janvrin, D., & Lowe, J. D. What factors influence auditors' use of computer-assisted audit techniques. *Advances in Accounting, incorporating Advances in International Accounting.* Retrieved from www.academia.edu/18877662/What_factors_influence_auditors_use_of_computer-assisted_audit_techniques

25. Rosli, K., Yewo, P.H., & Siew, E.G. (2012). Factors influencing audit technology acceptance by Audit Firms: A new I-TOE adoption framework. *Journal of Accounting and Auditing: Research & Practice.* Retrieved from http://ibimapublishing.com/articles/JAARP/2012/876814/876814.pdf

26. Singleton, T. W., & Singleton, A. J. (2011). *Fraud Auditing and Forensic Accounting.* Hoboken, NJ: John Wiley & Sons.

27. IAASB. (2015). *Handbook of International Quality Control, Auditing, Review, Other Assurance, and Related Services Pronouncements.* Volume 1. Retrieved from www.ire.lu/fileadmin/media/Env_normatif_ISA/IAASB-2015-Handbook-Volume-1.pdf

28. IIA-IPPF. (2017). International Standards for the Professional Practice of Internal Auditing (Standards). Retrieved from https://na.theiia.org/standards-guidance/Public%20Documents/IPPF-Standards-2017.pdf

29. ISACA. (2009). IT Standards, Guidelines, and Tools and Techniques for Audit and Assurance and Control Professionals. Retrieved from www.isaca.org/knowledge-center/standards/documents/it-audit-assurance-guidance-1march2010.pdf

30. Lala, S., Gupta, M., & Sharman, R. (2014). Fraud Detection through Routine Use of CAATTs. Retrieved from https://pdfs.semanticscholar.org/11b8/974bc40e42382465ed2a86d4f8d3021869c3.pdf

31. Albrecht, C. C. (2008). *Fraud and Forensic Accounting in a Digital Environment.* Brigham Young University. Retrieved from www.theifp.org/research-grants/IFP-Whitepaper-4.pdf

32. Maciejewska, I. (2015). Computer-Assisted Audit Tools in Relation with International Standard on Quality Control 1 (ISQ1): (Based on Experiences from Polish Small Audit Practices). DOI: 10.1109/CISTI.2015.7170617

33. ICAEW. (2016). Data Analytics for External Auditors International Auditing Perspectives. Retrieved from www.icaew.com/-/media/corporate/files/technical/audit-and-assurance/audit-and-assurance-faculty/publications/international-auditing-perspectives/web_tecpln14725_aaf_data_analytics.ashx?la=en

34. Turnbull, C. (2003). *Fraud Investigation Using IDEA* (1st Edition, pp. 9, 20–27, 84). Vancouver, BC: Ekaros Analytical Inc.

35. Coderre, D. G. (2009). *Computer-Aided Fraud Prevention and Detection: A Step-By-Step Guide.* Hoboken, NJ: John Wiley & Sons.

36. Byrnes, P. E., Al-Awadhi, A., Gullvist, B., Brown-Liburd, H., Teeter, R., Warren Jr., J. D., & Vasarhelyi, M. (2012). Evolution of Auditing: From the Traditional Approach to the Future Audit. Retrieved on May 31, 2017, from www.aicpa.org/interestareas/frc/

assuranceadvisoryservices/downloadabledocuments/whitepaper_
evolution-of-auditing.pdf

37. Mahzan, N., & Lymer, A. (2010). Adoption of Computer Assisted Audit Tools and Techniques (CAATTs) by Internal Auditors: Current issues in the UK. Retrieved from http://citeseerx.ist.psu.edu/viewdoc/download?doi=10.1.1.469.4899&rep=rep1&type=pdf

38. Venkatesh, V., Morris, M. G., Davis, G. B., & Davis, F. D. (2003). User acceptance of information technology: Toward a unified view. *MIS Quarterly, 27*(3), 425–478.

39. Ghani, R., Ismail, N. A., & Saidin, S. Z. (2016). Adoption of computer-assisted audit tools and techniques (CAATTs): An exploratory study in audit firms. *International Conference on Accounting Studies (ICAS)* 2016. Langkawi, Kedah, Malaysia.

40. BBVA. (2012). Fraud and internal audit: Current views, examples, and resources. *Institute of Internal Auditors, Birmingham Chapter,* Retrieved on June 6, 2017, from https://chapters.theiia.org/birmingham/Documents/Fraud___Internal_Audit_IIA_6Sep2012.pdf

41. CGMA. (2012). CGMA Report Fraud Risk Management A Guide to Good Practice. Retrieved on June 5, 2017, from www.cgma.org/Resources/Reports/DownloadableDocuments/fraudriskmanagement.pdf

42. CIMA. (2008). Fraud Risk Management A Guide to Good Practice. Retrieved on June 5, 2017, from www.cimaglobal.com/documents/importeddocuments/cid_techguide_fraud_risk_management_feb09.pdf.pdf

7

Audit Test Manual for ACFE Fraud Tree Schemes Using IDEA®

This final practice-based section aims to familiarize readers with the basics of Interactive Data Extraction and Analysis (IDEA) software as one of the audit Computer-Assisted Audit Tools and Techniques (CAATT). The chapter is organized into three main sections:

a. *Data Import*: This first phase is a very important one as the auditor cannot perform a CAATT-based audit test if he/she is unable to successfully import the data into the software. In this section, readers are provided with three common data import scenarios: importing data in Microsoft Excel, Microsoft Access, and text data.

b. *Audit Procedures*: A step-by-step tutorial covering ten common audit tests organized by fraud scheme category are presented. These tests are basic in nature and are intended to provide audit or fraud professionals with no or little CAATT experience with some audit test practice opportunities. The IDEA software includes some basic dummy (test) data to accommodate practice opportunities. However, the reader may want to use his/her organizational test/training data for some or all of these tests.

c. *Report Creation*: This last section deals with output (report) creation phase of an audit test.

Furthermore, just about all CAATT audit analysis vendors offer elaborate training resources on their sites allowing professionals access to more advanced training material, white papers, and other useful resources. Professionals seeking to attain an expert level in the use of CAATT audit analysis software are encouraged to familiarize themselves with the training resources offered through their chosen CAATT software provider.

Section I: Performing Basic Tasks with IDEA

 a. Creating a new Project in IDEA
 b. Data Import: Microsoft Excel format
 c. Data Import: Microsoft Access format
 d. Data Import: Text Data format

a. Creating a new Project in IDEA

Objective: Creating a new project using IDEA V.10

  The objective of creating an individual new project for each audit test is that all information related to that specific audit test will be stored in a separate project. To create a new project:

Step 1. Select "Home" and click "Create" (a dialog box will appear).

Step 2. Select "Managed Projects" and enter the project name as "Fraud Auditing."

Step 3. Click "OK."

A new project will be created with the name "Fraud Auditing." The location of the created project will be

C:\Users\LastName   FirstName\Documents\My   IDEA Documents\IDEA Projects\Fraud Auditing

To perform audit test, copy test data "Source Files.ILB"

C:\Users\LastName   FirstName\Documents\My   IDEA Documents\IDEA Projects\Fraud Auditing\Source Files.ILB

Note 1: Properties such as "Report Name," "Report Period," and "Locked By" can be changed by clicking the Properties button on the home screen.

Note 2: The path of the project will differ because of the location (e.g., computer name). Once a new project is created, data is copied to the default location. The next step is to import that data into IDEA.

b. Data Import: Microsoft Excel format

Objective: Importing "Microsoft Excel" data into IDEA for analysis

Step 1. Select "Home" and click "Desktop."

The "Import Assistant" dialogue box showing the format, location, and file name will appear. Select the appropriate format of the data.

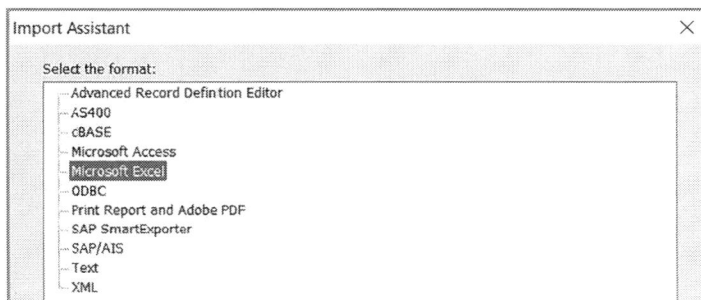

Step 2. From the "Select the format" of the dialogue box, select "Microsoft Excel," and click ▢ (i.e., on the right corner of the "File Name") to select the default location of the file **(C:\C:\Users\ LastName FirstName\Documents\My IDEA Documents\ IDEA Projects\Fraud Auditing\Source Files.ILB).**

Step 3. From the "Select File" window, select "Sample Data for Analysis."

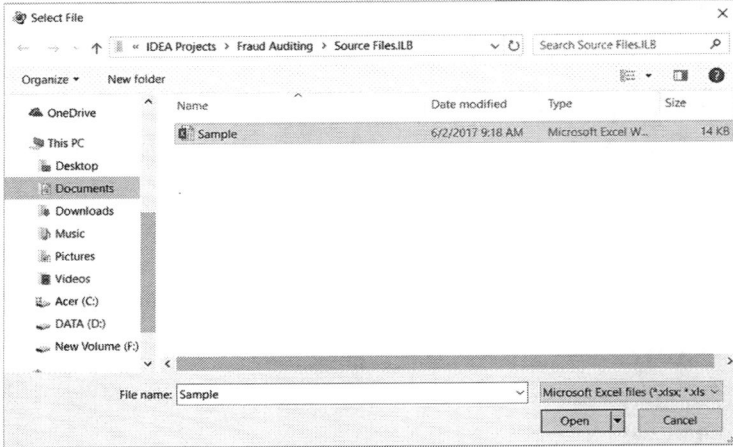

Step 4. Click "Open" followed by "Next."
- The "Sample" file contains three different sheets (i.e. Credit Card, Month 1, Month 2). An investigator can select different sheets depending on the investigation.
- Select the Checklist button "First Row is Field Name."

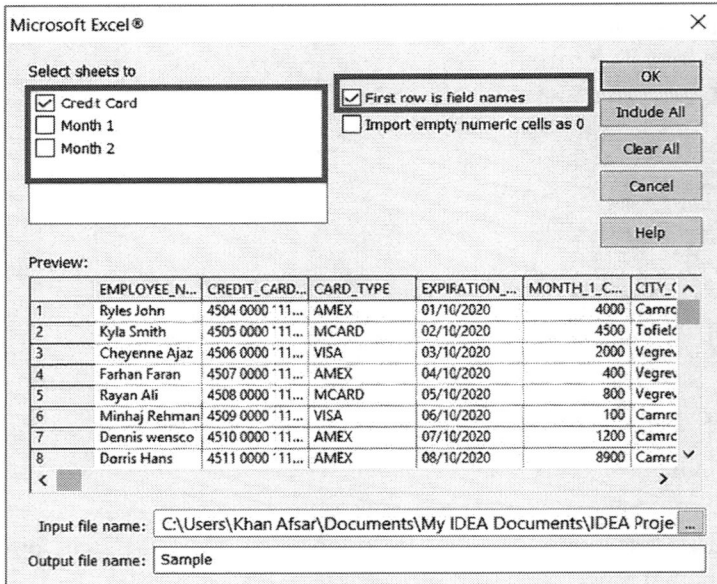

Step 5. Click "OK" to import the data.

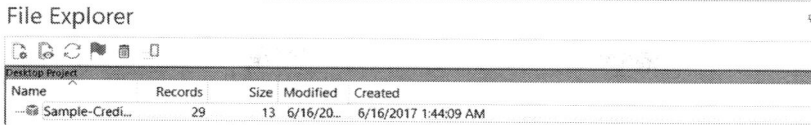

File Explorer

Name	Records	Size	Modified	Created
Sample-Credi...	29	13	6/16/20...	6/16/2017 1:44:09 AM

"Sample Credit Card" Data is therefore imported into IDEA for analysis.

Sample-Credit Card ×

EMPLOYEE_NAME	CREDIT_CARD_NUMBER	CARD_TYPE	EXPIRATION_DATE	MONTH_1_CREDIT_CARD_BILL	CITY_OF_WORK
1 Ryles John	4504 0000 1111 2222	AMEX	10/1/2020	4000	Camrose
2 Kyla Smith	4505 0000 1111 2233	MCARD	10/2/2020	4500	Tofield
3 Cheyenne Ajaz	4506 0000 1111 3322	VISA	10/3/2020	2000	Vegreville
4 Farhan Faran	4507 0000 1111 2112	AMEX	10/4/2020	400	Vegreville
5 Rayan Ali	4508 0000 1111 4422	MCARD	10/5/2020	800	Vegreville

c. Data Import: Microsoft Access format

Objective: Importing Microsoft Access data into IDEA for analysis

Step 1. Select "Home" and click "Desktop."

CaseWare IDEA

File | Home | Data | Analysis | View | Macros | SmartAnalyzer

Project Overview | Create | Select | Archive | Properties | Desktop | IDEA Server | Export • | Save As | Send Using E-mail | Project Administration | Select Server | Passport

Projects | Import | Export | IDEA Server | CaseWare

The "Import Assistant" dialogue box showing the format, location, and file name will appear.

Step 2. From "Select the format" of the dialogue box, select "Microsoft Access."

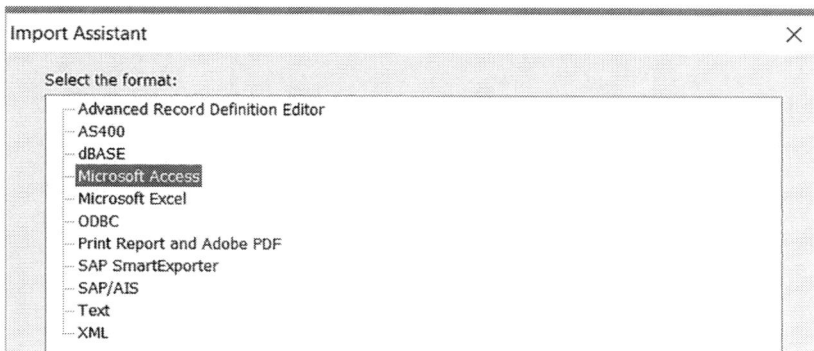

Import Assistant ✕

Select the format:

- Advanced Record Definition Editor
- AS400
- dBASE
- Microsoft Access
- Microsoft Excel
- ODBC
- Print Report and Adobe PDF
- SAP SmartExporter
- SAP/AIS
- Text
- XML

Step 3. Select "Microsoft Excel," and click ⬚ on the right corner of the file name to select the default location of the file.

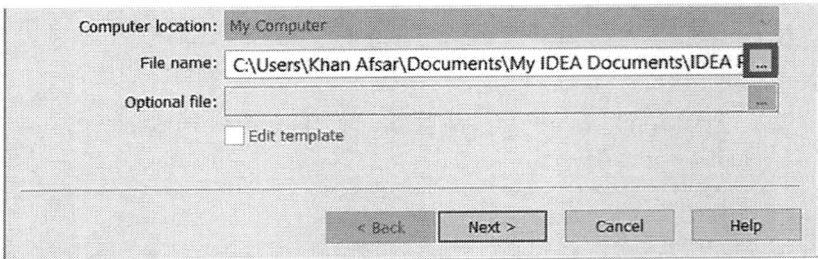

Computer location:	My Computer	
File name:	C:\Users\Khan Afsar\Documents\My IDEA Documents\IDEA F	...
Optional file:		...

☐ Edit template

< Back	Next >	Cancel	Help

Step 4. Select the location where the data is saved.

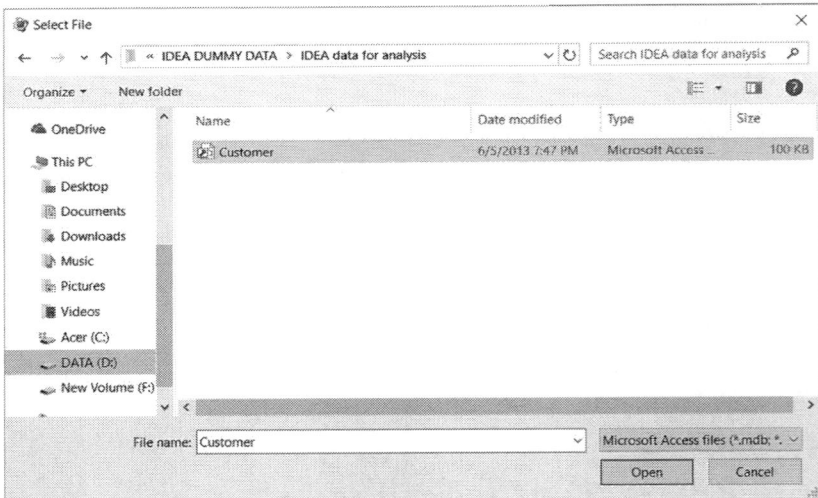

Select File					✕
← → ∨ ↑ ▯ « IDEA DUMMY DATA › IDEA data for analysis		∨ ↻	Search IDEA data for analysis	✕	🔎

Organize ▾   New folder   ☰ ▾   ▯   ❷

	Name ⌃	Date modified	Type	Size
☁ OneDrive				
💻 This PC	🔲 Customer	6/5/2013 7:47 PM	Microsoft Access ...	100 KB
🖿 Desktop				
🗎 Documents				
⬇ Downloads				
🎵 Music				
🖼 Pictures				
🎬 Videos				
💽 Acer (C:)				
💽 DATA (D:)				
💽 New Volume (F:)				

File name:	Customer		Microsoft Access files (*.mdb; *. ∨
			Open Cancel

Step 5. Click "Open."

Step 6. Click "Next."

Step 7. From the Microsoft Access box, in "Select Tables," select "Database1."

Step 8. Enter the output file name.

Microsoft Access®   ×

Select tables: ☑ Database1   [OK]

                                                         [Include All]

                                                         [Clear All]

                                                         [Cancel]

                                                         [Help]

Character Field Options

☑ Scan records for field length

○ Scan all

◉ Scan only 10000

☐ Create a record number field

Output file name: Customer Database

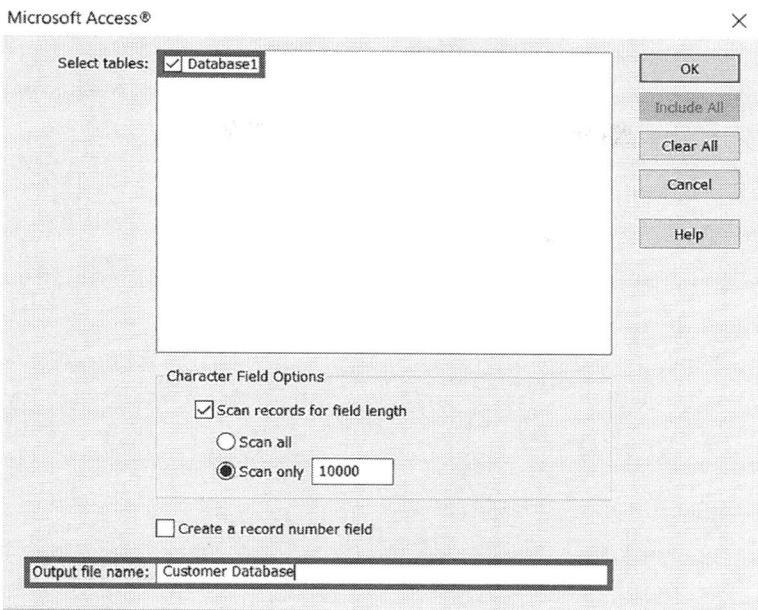

Step 9. Click "OK." Microsoft Access data will be imported.

Customer Database-Datab... ×

	CUST_NO	FIRST_NAME	LAST_NAME	COUNTRY	STATUS	CREDIT_LIM
1	10000	DIANE	BURROWS	SOUTH AFRICA	M	4000
2	10003	KEVIN	NICHOLSON-KNOWLES	SOUTH AFRICA	M	20000
3	10004	JENNIFER	DE FREITAS	SOUTH AFRICA	M	12000
4	10005	CHABIRAJI	SAWYER	SOUTH AFRICA	F	10000
5	10006	KATHARINE	BURROWS	SOUTH AFRICA	F	13000
6	10007	DONGJIAN	ELLIS	NIGERIA	M	8000
7	10101	MALINDA	JOHNSTON	NIGERIA	M	3000
8	10102	TANYA	PLOUFFE	NIGERIA	M	2000
9	10201	NATASHA	MCDONALD	NIGERIA	R	280000
10	10203	KENNETH	HIGGS	NIGERIA	M	10000

a. Data Import: Text Data format

Objective: Importing "Text" data into IDEA for analysis

Step 1. Select "Home" and click "Desktop."

CaseWare IDEA

File   Home   Data   Analysis   View   Macros   SmartAnalyzer

Project   Create   Select   Archive   Properties   Desktop   IDEA   Export   Save As   Send Using E-mail   Project   Select   Passport
Overview   Server
          Projects   Import   Export   IDEA Server   CaseWare

The "Import Assistant" dialogue box showing the format, location, and file name will appear.

Step 2. From the "Select the format" of the dialogue box, select "Text."

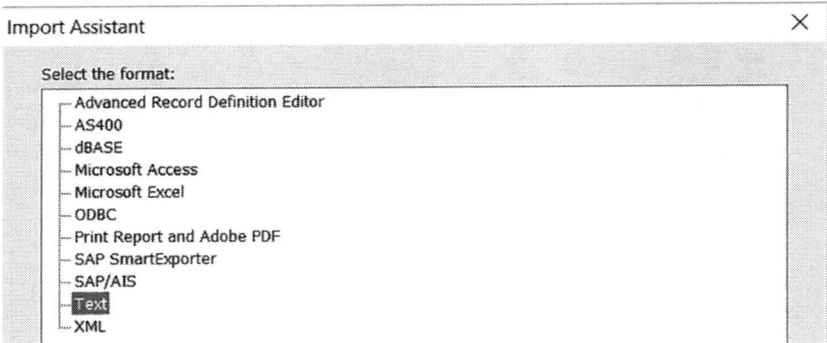

Import Assistant   ✕

Select the format:

- Advanced Record Definition Editor
- AS400
- dBASE
- Microsoft Access
- Microsoft Excel
- ODBC
- Print Report and Adobe PDF
- SAP SmartExporter
- SAP/AIS
- Text
- XML

Step 3. Select "Text," and click ⊡ on the right corner of the "File Name" to select the default location of the file.

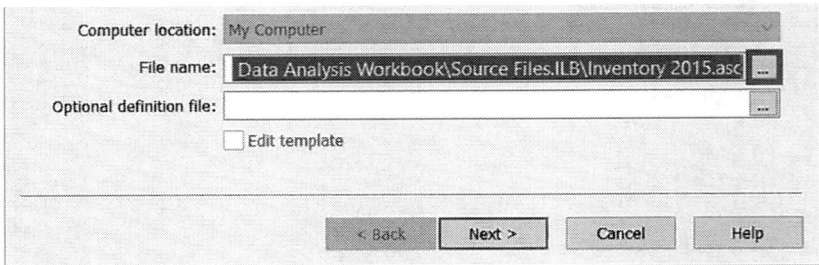

Computer location:	My Computer
File name:	Data Analysis Workbook\Source Files.ILB\Inventory 2015.asc
Optional definition file:	
	☐ Edit template

< Back   Next >   Cancel   Help

Step 4. Select the location where the data is saved.

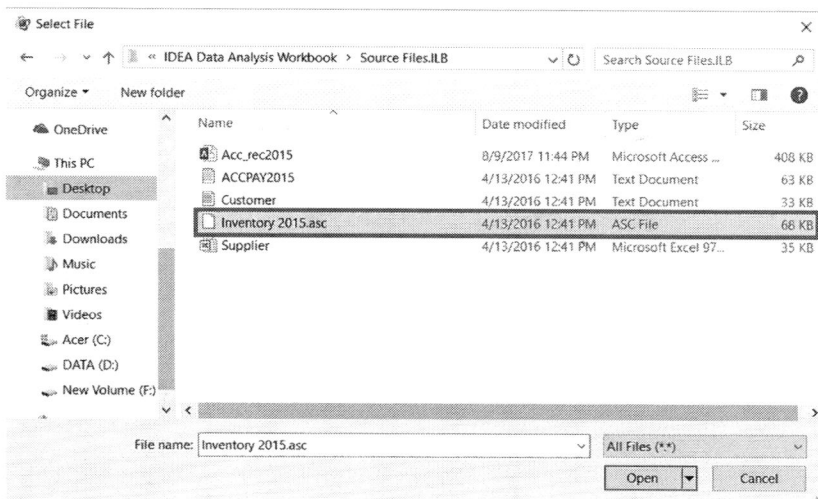

Step 5. Click "Open."

Step 6. Click "Next."

Step 7. From the "Import Assistant – File Type" dialogue box, select the correct file type. In this case, select "Delimited."

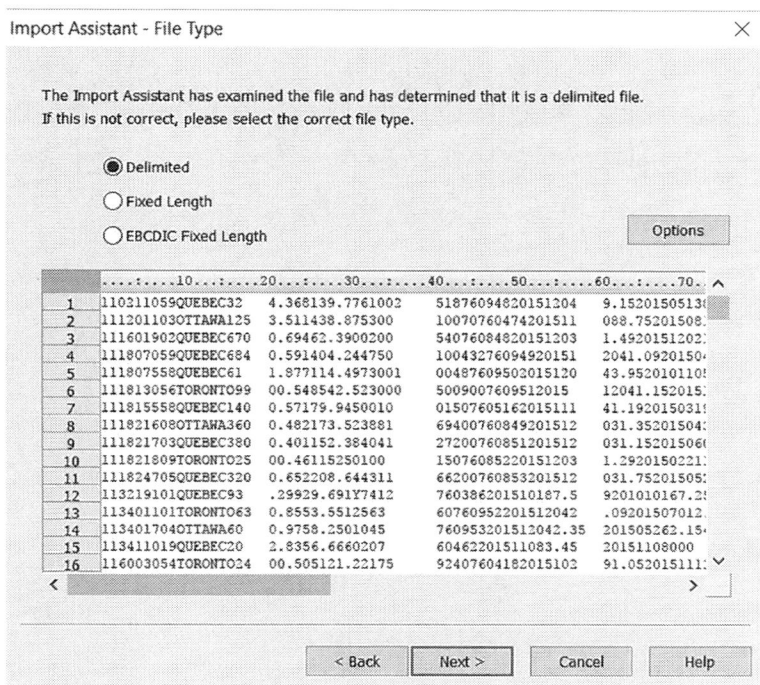

Step 8. Click "Next."

Step 9. From the "Import Assistant – Specify Field Separator" and "Text Encapsulator" to accept the default setting, or select the option that better suits your data's format.

Step 10. Click "Next."

Import Assistant - Specify Field Separator and Text Encapsulator   ×

Please inspect the file displayed in the preview and make changes, if required, in the options below.

Field Separator
Delimited files use a special character to separate fields. Please inspect the file below and, if required, change the Field Separator selected.

○ Comma   ○ Colon   ○ Semicolon   ● Tab   ○ Space   ○ Other |

Text encapsulator: | "   ∨   Header lines to ignore: 0

☐ First visible row is field names

1	110211059	QUEBEC	32	4.368	139.776	100	25	18	760948	20151204	9.15	2C
2	111201103	OTTAWA	125	3.511	438.875	300	100	70	760474	20151108	8.75	2C
3	111601902	QUEBEC	670	0.69	462.3	900	200	540	760848	20151203	1.49	2C
4	111807059	QUEBEC	684	0.591	404.244	750	100	432	760949	20151204	1.09	2C
5	111807558	QUEBEC	61	1.877	114.497	300	100	48	760950	20151204	3.95	2C
6	111813056	TORONTO	990	0.548	542.52	3000	500	900	760951	20151204	1.15	2C
7	111815558	QUEBEC	140	0.571	79.94	500	100	150	760516	20151114	1.19	2C
8	111821608	OTTAWA	360	0.482	173.52	388	169	400	760849	20151203	1.35	2C
9	111821703	QUEBEC	380	0.401	152.38	404	127	200	760851	20151203	1.15	2C
10	111821809	TORONTO	250	0.46	115	250	100	150	760852	20151203	1.29	2C
11	111824705	QUEBEC	320	0.652	208.64	431	166	200	760853	20151203	1.75	2C
12	113219101	QUEBEC	9	3.299	29.691	Y 7	4	12	760386	20151018	7.59	2C
13	113401101	TORONTO	63	0.85	53.55	125	63	60	760952	20151204	2.09	2C

[< Back]   [Next >]   [Cancel]   [Help]

Step 11. Enter "Field Name" and "Description" and select the appropriate data type.

Field name: PRODCOD
Type: Numeric
Description: Product Code
Number of decimals: 0
☐ Do not import this field
☐ Implied decimals
Converted Example
110,211,059

PRODCOD	DEPT	QTY	AV_COST	T._COST	DI	MAX	MIN	DELQTY	ORDE

Field name: QTY
Type: Numeric
Description: Quantity on Hand
Number of decimals: 0
☐ Do not import this field
☐ Implied decimals
Converted Example
32

PRODCOD	DEPT	QTY	AV_COST	T._COST	DI	MAX	MIN	DELQTY	ORDE

Field name: DEPT
Type: Character
Description: Depot Name
☐ Do not import this field
Converted Example
QUEBEC

PRODCOD	DEPT	QTY	AV_COST	T._COST	DI	MAX	MIN	DELQTY	ORDE

Field name: DELDATE
Type: Date
Description: Last Delivery Date
Date Mask (e.g., YYMMDD): YYYYMMDD
☐ Do not import this field
Converted Example
20151204

MAX	MIN	DELQTY	ORDERNO	DELDATE	CURPRI	REFDAT	RESELPRI

Step 12. Click "Next."

Step 13. "Import Assistant – Create Fields" allows the creation of new fields.

Step 14. Click "Next."

Step 15. The "Import Assistant – Import Criteria" screen will appear.

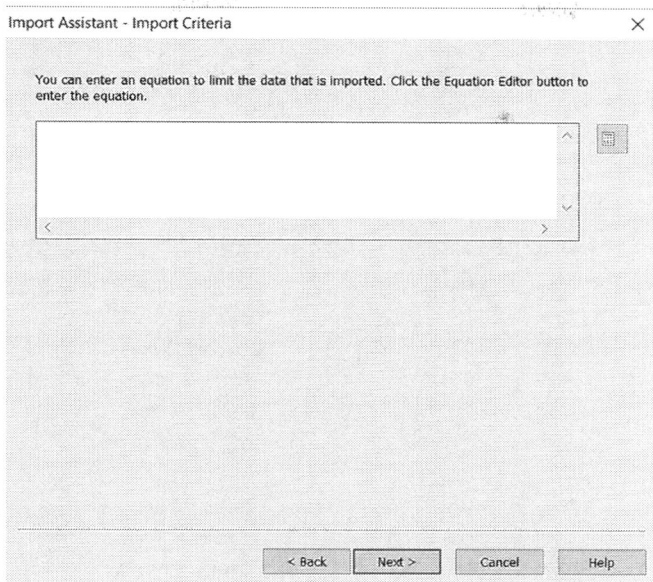

Import Assistant - Import Criteria   ✕

You can enter an equation to limit the data that is imported. Click the Equation Editor button to enter the equation.

< Back   Next >   Cancel   Help

Step 16. Click "Next."

Step 17. Enter the file name and click "Generate Field Statistics."

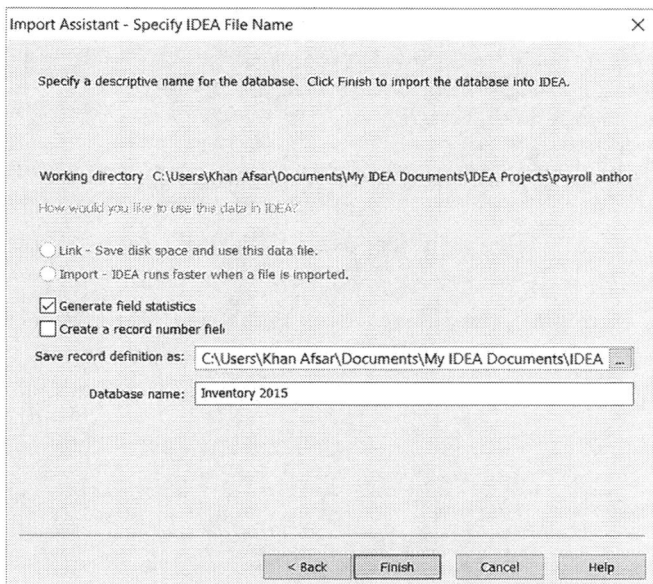

Import Assistant - Specify IDEA File Name   ✕

Specify a descriptive name for the database. Click Finish to import the database into IDEA.

Working directory C:\Users\Khan Afsar\Documents\My IDEA Documents\IDEA Projects\payroll anthor

How would you like to use this data in IDEA?

◯ Link - Save disk space and use this data file.
◯ Import - IDEA runs faster when a file is imported.
☑ Generate field statistics
☐ Create a record number fiel

Save record definition as: C:\Users\Khan Afsar\Documents\My IDEA Documents\IDEA ...

Database name: Inventory 2015

< Back   Finish   Cancel   Help

Step 18. Click "Finish."

Inventory data will now be imported to IDEA.

Section II: Performing Ten Common Audit Tests Using IDEA

AUDIT TEST NUMBER	SCHEME CATEGORY
Audit Test # 01	Fictitious Revenues
Audit Test # 02	Fictitious Revenues
Audit Test # 03	Fictitious Revenues
Audit Test # 04	Billing Schemes
Audit Test # 05	Billing Schemes
Audit Test # 06	Payroll Schemes
Audit Test # 07	Purchases Schemes
Audit Test # 08	Conflict of Interest
Audit Test # 09	Conflict of Interest
Audit Test # 10	Non-cash Larceny

a. Audit Test # 01: Fictitious Revenues

Association of Certified Fraud Examiners' (ACFE) Fraud Tree Subcategory:
Fictitious Revenues
Purpose: To detect schemes related to fictitious revenues.
Audit Test Procedure: Identify duplicate items or serial numbers.
Assertion(s) Tested: Occurrence.
CAATT Expression: Duplicates.
Possible Red Flag: Duplicate serial numbers for different items.

Step 1. Create a new Project (follow "Creating New Project in IDEA" in Section I).
Step 2. Import "Sales Data 2" for Analysis (follow "Importing Audit Data for Analysis").
Step 3. Select "Duplicate" and click "Detection."

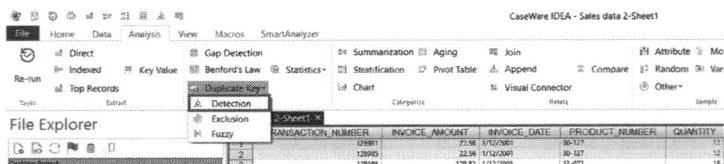

Step 4. From the "Duplicate Key Detection" window, select "Output duplicate records" and click "Key."

Step 5. In the "Define Key" window, select the field that will be used as base for duplicate detection and click "OK." Select "TRANSACTION_NUMBER" and "PRODUCT_ NUMBER" (Transaction number will be tested against Product number).

Note: Different combinations can be selected depending on the nature of test and data.

Step 6. Enter the file name "Dup. Transaction & Product Num."

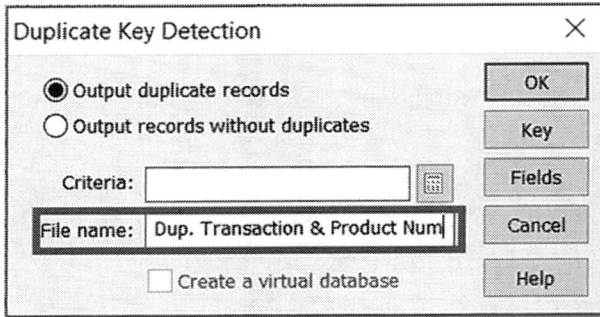

Step 7. Click "OK."

The duplicate transaction and product number window shows that for product numbers 33–083 and 35–111, transactions are twice recorded.

b. Audit Test # 02: Fictitious Revenues

ACFE Fraud Tree Subcategory: Fictitious Revenues.
Purpose: To detect schemes related to fictitious revenues.
Audit Test Procedure: Identify customer accounts with no address or telephone information.
Assertion(s) Tested: Existence.
CAATT Expression: Expression/Equation.
Possible Red Flag: High balance receivables without customer information.

Step 1. Create a new Project for "Fictitious Revenues."
Step 2. Import "Customer" Data for analysis.
Step 3. Under the "Analysis" tab, select "Direct."

Step 4. Change the file name to "Receivables without Customer Information."

Direct Extraction ✕

Records to extract: ● All   Starting record #: 1

       ○ Range   Ending record #: 26

       ☐ Create a virtual database

Database order: No index

	File Name		Criteria
1	Receivables without Customer Information	▦	
2			

OK | Create Fields | Fields | Delete | Cancel | Help

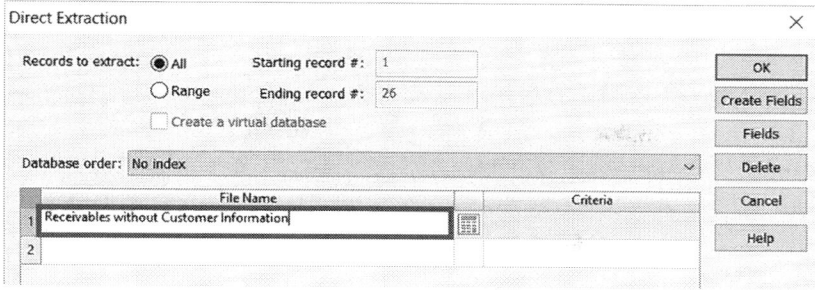

Step 5. Click ▦. The "Equation Editor" dialogue box will appear. Enter the equation as "ADDRESS=.OR. TELEPHONE_NUMBER="

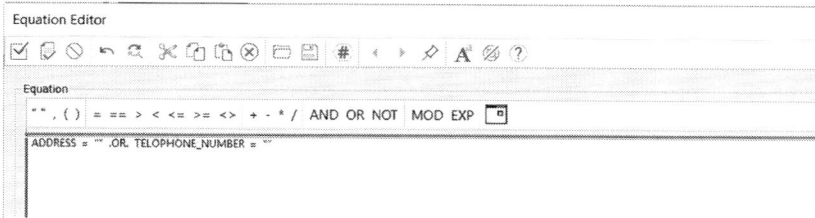

Equation Editor

☑ ▢ ⊘ ↰ ⌕ ✂ ▤ ▣ ⊗ ▭ ▣ # ‹ › ✎ A ⊘ ?

Equation

" " , ( ) = == > < <= >= <> + - * / AND OR NOT MOD EXP [▫]

ADDRESS = " " .OR. TELOPHONE_NUMBER = " "

Step 6. Once the criteria is defined, click ☑ or press "Ctrl+U" to validate and exit from the equation editor.

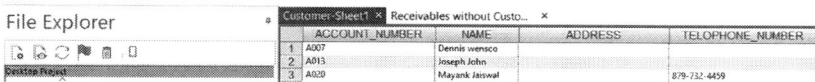

File Explorer

	ACCOUNT_NUMBER	NAME	ADDRESS	TELOPHONE_NUMBER
1	A007	Dennis wensco		
2	A013	Joseph John		
3	A020	Mayank Jaiswal		879-732-4459

Results show that three customers don't have an address and/or telephone number in the company registry.

c. Audit Test # 03: Fictitious Revenues

ACFE Fraud Tree Subcategory: Fictitious Revenues.

Purpose: To detect schemes related to fictitious revenues.

Audit Test Procedure: Credits, receipts, and invoices not in proper sequence or range.

Assertion(s) Tested: Completeness.

CAATT Expression: Gaps or Sort.

Possible Red Flag: Transactions which are not in proper sequencing and range.

Step 1. Create a new project for "Fictitious Revenues."

Step 2. Import "Sales Data 2" for analysis.

Step 3. Under the "Analysis" tab, click "Gap Detection."

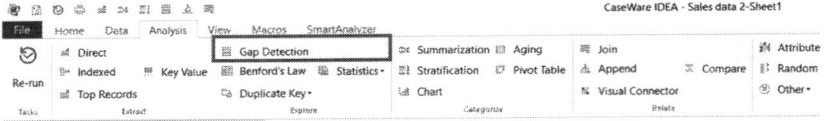

Step 4. From the "Field to Use" drop-down menu, select "TRANSACTION_NUMBER."

Step 5. In the "Result Name," enter "Missing Transaction Number" and click "OK."

Step 6. Shows the results of the missing transaction.

Sales data 2-Sheet1

From TRANSACTION NUMBER	To: TRANSACTION NUMBER	Number
132,173	132,173	1
132,175	132,179	5
132,182	132,186	5
132,188	132,188	1
132,191	132,191	1
132,193	132,194	2
132,196	132,210	15
132,212	132,219	8
132,222	132,223	2
132,225	132,225	1
132,227	132,228	2
132,230	132,230	1
132,232	132,233	2
132,236	132,240	5
132,242	132,275	34
132,277	132,292	16
132,294	132,321	28
132,323	132,339	17
132,341	132,359	19
132,361	132,378	18
132,380	132,392	13
132,394	132,416	23
132,418	132,517	100
132,519	132,528	10
132,530	132,542	13
132,544	132,545	2

Total number of items detected	2,588
Total number of gaps detected	670

Step 7. Analyze the missing transaction numbers. For example, from transaction numbers 128,982–128,984, three transactions were not recorded.

From: TRANSACTION NUMBER	To: TRANSACTION NUMBER	Number
128,982	128,984	3
128,982		
128,983		
128,984		

Missing transaction may be a red flag for fraud. The fraud investigator should further investigate that the red flag is due to an error or not as a result of fraud.

d. Audit Test # 04: Billing Schemes

ACFE Fraud Tree Subcategory: Billing Schemes.

Purpose: To detect schemes related to a shell company.

Audit Test Procedure: Summarize large invoices without purchase orders (by vendor).

Assertion(s) Tested: Occurrence and Authorization.

CAATT Expression: Filter/Display Criteria and Expression/Equation.

Possible Red Flag: Presence of large invoices without any purchase orders in organization records.

Step 1. Create a new Project for "Billing Schemes."

Step 2. Import "Payable Vendor Data" for analysis.

Step 3. Select "Direct" under the "Analysis" tab.

Step 4. In the dialogue box, change the default name to "Invoices without Purchase Order."

Step 5. Click ▦; the "Equation Editor" dialogue box will appear to enter the equation below:

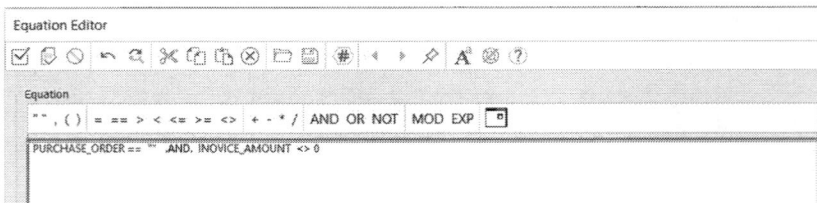

PURCHASE_ORDER == "" .AND. INVOICE_AMOUNT <> 0

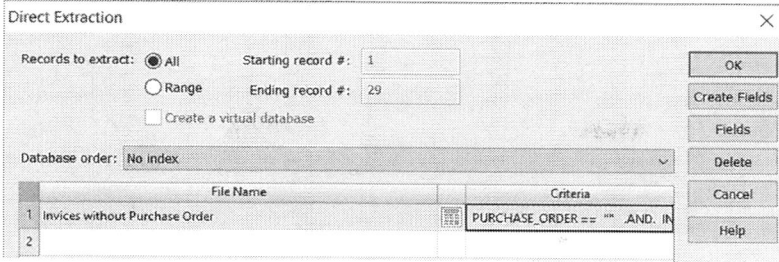

Step 6. Click "OK" to close the "Direct Extraction" dialogue box and run the equation.

Results show that two transactions do not have purchase order numbers. Furthermore, invoice amounts 15,000 and 10,119 are paid, indicating a fraud red flag.

e. Audit Test # 05: Billing Schemes

ACFE Fraud Tree Subcategory: Billing Schemes.

Purpose: To detect schemes related to a shell company.

Audit Test Procedure: Identify duplicate purchase order number, credit and invoices.

Assertion(s) Tested: Occurrence.

CAATT Expression: Duplicates.

Possible Red Flag: Multiple duplicate order numbers.

Step 1. Create a new Project for "Billing Schemes."

Step 2. Import "Payable Vendor Data" for analysis.

Step 3. Select "Duplicate Key > Exclusion" under the "Analysis" tab.

Step 4. Define criteria for duplicate key exclusion and check the fields to match as shown in the figure.

Step 5. Enter file name as "Dup. Pur. Order & Invoices."

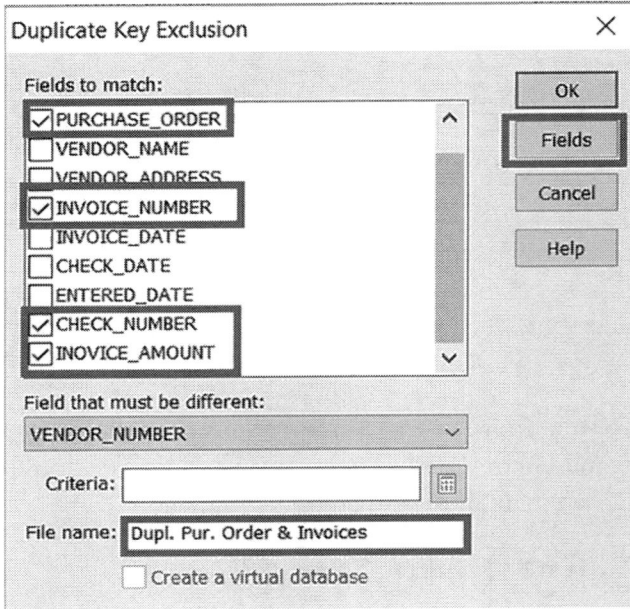

Step 6. Select Fields and click "OK."

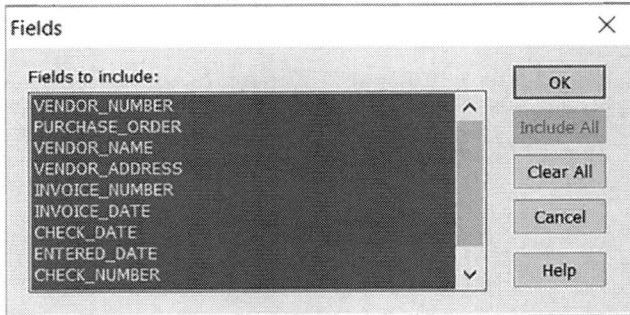

Two transactions were found with the same "Purchase Order" and "Invoice Amount."

f. Audit Test # 06: Payroll Schemes

ACFE Fraud Tree Subcategory: Payroll Schemes.
Purpose: To detect schemes related to a ghost employee.
Audit Test Procedure: Compare payroll date with employee start and termination dates.
Assertion(s) Tested: Accuracy and Occurrence.
CAATT Expression: Join/Relate and Expression/ Equation.
Possible Red Flag: Anomalies found in the payroll file when compared to employee master file in the HR division.

Step 1. Create a new project for "Payroll Schemes."

Step 2. Import "Payroll Record Register & Employee Information" for analysis.

Step 3. Under the "Analysis" tab, select "Join."

Step 4. Select "Secondary Database."

Step 5. Select "Payroll Record Register" as the "Secondary Database."

Note: If the active database is "Payroll Record Register," select "Employee Information" as the "Secondary Database."

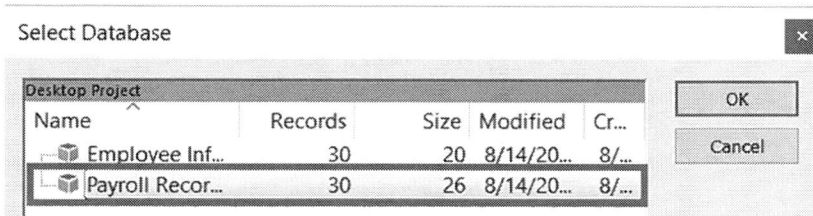

Step 6. Once the secondary database is selected, click | Fields | to define which fields will be imported from the secondary database to "Employee info. & Payroll Database." Select desired fields and click "OK."

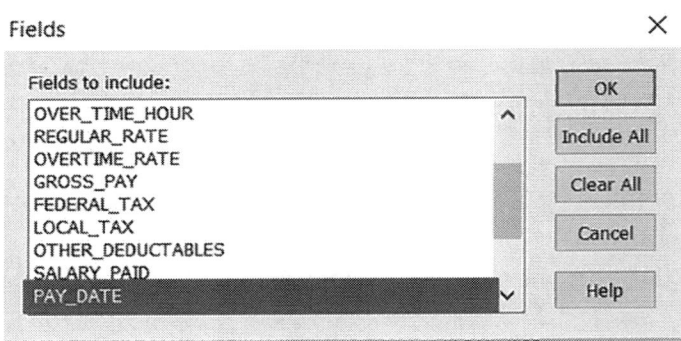

Fields		✕
Fields to include:		OK
OVER_TIME_HOUR REGULAR_RATE OVERTIME_RATE GROSS_PAY FEDERAL_TAX LOCAL_TAX OTHER_DEDUCTABLES SALARY_PAID PAY_DATE		Include All Clear All Cancel Help

Step 7. Enter the file name as "Employee info. & Payroll Database."

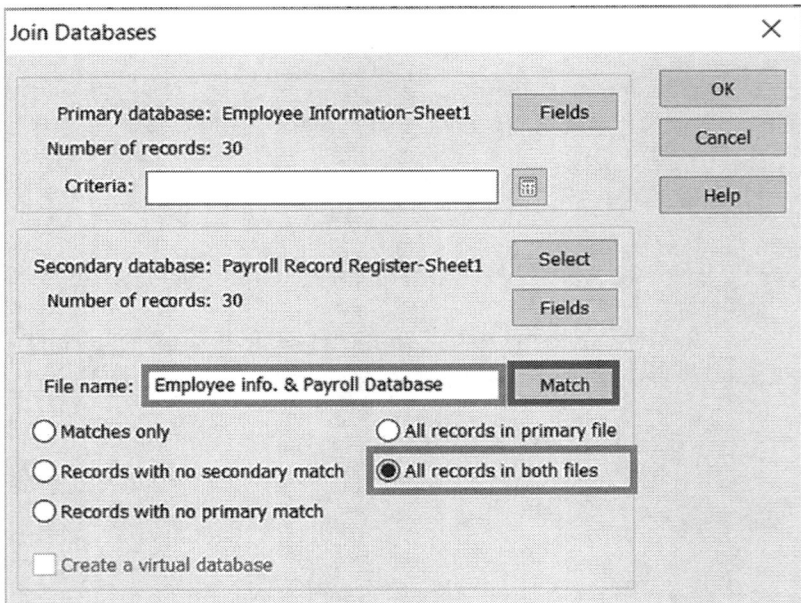

Join Databases		✕
Primary database: Employee Information-Sheet1	Fields	OK
Number of records: 30		Cancel
Criteria: [ ] 🔲		Help
Secondary database: Payroll Record Register-Sheet1	Select	
Number of records: 30	Fields	
File name: [Employee info. & Payroll Database]	Match	
○ Matches only ○ All records in primary file		
○ Records with no secondary match ⦿ All records in both files		
○ Records with no primary match		
☐ Create a virtual database		

Step 8. Click "Match" to define the match criteria, select "EMPLOYEE_NUMBER" as the primary field and "EMP_ID" as the secondary field and click "OK."

Match Key Fields			×
Primary	Order	Secondary	OK
EMPLOYEE_NUMBER (N)	Ascending	EMP_ID (N)	Delete

Step 9. Under "Properties," select "Criteria."

Properties

▼ Database

- ✓ Data
- History
- Field Statistics
- Control Total
- Criteria

Step 10. In the "Equation Editor" dialogue box, select "Enter."

Equation Editor

Equation

`" ", ( ) = == > < <= >= <> + - * / AND OR NOT MOD EXP`

`@Age(HIRE_DATE, PAY_DATE) > 0`

EMPLOYEE_NUMBER	FULL_NAME	ADDRESS	PHONE_NUMBER	PAY_TYPE	PAY_DAY	HIRE_DATE	SALARY_PAID	PAY_DATE
1	10120133 Joseph John	-	879-732-4448	H	Wednesday	8/27/2017	920.00	7/24/2017
2	10120149 Faran Fashon	60 School Road	879-732-449	H	Wednesday	8/13/2017	886.10	7/24/2017

Results show that two employees were hired in August 2017, but were getting paid for July 2017.

g. Audit Test # 07: Purchasing Schemes

ACFE Fraud Tree Subcategory: Purchasing Schemes.
Purpose: To detect schemes related to purchasing schemes and identify possible employee fraud.
Audit Test Procedure: Compare rates for similar products from other vendors-ratio analysis on unit price by product (check high-ratio details).
Assertion(s) Tested: Existence and Validity.
CAATT Expression: Duplicate, Ratio Analysis, and Expression/Equation.
Possible Red Flags: Duplicate supplier and/or invoices number.

Step 1. Create a new Project for "Purchasing Schemes."
Step 2. Import the *"ACCPAY2012.txt"* data file for analysis.
Step 3. Select "Duplicate Key > Detection" under the "Analysis" tab.

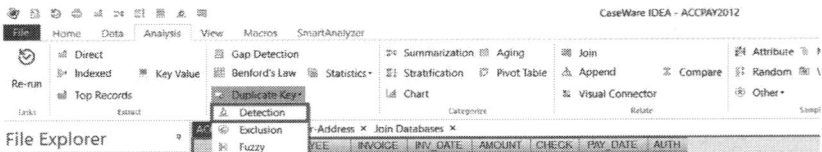

Step 4. From the "Duplicate Key Detection" window, select "Output Duplicate Records" and click "Key."

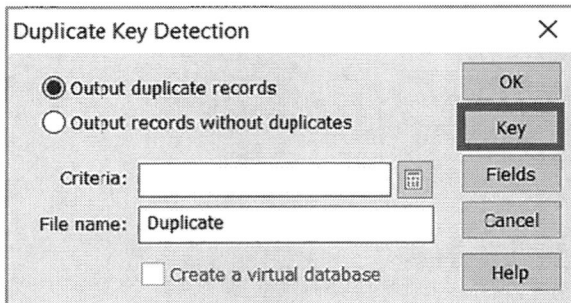

Step 5. In the "Define Key" window, select the field that will be used as base for duplicate detection and click "OK."

Define Key

Base index on:

NEW INDEX

Field	Direction
SUP_NO	Ascending
AMOUNT	Ascending

OK

Delete Key

Cancel

Help

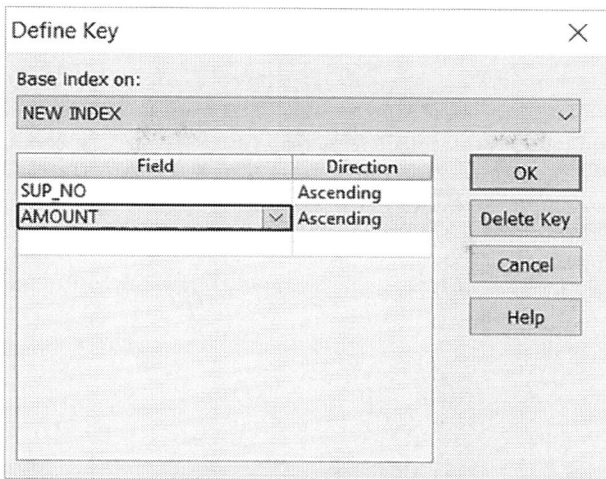

Step 6. Enter the file name "Dup. Supplier and Amount."

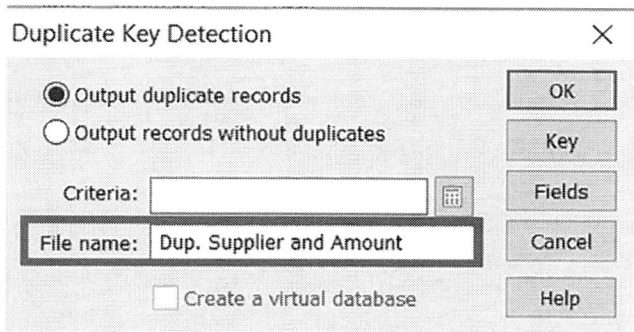

Duplicate Key Detection

- ● Output duplicate records
- ○ Output records without duplicates

Criteria:

File name: Dup. Supplier and Amount

☐ Create a virtual database

OK

Key

Fields

Cancel

Help

Step 7. Click "OK."

File Explorer

ACCPAY2012 × Supplier-Address × Join Databases × Dup. Supplier and Amount ×

	SUP_NO	PAYEE	INVOICE	INV_DATE	AMOUNT	CHECK	PAY_DATE	AUTH
1	M100	M Cash Inc	UP-76409	10/3/2012	75,000.00	701774	10/8/2012	HMV
2	M100	Cash Inc	CS - 717 -97	9/15/2012	75,000.00	701728	9/17/2012	VST
3	M100	Co Cash Inc	T5352	10/19/2012	75,000.00	701849	10/22/2012	V.S.T
4	P007	Nellie Dunn	000528CJW	6/26/2012	145.50	701531	7/21/2012	VST
5	P007	Nellie Dunn	000526CJW	6/12/2012	145.50	701490	7/12/2012	CW

Desktop Project

Name	Records
ACCPAY2012	999

Results show that five transactions have the same supplier and amount. Also, two transactions have the same invoice numbers.

h. Audit Test # 08: Conflict of Interest

ACFE Fraud Tree Subcategory: Conflict of Interest

Purpose: To test the validity of payments to authorized suppliers.

Audit Test Procedure: Check the total purchases made by the ordering clerk and vendor to find out if there were purchases made from suppliers that are not on the company's supplier's list.

Assertion(s) Tested: Existence, Occurrence, Authorization, and Validity

CAATT Expression: Join and Summarize

Possible Red Flag: Transactions with unapproved supplier(s).

Step 1. Create a new Project for "Conflict of Interest."

Step 2. Import "ACCPAY2012 & SUPPLIER" data for analysis.

Step 3. Under the "Analysis" tab, select "Join."

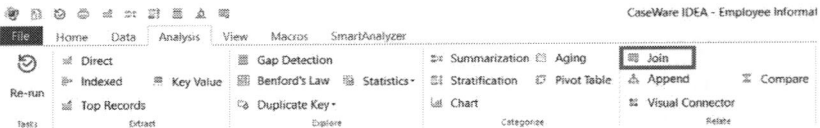

Step 4. Select "Secondary Database."

Step 5. Select "Supplier" as the secondary database.

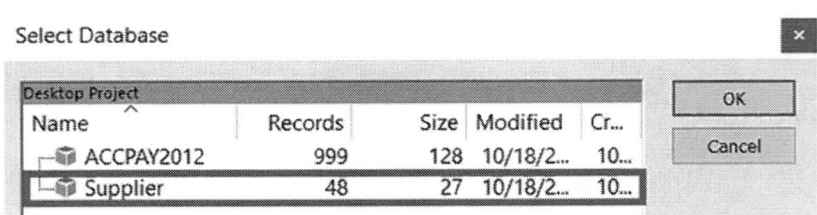

Step 6. Enter the file name as "Unauthorized Supplier."

Join Databases ×

Primary database: ACCPAY2012	Fields	**OK**
Number of records: 999		Cancel
Criteria: [ ] 🔢		Help
Secondary database: Supplier	Select	
Number of records: 48	Fields	

File name: Un-Authorized Supplier   Match

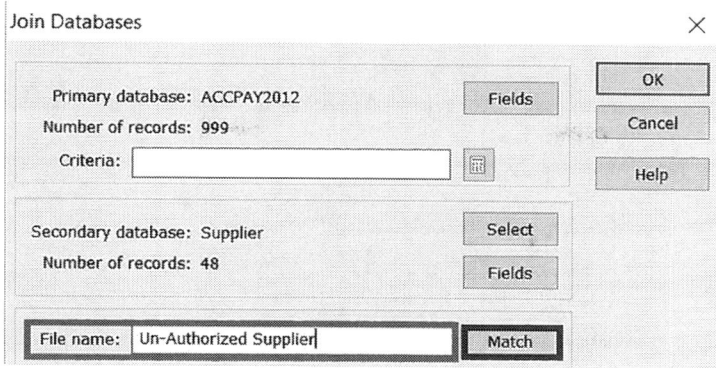

Step 7. Click "Match" and select "SUP_NO (C)" as the primary field and "SUPPNO (C)" as the secondary field.

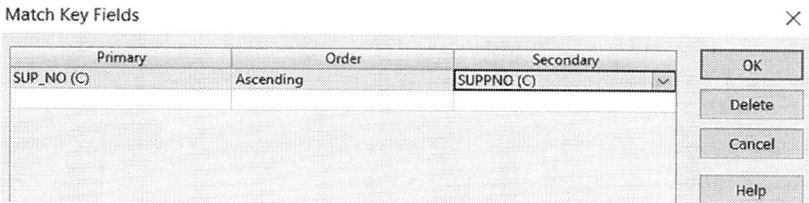

Match Key Fields ×

Primary	Order	Secondary	
SUP_NO (C)	Ascending	SUPPNO (C)	**OK**
			Delete
			Cancel
			Help

Step 8. Select "Records with no secondary match."

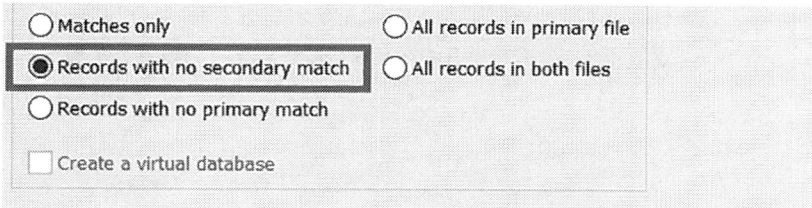

○ Matches only   ○ All records in primary file

● **Records with no secondary match**   ○ All records in both files

○ Records with no primary match

☐ Create a virtual database

Step 9. Click "OK."

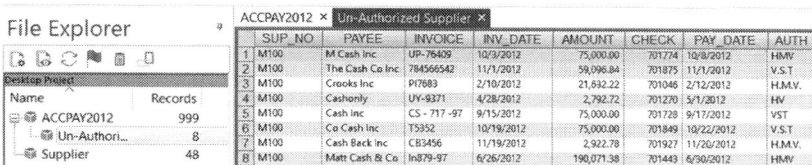

File Explorer

ACCPAY2012 × | Un-Authorized Supplier ×

	SUP_NO	PAYEE	INVOICE	INV_DATE	AMOUNT	CHECK	PAY_DATE	AUTH
1	M100	M Cash Inc	UP-76409	10/3/2012	75,000.00	701774	10/8/2012	HMV
2	M100	The Cash Co Inc	784566542	11/1/2012	59,096.84	701875	11/1/2012	V.S.T
3	M100	Crooks Inc	P17683	2/10/2012	21,632.22	701046	2/12/2012	H.M.V.
4	M100	Cashonly	UY-9371	4/28/2012	2,792.72	701270	5/1/2012	HV
5	M100	Cash Inc	CS - 717 -97	9/15/2012	75,000.00	701728	9/17/2012	VST
6	M100	Co Cash Inc	T5952	10/19/2012	75,000.00	701849	10/22/2012	V.S.T
7	M100	Cash Back Inc	CB3456	11/19/2012	2,922.78	701927	11/20/2012	H.M.V.
8	M100	Matt Cash & Co	In879-97	6/26/2012	190,071.38	701443	6/30/2012	HMV

Name	Records
ACCPAY2012	999
Un-Authori...	8
Supplier	48

Results show that the M100 record is fictitiously added to the supplier list, because it doesn't have a secondary record.

i. Audit Test # 09: Conflict of Interest

ACFE Fraud Tree Subcategory: Conflict of Interest.
Purpose: To identify any unusual trends and to determine the high-value payment amount by extractions.
Audit Test Procedure: Match contract price to invoice and report on Variances.
Assertion(s) Tested: Existence, Occurrence, Authorization, and Validity.
CAATT Expression: Join/Relate, Summarize, and Expression.
Possible Red Flags: Unusual trends and the high-value payment amount.

Step 1. Create a new Project for "Conflict of Interest."
Step 2. Import the "ACCCPAY2012" and "SUPPLIER" data files for analysis.
Step 3. Under the "Analysis" tab, select "Join."

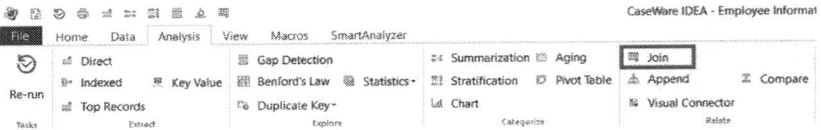

Step 4. Select "Secondary Database."

Step 5. Select "Supplier" as the secondary database.

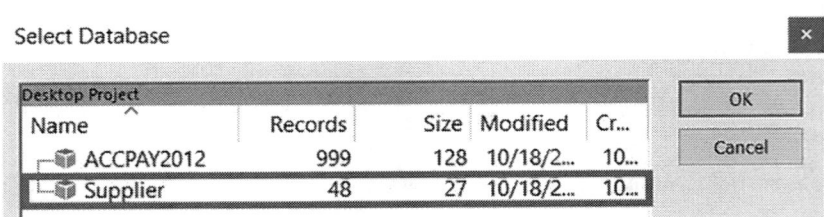

Step 6. Enter the file name as "High Payments."
Step 7. Click "Match" and select "SUP_NO (C)" as the primary field and "SUPPNO (C)" as the secondary field.

Step 8. Click "OK."

Step 9. Under the "Analysis" tab, click "Stratification."

Step 10. Select "Amount" in both "Field to Stratify" and "Field to Total on" and enter file name as "Unusual High Payments."

Note: For the 1–10 rows, select "Increment" as 10,000, and then as 50,000.

Step 11. Click "OK."

Totalled on: AMOUNT

Stratum #	>= L Limit	< U Limit	# Records	(%) # Records	AMOUNT	(%) AMOUNT
1	0.00	10,000.00	281	28.10	1,200,650.85	3.52
2	10,000.00	20,000.00	149	14.90	2,257,164.61	6.61
3	20,000.00	30,000.00	116	11.60	2,912,354.72	8.53
4	30,000.00	40,000.00	82	8.20	2,881,028.82	8.44
5	40,000.00	50,000.00	78	7.80	3,521,137.79	10.31
6	50,000.00	60,000.00	72	7.20	3,913,479.17	11.46
7	60,000.00	70,000.00	61	6.10	3,926,579.42	11.50
8	70,000.00	80,000.00	84	8.40	6,363,260.83	18.64
9	80,000.00	90,000.00	36	3.60	3,069,755.59	8.99
10	90,000.00	100,000.00	38	3.80	3,612,217.66	10.58
11	100,000.00	150,000.00	1	0.10	104,112.83	0.30
12	150,000.00	200,000.00	2	0.20	383,558.60	1.12
13	200,000.00	250,000.00	0	0.00	0.00	0.00
		Lower limit exceptions:	0	0.00	0.00	0.00
		Upper limit exceptions:	0	0.00	0.00	0.00
		Totals:	1,000	100.00	34,145,300.89	100.00

As the limit increases, the number of records decreases.

Step 12. Click the ▦ button to view the graphic representation to analyze the trend.

Note: As the number of records decreases, there is unusual trend in strata no. 8.

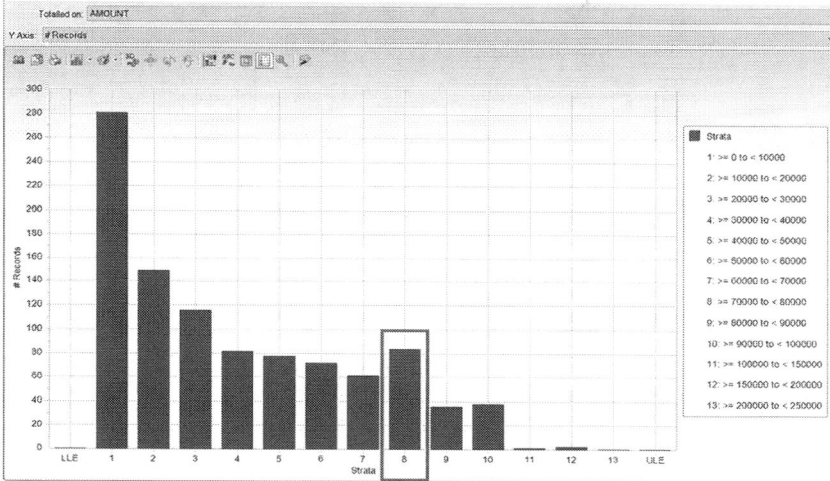

Results show that there are many payments between 70,000 and 80,000. This can be investigated further by also taking a closer look at records or transactions between 70,000 and 80,000.

Step 13. Click the ▦ button to go back to the grid view.

Step 14. Click the no. 8 record in "# Records" and select "Display Records."

8	70,000.00	80,000.00	Extract Records	5,363,280.83	18.64
9	80,000.00	90,000.00	Display Records	3,069,755.59	8.99
10	90,000.00	100,000.00	Display Field Statistics	3,612,217.66	10.58
11	100,000.00	150,000.00		104,112.83	0.30

Preview Database

	SUP_NO	PAYEE	INVOICE	INV_DATE	AMOUNT	CHECK	PAY_DATE	AUTH	SUPPNO	SUPPNAME	ADDRESS1
1	A128	A Meadow	117-2393	9/7/2012	75,777.62	701773	10/3/2012	BC	A128	Ivan Aker	149 1 AVE.
2	A128	A Meadow	117-2395	9/7/2012	70,979.93	701802	10/6/2012	BC	A128	Ivan Aker	149 1 AVE.
3	B008	A Raid	3501068	4/25/2012	76,113.99	701256	5/31/2012	WIT	B008	Denise Bent	43-191 67 AVE.
4	B010	Carter Bout	971077A	11/3/2012	70,825.47	701970	12/3/2012	H.M	B010	Carter Bout	869 KENSIGNTON AVE.
5	C202	P Crook	JFM.1256	10/3/2012	78,794.09	701801	10/6/2012	HMV	C202	Cash Inc	3124 TOWER ST.
6	C202	Cary S Matic	CS - 589 - 97	3/24/2012	79,217.47	701241	4/18/2012	H.M.V.	C202	Cash Inc	3124 TOWER ST.
7	C202	Cary S Matic	CS - 599 - 97	4/10/2012	75,819.56	701287	5/7/2012	H.M.V.	C202	Cash Inc	3124 TOWER ST.
8	C202	Cary S Matic	CS - 620 - 97	5/22/2012	76,220.09	701414	6/20/2012	HMV	C202	Cash Inc	3124 TOWER ST.
9	D014	Cary S Matic	CS - 705 - 97	10/26/2012	70,907.38	701942	11/26/2012	VMH	D014	William Ditt	151 MAGNUS AVE.
10	D025	Denise Bent	81340	1/5/2012	75,373.66	701003	2/2/2012	BC	D025	Nellie Dunn	957 QUEEN ST.
11	F123	Dick Tate	35284DUF	8/29/2012	76,992.02	701747	9/25/2012	HMV	F123	Wanda Farr	599 23 E AVE.
12	F123	Dick Tate	35239DUF	5/22/2012	78,105.10	701334	6/22/2012	VMH	F123	Wanda Farr	599 23 E AVE.
13	F128	Em Payed	82 951	2/17/2012	79,826.53	701148	3/15/2012	WIT	F128	Fixes	533 DOMINIC ST.
14	F128	Em Payed	82 981	3/6/2012	75,553.42	701200	4/3/2012	HMV	F128	Fixes	533 DOMINIC ST.
15	F128	Edward Zoff	99805ABC	4/3/2012	70,403.18	701276	5/3/2012	BC	F128	Fixes	533 DOMINIC ST.
16	F130	1 Moore	IN 6428 97	1/12/2012	78,262.98	701020	2/9/2012	CW	F130	Farmer	455 39 E AVE.
17	F130	1 Moore	IN 6497 97	8/9/2012	74,935.34	701579	8/4/2012	BC	F130	Farmer	455 39 E AVE.
18	G010	Fixes	871539BUZ	7/20/2012	74,918.27	701613	8/14/2012	WIT	G010	Polly Gunn	141 58 ST.
19	G010	Fixes	871538BUZ	7/3/2012	72,809.45	701568	7/31/2012	WIT	G010	Polly Gunn	141 58 ST.
20	G020	Fixes	871552BUZ	9/25/2012	76,758.03	701838	10/23/2012	WIT	G020	P Green	72-930 QUEEN ST.

Three transactions were paid above 100,000 and HMV autho-rized all the transactions. Also, supplier no. M100 is not in authorized supplier list, suggesting a ghost supplier scheme.

SUP_NO	PAYEE	INVOICE	INV_DATE	AMOUNT	CHECK	PAY_DATE	AUTH	SUPPNO	SUPPNAME	ADDRESS1	ADDRESS2	ADDRESS3	ZIP_CODE	TOT_PREV_YR
1	W007	Cash Inc	AB 3265 M	3/19/2012	104,112.83	701106	3/25/2012	HMV	W007	The Matt Cash Co	1596 1 N AVE	OTTAWA	ONTARIO	N8W 3P4	1,397,587.00

SUP_NO	PAYEE	INVOICE	INV_DATE	AMOUNT	CHECK	PAY_DATE	AUTH	SUPPNO	SUPPNAME	ADDRESS1	ADDRESS2	ADDRESS3	ZIP_CODE	TOT_PREV_YR
1	K001	Joyce Tick	54588	3/12/2012	191,887.22	701213	4/7/2012	HMV	K001	O Kay Vans	875 98 AVE	OTTAWA	ONTARIO	P6Z 5K7	998,678.23
2	M100	Matt Cash & Co	In079-97	5/28/2012	190,071.38	701443	6/30/2012	HMV							0.00

j.   Audit Test # 10: Non-cash Larceny

ACFE Fraud Tree Subcategory: Non-cash Larceny.

Purpose: To detect schemes related to false sales and shipping.

Audit Test Procedure: Identify duplicate invoices, credits, or receipts.

Assertion(s) Tested: Existence.

CAATT Expression: Duplicate.

Possible Red Flag: Duplicate documents.

Step 1. Create a new Project for "False Sales and Shipping Schemes."

Step 2. Import "Invoice" data for analysis.

Step 3. Select "Duplicate Key > Detection" under the "Analysis" tab.

Step 4. From the "Duplicate Key Detection" window, select "Output duplicate records" and click "Key." Enter the file name "Duplicate Invoices."

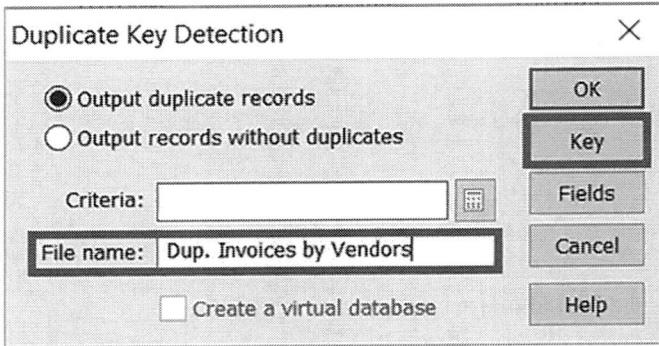

Step 5. In the "Define Key" window, select the fields that will be used as a base for duplicate detection.

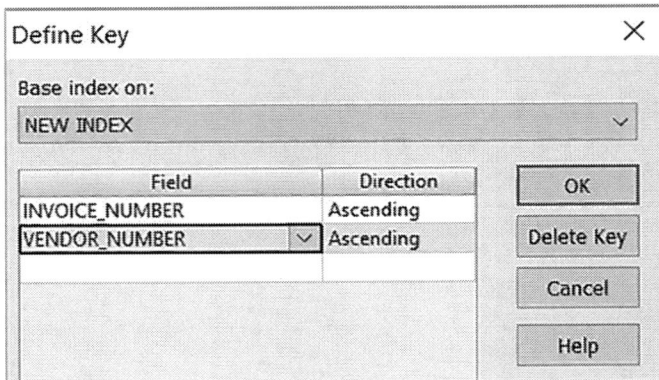

Step 6. Click "OK."

Results indicate that several duplicate invoices have been issued by the same vendor.

Section III: Creating Reports in IDEA

Step 1. From the "File" tab, select "Print" and "Create Report."

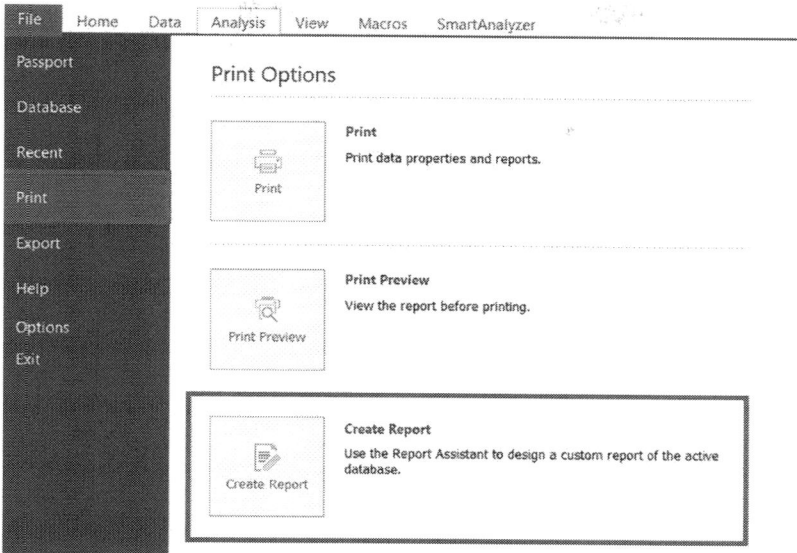

Step 2. From the "Report Assistant" dialogue box, accept the defaults.

Step 3. Click "Next."

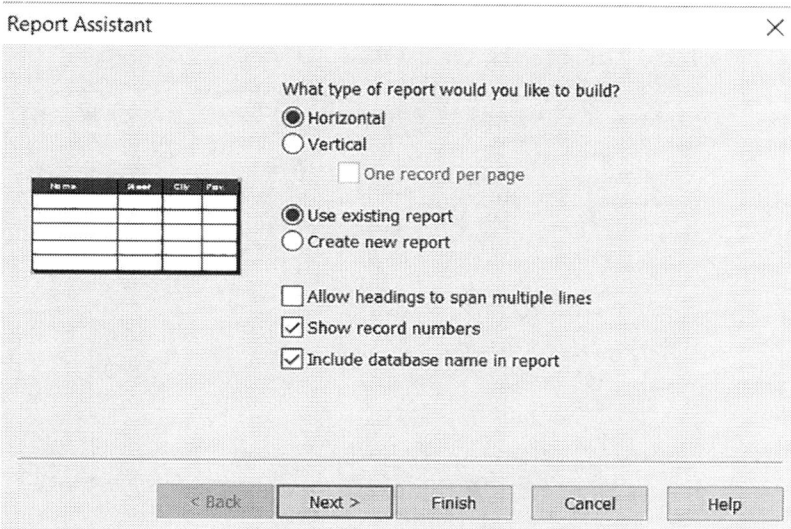

Step 4. From the "Report Assistant – Headings" window, modify the report headings.

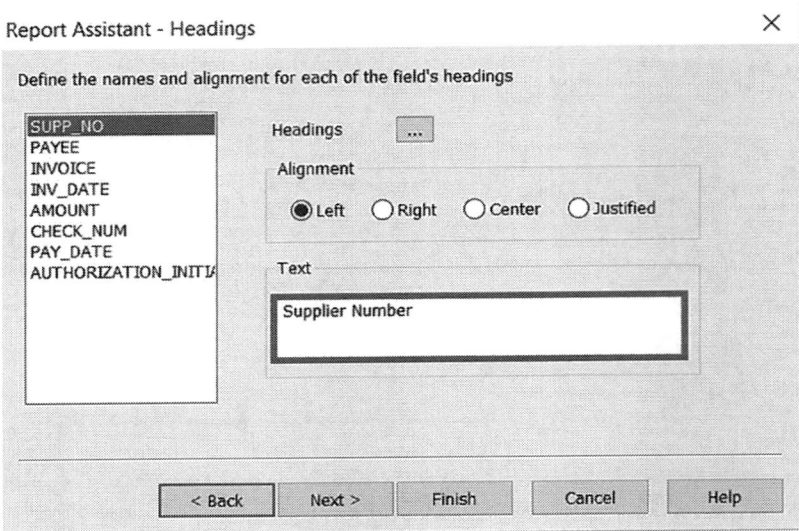

Step 5. Click "Next."

Step 6. From the "Report Assistant – Define Breaks" window, select the fields you prefer the report to break on.

Step 7. Click "Next."

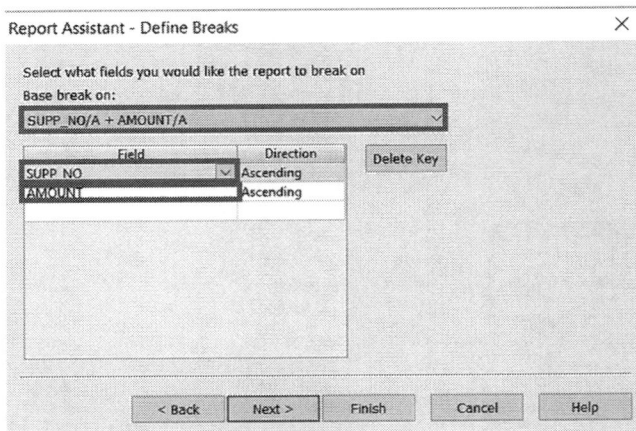

Step 8. Create a break in the "Report Assistant – Report Breaks" window as shown in the figure below, and click "Next."

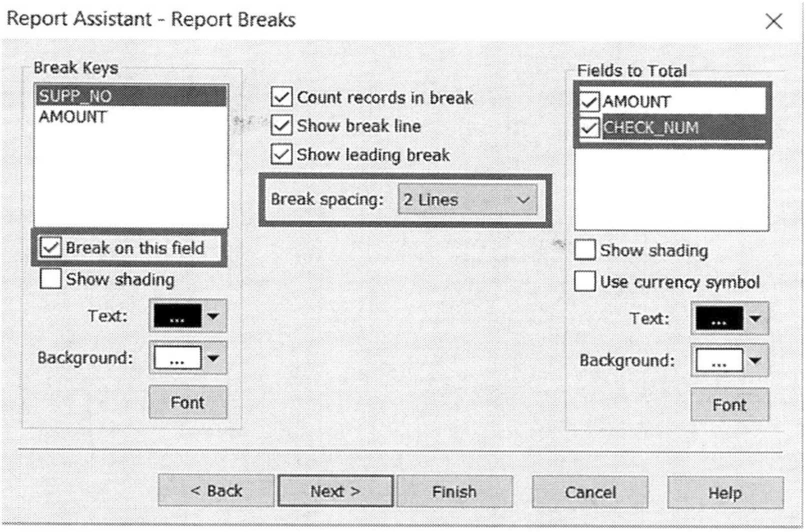

Report Assistant - Report Breaks   ✕

Break Keys

| SUPP_NO |
| AMOUNT |

☑ Count records in break
☑ Show break line
☑ Show leading break

Break spacing: 2 Lines ▼

☑ Break on this field
☐ Show shading

Text: ▪▪▪ ▼
Background: ... ▼
Font

Fields to Total

☑ AMOUNT
☑ CHECK_NUM

☐ Show shading
☐ Use currency symbol

Text: ▪▪▪ ▼
Background: ... ▼
Font

< Back   Next >   Finish   Cancel   Help

Step 9. From the "Report Assistant – Grand Totals" window create a grand total of "Amount."
Step 10. Click "Next."

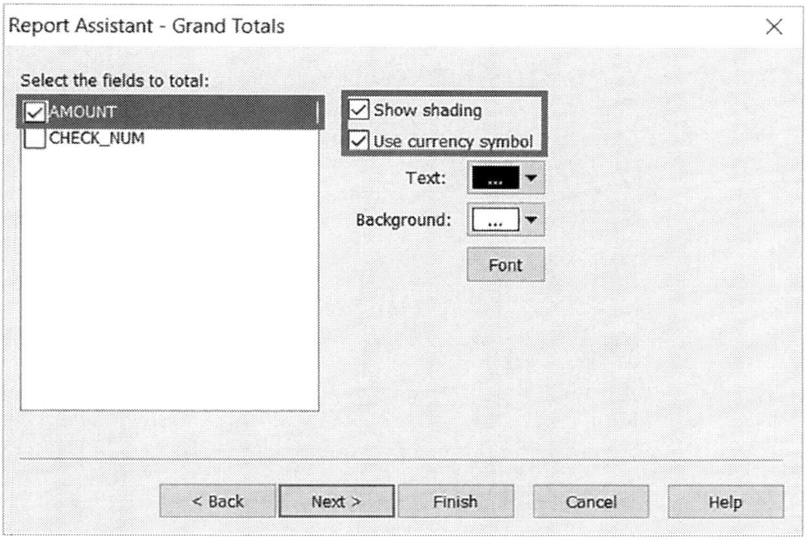

Report Assistant - Grand Totals   ✕

Select the fields to total:

| ☑ AMOUNT |
| ☐ CHECK_NUM |

☑ Show shading
☑ Use currency symbol

Text: ▪▪▪ ▼
Background: ... ▼

Font

< Back   Next >   Finish   Cancel   Help

Step 11. From the "Report Assistant – Header/Footer" window, select the "Print Cover Page" options.

Report Assistant - Header/Footer		×

☑ Print cover page

Title: Accounts Payable - Duplicate Payments

Comments: Ordered by Supplier Number and Amount

Prepared by: Khan Afsar   [Cover Page Font]

Header: MISAM Audit Test Manual (V   Date: Upper right

Footer: Time: Upper right

[Header/Footer Font]

[< Back]   [Next >]   [Finish]   [Cancel]   [Help]

Step 12. Click "Finish."

Note: IDEA will ask to preview the report. Click "Yes" to preview the report.

Bibliography

CaseWare IDEA. (2012). *IDEA Version Nine Tutorial A CaseWare IDEA Document*. Toronto, Ontario: CaseWare International. Retrieved from www.ideav9.caseware.com/pdf/idea-tutorial.pdf

CaseWare IDEA. (2016). *CI202 IDEA Data Analysis Workbo "OK" IDEA 10*. Toronto, Ontario: CaseWare International.

Free IDEA Videos. (n.d.). Retrieved October 16, 2017, from www.audimation. com/Resources/Video-Gallery/emodule/1675/egallery/17

Rutgers Accounting Digital Library. (2014, August 12). Advanced Auditing and Information Systems Lecture #8 1/2 7/31/2014. Retrieved October 25, 2017, from www.youtube.com/watch?v=ykk20T_bVYc

8

STUDENT CASE STUDY RESEARCH AND ORAL PRESENTATION PROJECT

Fraud examiners instructors or trainers can create an assignment where learners have to choose one of the case histories presented in this book and start researching its specifics, starting from the reference provided for the case at the end of the chapter.

The objective of this exercise is to conduct the research necessary to be able to create a 15- to 20-min, PowerPoint-based oral presentation that addresses/discusses the following:

a. What exactly transpired in the case history? Presenters need to be able to explain the fraud scheme to the audience in about five minutes! If the presenting group does not fully understand the scheme, they will not be able to explain it clearly to the audience!

b. How did the fraudster get caught?

c. What happened to the fraudster?

d. What weak (or non-existent) controls gave way to the fraud?

e. Analysis of the fraud based on the fraud triangle theory or other relevant framework.

f. What lessons can an auditor or fraud examiner learn from the case history presented?

g. What Computer-Assisted Audit Tools and Techniques (CAATT) audit test(s) could have revealed the fraud scheme? What would be the red flags associated with each audit test identified?

h. *Extra step for more in-depth presentations (optional)*: Take one of the audit tests discussed in step g (previous step), and demonstrate the CAATT audit steps using screenshots and directions, similar to the steps presented in the previous section of this book.

This is an excellent hands-on, group exercise that enables learners to study a case history in detail in order to assess the control gaps that gave rise to the scheme and to recommend the needed controls to help ensure that similar schemes do not happen again in the enterprise under study. The assignment can be further expanded to include a discussion of how the profile of the perpetrator(s) and the losses experienced are in line (or differ) from the statistics presented in the most recent Association of Certified Fraud Examiners (ACFE)'s Report to the Nations.

Index

A

Accounting scandal, Tesco, 92
ACFE, *see* Association of Certified
      Fraud Examiners (ACFE)
ACL, *see* Audit Command
      Language (ACL)
ActiveData, 2, 142
Active database, 159, 187
Adoption of fraud auditing, 152–
      157, 160–161
Aging analysis, 146, 160
Altered payee schemes, 54
American Psychological Association
      (APA), 9
Anti-bribery laws, 125–126
Anti-corruption
    management systems (ISO
      37001), 128
    organizations and laws, 125
Anti-fraud policy and strategy, 157
APA, *see* American Psychological
      Association (APA)
Artificial intelligence, 141, 145
Asset misappropriation, 47

audit tests worksheet, 21–45,
      58–89
billing schemes, 129
fraud
    risk mitigation, 19–21, 56–58
    schemes, 13, 15–18, 50, 52–55
victim organizations and society,
      11–12
Asset requisitions and transfers
      schemes, 18
Association of Certified Fraud
      Examiners (ACFE), 3,
      13, 18, 126, 157, 158,
      205, 206
audit tests worksheet
    asset misappropriation, 21–45,
      58–89
    corruption, 135–137
    fraud financial statement,
      101–120
fraud tree schemes, 3, 4
instructors/trainers cases,
      205–206
internal and external audit
      activities, 141–142